The Dream Deferred

THE DREAM DEFERRED

People, Politics, and Planning in Suburbia

Samuel Kaplan

A CONTINUUM BOOK

THE SEABURY PRESS · NEW YORK

The Seabury Press
815 Second Avenue
New York, N.Y. 10017

Printed in the United States of America

Library of Congress Cataloging in Publication Data
Kaplan, Samuel, 1935-
  The dream deferred : people, politics and planning in suburbia
  (A Continuum book)
  Bibliography: p.227
  Includes index.
  1. Local government—United States. 2. Suburbs—United States. I. Title.
JS341.K36   320.9′73′09733   75-35585
ISBN 0-8164-9282-4

DREAM DEFERRED

What happens to a dream deferred?

Does it dry up
Like a raisin in the sun?
Or fester like a sore—
And then run?
Does it stink like rotten meat?
Or crust and sugar over—
Like syrupy sweet?

Maybe it just sags
Like a heavy load.

Or does it explode?

—LANGSTON HUGHES

For Alison and Michael,
may they accept the challenge of change.
For Sherry, who has.

Contents

Acknowledgments

In the writing of this book I have drawn on seven years as a participant and observer of planning and political efforts in suburbia. As cited wherever possible in the text without breaking the flow of the narrative, I also have relied on numerous popular and professional articles and books. These sources and a bibliography that may be useful to students and professionals are included in *Notes and Sources.*

Many individuals contributed to the book by granting interviews, giving counsel, and providing insights. At the risk of offending some whom I do not mention, I want to thank for their assistance Stanley Buder of the City University of New York, Linda and Paul Davidoff of the Suburban Action Institute, Edwin Diamond of the Massachusetts Institute of Technology, David Laventhol of *Newsday,* Catherine Morrison of the Nassau-Suffolk Regional Planning Board, and the following residents of Port Washington: Norman Blankman, Myron H. Blumenfeld, Mrs. Toni Coffee, Mrs. Winifred Freund, Farrell Jones, Paul Jones, Mrs. Rosalie Jordan, Edward A. Lawrence, Ms. Amy Pett, Jill and Richard Sheinberg, William Schall, Michael F. Teitler, Dr. and Mrs. Stephen Zaslow, and the anonymous staff of the Port Washington Public Library.

A special note is due my other friends and neighbors in Port Washington, who may take exception to my portrait of our community, which I have woven into the fabric of my study of the suburban experience. To them I say it was immodestly done with the hope that through insights we could make Port Washington, and perhaps suburbia, a better place for all to live.

I am also grateful for the encouragement and professional advice of George Malko, Jerry and Frances Marton, Michael Roloff, J. George Lawler, Margot Shields, Charles Goldstein, Phyllis and Robert Seavey, Daniel Z. Nelson, and in particular to my literary agent, Phyllis Seidel. My gratitude also to Mrs. Sue Morgillo, who typed the manuscript and with me corrected it. The errors, of course, are mine.

To my wife, Sherry; my children, Alison and Michael; and my mother-in-law, Mrs. Dwaine Paxton Walther, who tolerated the unsettled life of our home while I compulsively pursued my writing, a special thanks. And my love.

September, 1975
Port Washington, New York

1
A Nation
of Suburbs

The quintessence of America is now suburbia. It is in suburbia where most Americans now live—an estimated 40 percent of our population, compared to about 30 percent in cities and 30 percent in rural areas. It is in suburbia that most of the nation's growth is occurring—in population, in jobs, and in power. And, it seems, it is in suburbia that most of the people, commerce, and industry want to be. Despite all the efforts to save our cities by planners, environmentalists, and reformers; despite the economic, energy-saving, social, and cultural arguments, and the clichés of the urban-oriented media and the jokes of comedians, suburbs are where most people seem to want to live. After growing from a nation of farms to a nation of cities, it is clear from all signs that America has become a nation of suburbs.

It is therefore in suburbia that many politicians, planners, and prognosticators believe that the quality of life for America will be determined, now and in the future, for better or worse. For along with the people has come the power: to vote, to legislate, to purchase, and to generally pursue the American dream. The fact is that suburbia is where the action is and will be.

As most sociologists, political scientists, and market and consumer analysts recognize, and as many intellectuals, tastemakers, and journalists resist, the dream of most Americans has never been one of a luxuriously appointed apartment high above an exciting and prestigious avenue or a quaint, tasteful brownstone set in a culturally stimulating, heterogeneous high-density city, but rather that of an attractively packaged comfortable single-family home set off from its neighbors on a well-landscaped plot in an economically, socially, and racially homogeneous community of good schools and convenient shopping. It is a dream not of a challenging, involved life-style rich in excitement, of the possibility of fantasies come true, but rather of a leisurely life-style, of privacy, health, security, status, and few conflicts. Whether one can reasonably expect to achieve this life-style in the suburbia that has evolved in the 1970s is questionable, but to the majority of Americans it is suburbia that still offers the greatest hope of that dream.

It is this dream that in the last 25 years has prompted the greatest migration in our country's history, and perhaps one of the greatest migrations in the history of man. It has caused mass disruptions in the economic, social, and racial balance of our cities, sending many into spirals of deterioration from which they may never recover. It has vastly altered, much for the worse, the metropolitan landscape, in many cases destroying the very amenities the people had sought in their migration further and further out of the central cities. Yet the migration and sprawl continues, for in comparison to the cities they are escaping from suburbia still harbors the hope of a better life for families. If indeed suburbia has become the harbinger of the hope of the American dream (or what is left of it), if suburbia in fact has become the focal point of the determinants that will shape our society, if it has become the quintessential America, then we must better understand it.

The word *suburbs* is defined as including all parts of all metropolitan areas outside of central cities, including suburban municipalities as well as unincorporated areas—in effect that vast area between our cities and our farms arbitrarily labeled suburbia by the United States Bureau of the Census. The definition is appropriately vague. If it is difficult to generalize about cities, the demography, economy, ecology, psychology, politics, and style of, say, San Francisco, as distinguished from New York City, or Los Angeles, Chicago, Atlanta, Buffalo, Boston, or Denver, it is even more difficult to generalize about suburbia.

Each separate metropolitan area has a variety of distinct suburbs. There are old suburbs that in reality could be classified as cities, except for their political status. There are the suburbs of popular repute, spreading subdivisions of sprawling three-bedroom, two-car-garage homes and one-stop shopping centers. There also are the more modest ticky-tacky tracts of green lawns, white fences, red bank balances, and two-tone station wagons. But also tucked here and there are the leafy enclaves with comfortable colonials set back on manicured lawns. And beyond the colonials, protected by even more restrictive zoning and ivy-covered stone walls, are the pleasant pseudo-English country estates, the zenith of suburbia. Less conspicuous are the black, Chicano, or poor-white suburbs, usually enveloping the old towns ignored by the thruways and real estate speculators carving up the countryside for shopping centers and subdivisions. These are the suburban slums, called slurbs, which are as much a racial and economic ghetto as an inner-city slum. And lately there are the attached garden-apartment developments, and even some high rises, many catering to singles or senior citizens, set off from the roadways by acres of asphalt parking lots. The high density developments have followed the industrial parks to suburbia, some of which are attractive sprawling corporate headquarters, but more and more of which have become manufacturing complexes belching polluted smoke and thousands of automobiles to clog the thruways at rush hour. And off the thruways, parkways, and roadways, and behind the billboards and struggling hemlock hedges, are the shopping centers and malls, the new main streets of America.

Suburbia has evolved into a mosaic of forms, constantly changing as it becomes less dependent on the inner city for its economic base and more dependent on the whims of speculators, real estate developers, corporate managers and highway engineers. Freed by the automobile and truck, and aided by the development of the highway system and the septic tank, suburbia is spreading. Its older communities are becoming more urbanized while its outer bucolic fringes, exurbia, is becoming suburban. Though the development of suburbia in the seventies has eased somewhat compared to the boom years of the fifties and sixties, the crush continues, with an estimated 1.5 million acres being "suburbanized" every year.

To try therefore to pin the wings of suburbia on a piece of graph paper and define it as a distinct physical area might be interesting to planners, architects, and real estate developers, but I question whether it would enhance our understanding of "it" as a phenomenon that has reshaped and reoriented America in the short span of a score of years. A descriptive narrative of its myriad forms further wanes when presented with the fact that there are approximately 20,000 suburban communities, as defined by the

Bureau of the Census. I am afraid the result would be a collection of clichés or, worse, an academic extrapolation of the latest census figures, with some opinion polls added for "depth." Having attacked these approaches in the past as both a critic and teacher for their lack of focus and empathy, I now hope to avoid the same pitfalls of blandness and boredom.

In my various readings I found the most interesting descriptions of suburbia not in the general surveys, but in the microstudies of individual communities, such as the portrait of Park Forest, Illinois by William H. Whyte, Jr. in his *The Organization Man*, and the dissecting of Levittown, New Jersey, by Herbert J. Gans. These studies defined suburbia for me as a union of people giving their communities a form through their possessions and a style through their attitudes.

Questions of planning and design, debates on educational policies, concerns of environmental quality, conflicts over open housing and zoning, discrimination and political battles—all issues in suburbia—mean nothing unless they can be related to people and places. It is only through specifics that they become relevant. I therefore decided not to do a broad objective survey. Instead, I chose the approach of an individual taking part in the phenomenon as an activist in my immediate community, with perspectives on the national level to place my observations in context and hopefully add depth. Because I care about the issues I have made no pretense to be anything but a biased participant and observer.

My interest in suburbia follows in many ways the shift in the last decade of our national focus from the city to suburbia. Born and raised in New York City, I had worked for *The New York Times* from 1958 to 1966 as a reporter, covering city problems, with a specialty in housing and planning. I lived most of these years in East Harlem, where I took part with my wife in a variety of community activities, even serving for a time as vice-chairman of the local planning board. To us, East Harlem was then an exciting, heterogeneous community, as was New York City, and we considered ourselves confirmed urbanites. In fact, I had co-authored a very upbeat city book at the time, *The New York City Handbook*, the opening sentence of which declared that "the premise of this book is that New York City *is* a great place to live." My only contact with suburbia during these years was a rare assignment beyond the city limits or to visit my wife's family in Port Washington, a pleasant, secure, settled community of then around 30,000 persons on Long Island's North Shore, about 20 miles, or 45 minutes, from Manhattan. They had moved to Port in

1953, after a brief tenure in Levittown, Long Island, a sprawling subdivision of modest homes considered by many as the epitome of suburbia.

My view of suburbia at the time was flavored by the popular public images created by such best sellers as *The Crack in the Picture Window,* by John Keats, *The Exurbanites,* by A. C. Spectorsky, and *The Organization Man.* Suburbia to me was synonymous with conformity; a dreary, deadening environment. I assumed that it, and most of the people who lived there, would be boring, except, of course, the people I knew, such as my in-laws. But before they moved to Levittown, before my 14-year-old brother-in-law had his third football stolen from him in Riverside Park, they had lived on the West Side of Manhattan, which explained the exception to me. (I did not realize then, as I do now, that the many and varied neighborhoods of suburbia are in fact low-density, leafy extensions of neighborhoods of the city from which its residents had moved.)

Tired of writing about city problems and anxious instead to do something about them, I left the secure *Times,* the civil service of journalism, early in 1966 and moved to New Haven, Connecticut, to become that city's downtown urban renewal director. We lived in New Haven, which city had a population of 150,000, just about the same size as East Harlem, and we experienced for the first time the pleasures of a single-family home with a backyard for our child and dog. Another child and a year and a half later we were in another house, this one in Princeton, New Jersey, where I was a consultant to the state for housing development. Princeton is considered by some a suburban community, but the dominance of the university and the town's setting, much like a well-planned, wealthy oasis in exurbia, makes it very much the exception. We found Princeton a very comfortable community. In fact, it was too comfortable, almost unreal, and its airs of self-satisfaction became boring to me very shortly. My job with the state also became boring, for the state just seemed to want to study the problem of housing development and not necessarily do anything about it. I had left the *Times* because I was tired of writing about problems, but I now found myself writing once again, this time memoranda instead of articles. So when a job promising a challenge in New York City was offered to me, I accepted, with the hope we could also move back to the city. This resolve was heightened by the three hours daily commuting between Princeton and New York City.

However, having a comfortable house with space in and around it for our two children and my wife and me to feel open and free in had spoiled us. The cost of comparable space in a Manhattan apartment was prohibitive dollar for dollar, and as an investment, a single-family home in suburbia could not be matched by any city dwelling, including a cooperative or condominium. In addition, there was now the problem of schools. New York City's public schools were in turmoil, and we did not like, nor could we afford, private schools. Of course, surburban schools had their problems, but they were relatively minor compared to those besetting the city's. The decision therefore was to move to a suburb closer to New York City, which we still viewed as the source of our economic and cultural lives. And we decided that the suburb would not be in New Jersey or Connecticut, but New York, for the job I had taken, Director of Development for the newly created New York City Educational Construction Fund—a public benefit corporation which plans, finances, and constructs schools in combination with residential or commercial structures—was in effect a state authority. The least we could do was live and pay taxes in the state.

Scouring the real estate section of a local paper in July of 1968, I came across a classified advertisement by someone who wanted to swap his "Pre-Revolutionary War Five Bedroom Home on a half acre overlooking Manhasset Bay in Port Washington" for a house in Princeton, where he was being transferred to by his company. My wife knew of the house, a town landmark of sorts in the old section of town sitting unceremoniously on a slight knoll facing the waterfront, with a busy roadway on one side and a pleasant duck pond on the other. Also appealing, at least to us, was that the rambling structure bordered an active, somewhat quaint neighborhood of small shops and bars, and was in walking distance of the public school, a new library, stores, and the train station. With my wife's mother still living and active in town, as were a few of my wife's old friends, it also would not be like moving into a strange, new, unsettled community, but one in which we already had some roots. Despite some trepidation about the physical condition of the house, we contracted to swap, and on September 1, 1968, some money, the mortgages, and titles were exchanged and we moved to Port Washington. We had become suburbanites, another statistic in the great migration in the 1960s.

After spending an exhausting day moving in, we gratefully accepted an invitation from a couple we knew who lived in town to bring the kids over and have dinner. Another couple also was invited, ostensibly to greet us, and after dinner and a few drinks the conversation turned to our new common interest, the community. The wives were quite involved in a number of community concerns, and as the discussion became more animated it reminded me very much of some of the meetings I had attended when I was an active resident of East Harlem. The broad issues were the same: quality education, housing, ethnic politics, zoning, and planning. Only this was suburbia, supposedly the secure, protected enclave of the bored bourgeois, the uncommitted, not an inner-city neighborhood in the throes of change and constant crisis.

As the evening and drinks wore on, I found myself drawn into debating the latest community crisis, the public review of a draft master plan for the Town of North Hempstead, of which Port Washington is a part. One of the women was serving on a Citizens Advisory Committee on the Master Plan as a representative of Port, but despite her good intentions, I sensed from our discussion that she and the committee were probably being pressured by the local politicians and paid planning professionals into a rubber-stamping act. When I told her this, she suggested somewhat defensively that I should serve on the committee and, if I really was interested, she would nominate me. I replied that I was interested and that I would be pleased to serve. Despite the fact that I had not been a resident of the town for one day, my foot was already in the door. And what lay behind that door, and the doors beyond, was the morass of suburbia, the new America.

2
A Bit of History

Ever since a few settlers decided to move beyond the walls of the fort, there has been a suburbia. Though most of the settlers recognized that the fort, then later the trading post, village, town, and ultimately the city, was their source of commerce and culture, they sought the promise of privacy and space of a home in a bucolic setting where they could more easily pursue their hopes of a better life. The early American dream was that of the agrarian populists, from Thomas Jefferson to William Jennings Bryan, who envisioned a continent of farmers, each on his own acres, independent and prosperous. The agrarian myth mixed with a bit of greed spurred the move west, until the official closing of the frontier in 1890. With the cities then industrializing and suffering the strain of immigration, which created problems not unlike those of today, political philosophers, social reformers, and the omnipresent real estate speculators adopted and adulterated the agrarian myth and turned their view toward a new area for settlement and development, the so-called middle landscape between town and country, what we now label as suburbia.

The suburbs of New York already were being settled before the turn of the century, aided first by the coach and ferry, then by the development of the railroad and the imported ideal of the English country manor. Such suburbs as those on the North Shore of Long Island, the so-called Gold Coast made infamous a few decades later by F. Scott Fitzgerald in *The Great Gatsby,* allowed the wealthy to pursue their leisure-time activities of yachting and hunting while living in reasonable distance to New York City, and

Wall Street, where they could keep an eye on their fortunes. Importing designs and decorations from Europe, great estates spotted the Long Island landscape, with those who pursued yachting settling near the Sound and the Seawanhaka and Knickerbocker Yacht Clubs on Oyster and Manhasset Bays, and those who fancied hunting in the mid-Island on the Hempstead Plains, close to the Meadow Brook Club. The clubs were formed in the 1870s. To be sure, the development of the area at the time was sparse, and its economic base was still agriculture. However, the construction and care and feeding of the estates did give suburbia a new perspective. Now not only did its residents look to the central city as a market for their produce, but also to its population as potential consumers of suburbia's basic commodity—land.

The wealthy of Philadelphia and Boston also were moving out to their country estates and clubs in the late nineteenth century. A wealthy Bostonian was quoted at the time giving the following advice to his son: "Boston holds nothing for you except heavy taxes and political misrule. When you marry, pick out a suburb to build your house in, join the Country Club, and make your life center about your club, your home, and your children." The city was viewed as a necessary evil; a place to carry on commerce and to make money. The ideal remained the values of the Founding Fathers, the values of rural America; the gentleman farmer and sportsman, at peace with nature, away from the masses of the burgeoning cities.

The state of the cities at the time also was disturbing the political philosophers and social reformers, and they too were looking at the so-called middle landscape, between town and country, for solutions. "The 'rise of the suburbs' it is, which furnishes the solid basis of a hope that the evils of city life, so far as they result from overcrowding, may be in large part removed . . ." wrote Adna F. Weber in 1899, echoing a theme being debated in the settlement house movement and in academia. Spurred by the publication in 1898 of Ebenezer Howard's *Garden Cities of Tomorrow,* suburbia was being viewed as a practical resolve of the American paradox of rural values and urban wealth. "Town and Country must be married, and out of this joyous union will spring a new hope, a new life, a new civilization," stated Howard as he laid out his plan for the development of new towns.

The development of suburbia at the turn of the century depended on the trolley and the railroad, and along every line and spur leading out of the cities distinct settlements grew. Describ-

ing the phenomenon at the time in *The Big Change,* Frederick
Lewis Allen noted that "each city had its outlying residential
areas; long blocks of single-family or two-family houses, rising
bleakly among the vacant lots and fields; comfortable lawn-sur-
rounded houses for the more prosperous. And there were many
who made a cindery railroad journey to work from the suburban
towns . . ."

"The open fields about the city are inviting occupancy, and
there the homes of the future will surely be. The city proper will
not remain the permanent home of the people. Population must
be dispersed," wrote Frederick C. Howe, in his 1905 book oddly
entitled, *The City: The Hope of Democracy.* Despite the title, it
was clear that Howe considered not the city, but suburbia as the
hope of democracy in the future. And there were many others at
the time, such as the Harvard philosophers Josiah Royce and
George Santayana, the sociologist Robert Park and educator John
Dewey, who also viewed the potential of suburbia as the bulwark
of individuality and democracy. But while the wealthy continued
to pursue their genteel life-style on imitation European estates,
and while the philosophers and reformers discussed and debated
plans of what new landscape forms and economic and government reorganizations would be needed to free the workers wal-
lowing in the cities so they could better participate in the democratic process, bankers, builders, and real estate speculators were
at work, watching with principal and interest what villages
would be blessed by each new spur of the commuter railroads
being laid beyond the city limits.

The railroad came to Port Washington in 1898, ostensibly to
serve the Gold Coast estates of Sands Point, known later to Fitzgerald readers as East Egg, and the farmers supplying the markets of New York City. The town itself was inhabited at the time
by less than 2,000 people, mostly tradesmen servicing the estates,
the area's farmers, and the laborers mining the peninsula's high-
grade gravel and sand pits. Dairy farming still dominated the
peninsula, as it had since it was settled by a small band of English
farmers who had rowed across the Long Island Sound in 1643 to
escape religious persecution in Connecticut. The settlers found
the sloping hills, abundant water supply, and salt marshes ideal
for cattle grazing, and in 1658 they built a pasture fence of 11-foot
panels across the neck of the peninsula for 5 miles, from Hempstead Harbor to Manhasset Bay, which was then called Sint Sink
Bay by the Matinecock Indians. In deference to their source of

sustenance, the settlers named the bay Cow Bay and the peninsula Cow Neck, which they then divided up in parcels among
themselves according to the number of fence panels each had
built. The names and the principal occupation of dairy farming
remained for nearly 200 years, until 1857, when the state legislature approved a petition of the residents to rename the area Port
Washington, in honor of the first president, who had passed
through the tiny settlement on the bay in 1790. Local folklore has
it that the petition had been pressed by the bay's fishermen, as an
act to affront the peninsula's dairymen and their beloved, some
felt sacred, cows. The fishermen were newcomers to the area,
most making a living from oyster farming. Still, the town's population only hovered around 200, until two developments immediately after the Civil War pushed the total to 1,200.

The first was the discovery in 1865 of the high-quality sand and
gravel, which quickly attracted cement and asphalt contractors
and their laborers from New York City. Soon scows were convoy-
ing to Manhattan with the sand and gravel, and back to Port
Washington with manure for the farms, an efficient exchange of
materials of a significance and symbol undoubtedly noted by the
fishermen. The second development was the extension of the
Long Island Railroad in 1867 to Great Neck, which was a short
stagecoach ride from Port. The estates soon followed, and in time
the North Shore became very much the fashionable playground
of the robber barons and the privileged. However, the cows remained in the majority, despite occasional mistakes by weekend
hunting parties stumbling off the estates. Even when the railroad
line was extended to Port Washington in 1898, the train was still
driven by a slow steam engine, good for hauling produce to market and passengers who did not have to worry about getting to
work on time or every day. Only when the railroad was electrified
in 1913, cutting down commuting time to New York City to less
than an hour, could real estate speculation begin in earnest to
make Port Washington the suburb it is today.

The pre-Revolutionary War house we live in had been the home
of a Captain Baxter, who, according to old maps, also had a small
farm and orchard. The house itself was sold around 1910 to an
architect, Addison C. Mizner, who designed a number of Sands
Point manor houses. However, the Baxter farm and orchard were
subdivided for custom-built homes. The Baxter Homestead became Baxter Estates to readers of the real estate ads in the New
York City newspapers of the day. Other farms also were subdi-

vided, some suffering the fate of a grid street pattern that ignored the community's hills and dales, and occasionally the brooks and swamps that come back to haunt homeowners on rainy days.

The town's growth was similar to what was happening across Nassau County, in Lower Westchester, and in the other near suburbs of large cities during the first 20 years or so of the century. It was a slow, steady, and unplanned growth, catering to the upper-middle class. The commuter railroad, trolleys, trams, and, now most of all, the automobile had, for this group, opened land that once had been only accessible to the wealthy. They could now follow the wealthy in pursuit not of the agrarian myth, as the political philosophers had hoped, but of a more leisurely life-style and a higher social status of which suburbia held the promise. If they could not achieve the opulence of the manor houses, at least they could fashion their own more modest style in proximity. It was a selling point not lost on the builders and real estate agents. The houses were large, most with a room or two for servants, and the lots were usually an acre. It was in this period that some of our better-known and wealthier suburbs were settled, including Bronxville and Scarsdale in Westchester, Old Greenwich in Connecticut, Great Neck and Glen Cove on Long Island, Shaker Heights outside of Cleveland, Grosse Point north of Detroit, Philadelphia's Main Line, and Evanston above Chicago. The houses were not designed for the masses, as some social reformers had hoped, but rather for the upper-middle class. A few attempts were made by socially conscious sponsors to build well-planned but modest developments to serve lower-income groups. However, when these homes went on the market, in planned communities such as Long Island's Garden City and Forest Hills, they were snapped up by middle-income families definitely on the way up.

A few more attempts were made after World War I to open up suburbia to a broader economic group and to bring some rationality to its unplanned growth. The time was ripe, for 1919 through 1921 were disastrous years for the nation's building industry. A combination of escalating labor and materials costs and prohibitive interest rates had created a housing crisis, with low vacancy rates and high rents. Few new housing units were being built, and the industry turned to the government for help. Social reformers saw their opportunity to push for legislation that would bring planning and the masses to suburbia. On the national level, Secretary of the Interior Franklin K. Lane urged resettlement legislation that would create on public lands "a new rural life with all the urban advantages," in effect, new towns in suburbia. The effort never got anywhere. Some attempts on the state level were more successful, such as the California Farm and Home Purchase Act of 1921, which did spur the purchase and construction of some 5,000 homes, and the creation of the New York State Commission of Housing and Regional Planning. Boston and Pittsburgh tried to pass legislation that would allow them to buy land in their suburban communities for low-cost housing (which Copenhagen and Stockholm were doing in Europe), but their attempts failed. One of the reasons for the various failures to subsidize the settlement of suburbia for low- and moderate-income families was that by the time legislation had been drafted, debated, redrafted, and, finally, considered, the housing crisis had abated, and private speculators, the banks and builders were again at work cutting up the landscape for middle- and upper-income families escaping the city.

By 1925 the growth of suburbia had become a national trend. Suburbanization was a demographic fact. The concerns of the social reformers did lead to the recognition of the need for metropolitan planning, and such groups as the Regional Planning Association of America were formed, but they did relatively little to shape the new landscape. Formless sprawl along the suburban commuter lines continued to spread, and despite the lack of planning, was praised by the social commentators of the day, such as Harlan Paul Douglas, who concluded in his *The Suburban Trend*, published in 1925, that a "crowded world must be either suburban or savage." The middle class of the late 1920s, however, did not need a philosophic justification for their move from the city to suburbia. All they needed was a down payment and reasonable financing terms.

The search for suburban real estate became a national pastime in the late twenties, buoyed by the Coolidge prosperity that persuaded "the four-thousand-a-year salesman that in some magical way he too might tomorrow be able to buy a fine house and all the good things of the earth," according to Allen in *Only Yesterday*, an informal account of the times. From 1926 to 1929, outstanding mortgage loans exceeded $5 billion annually, a figure not to be reached again until after World War II. The confidence was there and so was the financing. Then came the depression, and both were gone, along with the aspiring middle class. It was a time not of speculation in real estate, but of survival.

With the depression, the growth of suburbia that had spurted in the late twenties sputtered in the early thirties, once again prompting government to action. The most noteworthy attempt was the Resettlement Administration, headed by Rexford Tugwell, who saw in its establishment the hope of creating thousands of suburban garden cities serving the families being driven off the farm and those trying to escape the city slums. The 3,000 Tugwell set his goals on were cut to 25 in the Administration's proposal to Congress, then to 3 by Congress. They were Greenbelt, Maryland, outside of Washington, D. C.; Greendale, near Milwaukee; and Greenhills, outside of Cincinnati. The "cities" were planned as complete communities, offering a variety of housing types, community facilities, lavish open space, and some employment opportunities. The Resettlement Administration never saw the completion of the cities and was axed in 1937. The cities nevertheless were built, and they prospered. However, they were not, as hoped, self-contained communities, but attractive suburban villages catering to middle-income commuters, and remain so today. Once again, the garden-city concept failed, and with the economy recovering in the late thirties, suburbia went back to its familiar role as a land resource for speculators, banks, and builders and as an escape hatch for those in the city who could afford it.

Any hope of magnitude for suburbia to provide the setting for a new America combining the advantages of the country and the advantages of the city in well-planned, self-contained communities serving a cross section of economic groups dissipated at the end of World War II. The returning veterans and a new postwar prosperity created in effect one of the greatest land rushes in our country's history. Aiding and accelerating the demand was the development of the most important and strongest planning determinant in our history: the popularization of the private automobile and the parallel growth of our road system. With the spread and widening of accommodating concrete and asphalt cutting deeper and deeper into our landscape, settlements spread almost at the whim of speculators. Fed by easy financing backed in large part by the Federal Housing and Veterans' Administrations, a vast mosaic of single-family tracts and shopping centers sprawled across the countryside, from the city limit lines past the older and close-in suburbs of exurbia.

The lure of suburbia in the postwar period was first and foremost simply a place to live for returning veterans and the new families being formed in the euphoric flush of the times. The agrarian myth of the intellectuals at the turn of the century, the values of the leisure and status seekers culled by speculators and builders in the early part of the century and the garden-city ideals of planners and social reformers in the twenties and thirties might have been sounded in some real estate advertisements, but the real attraction of suburbia was the ability of developers to offer quickly and on easy financial terms a roof, four walls and a driveway.

The intellectuals and social commentators of the day took little solace in the fact that suburbia was finally being opened, for a time at least, for low- and moderate-income families, albeit for white families because of restrictive covenants and discriminatory practices of banks and the acquiescence of the F.H.A. Instead, they saw their hopes of a new middle-landscape setting for the Jeffersonian ideal or sites for greenbelt or garden cities crushed by rampaging bulldozers leveling the green hills, orchards, and forests, filling in the streams, brooks, and wetlands for bedroom communities of ticky-tacky homes. Wrote Mumford in *The City in History,* published in 1961:

While the suburb served only a favored minority, it neither spoiled the countryside nor threatened the city. But now that the drift to the outer ring (sparked by the twin elements of popularity and horsepower and spurred by government housing loans) has become a mass movement, it tends to destroy the value of both environments without producing anything but a dreary substitute, devoid of form and even more devoid of the original suburban values.

As documented by Scott Donaldson in his survey, *The Suburban Myth,* the intellectual and communication communities found suburbia wanting. Projecting their own prejudices, many critics created a public image of suburbia as the embodiment of a materialistic, conformist society. However, the negative publicity did little to deter the continuing migration to the suburbs. As the demand for suburban homes continued to increase in the late fifties and into the sixties, the suburbs became more and more economically segregated. The $7,990 modest Levittown house was now, with improvements, in the $25,000 class, and going higher. The families moving to the suburbs were now of the income bracket where they could make the choice of living in the city or the suburbs. They chose the suburbs because they wanted to live there, not because it was the only housing accommodations available, as had been the situation in the immediate postwar period. It seemed people liked living in suburbia. Their dream of the "good life" might just be a dream, but nonetheless it sustained them. Most declared in one form or other in various studies of the day that wherever they came from, the cities, the farms, or the older suburbs, they considered their life better where they were now living. Few contemplated a return to the farm or city, especially not to the city.

The migration to the suburbs throughout the sixties confirmed their choice, as millions followed them. The migration now was spurred not only by the attraction of "some breathing room for us and the kids," the most typical explanation given to interviewers, but more and more by the increasingly hostile city. The "lure" or pull of suburbia gave way to the push of the city. The riot-torn, racially troubled, overtaxed, polluted, crime-ridden central cities created in the sixties the largest migration in our history.

As an older community, closer to New York City, Port Washington actually experienced its greatest growth in the mid-fifties through the mid-sixties. In many ways, the growth of Port was a harbinger of the growth to occur a few years later in the more open regions of suburbia. Because large sections of the town already were settled, growth had to be manipulated. But manipulated it was. The one-acre building lots were cut to a half-acre, then a quarter-acre and, with the help of politically well-connected local lawyers, even less. Custom-designed houses were still being constructed on the larger lots, blending in with the pleasant rambling Tudor and frame homes that predominated in the older, settled sections of the town. But wherever they could, speculators, bankers, and builders, with the blessings of the local politicians, laid out tract developments of modest and marketable homes. A few garden and low-rise (3 stories) apartments on and near the waterfront also were built, and in a period of 10 years Port's population had increased 50 percent, from 20,000 to 30,000. The dramatic increase in the population of Port Washington reflected what was occurring in other suburban communities. A heavy demand for homes was filling out the older established suburban towns such as Port and pushing out the boundaries of newer settlements and subdivisions. Suburbia was booming.

Between 1960 and 1970 the nation's population increased about 12 percent, to around 205 million. About 75 percent of the growth occurred in the suburbs, putting the total suburban population at approximately 77 million. The newer cities in the South and

Southwest accounted for whatever urban growth there was, while most of the nation's older cities, in the East and Midwest, remained at best static. Taken together, the country's 25 largest cities gained a mere 710,000 persons, while their suburban areas gained 8.9 million, or 12 times more. New York City's suburbs passed in population New York City itself, growing to nearly 9 million to become, in effect, the largest "city" in America. The suburbs of Washington, D. C., gained 800,000; which was more than the population of the city itself. In Boston, San Francisco, and other metropolitan areas, the suburban population grew to outnumber the city population by 3 and 4 to 1.

The trend has continued into the seventies, with projections indicating a suburban population in 1980 of 93.6 million, or approximately 41 percent of the total projected United States population of 228 million. By the year 2000 the suburban population is expected to be about 126 million, close to 50 percent of the projected population of the United States. The planners and prognosticators are assuming that suburbia will continue to grow at the rate it is now growing. But from my experience in suburbia, and as each year passes, it seems to me that their assumption is becoming tenuous. A warning was sounded in 1968 by a President's Task Force on Suburban Problems, which reported that while millions of Americans were moving to the suburbs to find space, quiet, decency, and comfort, once there they were finding something else.

"In the rush to provide facilities that so many citizens wanted, suburban land has been cut too fine and built up too thick, and what should have been shapely towns have grown formlessly until the suburban sprawl has destroyed the sense of community and sense that the citizens could control their own environment." The report continued: "Blight and decay have begun to set in, as they do in any community that has lost the love of its inhabitants. Industry has been moving in, as it should in order to provide jobs near people's homes, but in the unordered and unprepared fashion, resulting in pollution of the air, water and landscape."

Growth, once considered the promise of an endless, prosperous future, is casting a shadow on suburbia. It has triggered a plethora of issues—environmental, economic, racial, and political—that is testing the nation. The dream of suburbia has become a dilemma.

My introduction to the dilemma came only three weeks after we had moved into Port Washington. Acting on the recommendation of Mrs. Winifred Freund, the woman I had met our first evening, the Port Washington Citizens Advisory Committee on the Master Plan invited me to its initial meeting of the autumn. The committee was one of about a half-dozen organized throughout the Town of North Hempstead, the Port Washington peninsula comprising about 15 percent, or 35,000, of the town's population of 235,000 and about 10 percent, or 5 square miles, of the Town's 54 square miles. The committee's purpose was to review and comment on a draft of a plan prepared by a private consultant firm, Community Housing and Planning Consultants, that had been hired by the Town Board of North Hempstead under a federal grant, one of a few the town had applied for. Our reviews and comments were to relate to the parts of the plan that affected the unincorporated areas of Port Washington, which came under the zoning jurisdiction of the town.

"The unincorporated areas?" I asked naively.

"Yes," replied the amiable chairman, an executive with the Long Island Lighting Company. "They're the areas outside the villages, but within our school district."

"I thought we would be reviewing a plan for all of Port Washington," I continued. "The name of the committee, The Port Washington Citizens Advisory Committee on the Master Plan, I think spells out the mandate clearly."

"But there is no Port Washington," stated Mrs. Freund, a thin smile of experience crossing her face.

3

Balkanization

The dot on the map on the North Shore of Long Island, the post office address, the railroad timetable, and the real estate ads in *The New York Times* all clearly state there is a Port Washington. Turning off Exit 36 of the Long Island Expressway and driving north on Route 101, a roadside sign reads that you are entering Port Washington and urges motorists, usually unsuccessfully, to reduce their speed to 40 miles per hour. According to maps, Route 101 is described as, and is commonly known as, Port Washington Boulevard, certainly a recognition that there is such a place.

The broad four-lane highway curves through pleasant, comfortable subdivisions hidden behind trimmed privet hedges and frontier fences, past a rambling golf course, a country club, a private school, a few stores, a police station, garish gasoline stations, the inevitable Carvel stand, a junior and senior high school complex of weathered brick buildings set back behind well-used and abused playing fields, the drive-in bank, a cluster of shops and a supermarket, a post office—an undistinguished utilitarian main street, typical of Long Island and suburban America.

A few blocks beyond, modest frame houses give way to gentle hills, tall trees, deep lawns, and large lots with attractive homes and two cars in the driveway. The hills to the west slope down to Manhasset Bay and the waterfront, along which sit three yacht clubs (each catering mainly to a major faith), a garden-apartment complex, boatyards, some shops and restaurants, a town dock and a bandshell (named after John Philip Sousa, one of the town's more famous residents), a few bars, a gas station, and some aging homes, one of which is ours. From my perspective as a planner it is a healthy mixture of uses, giving a diversity and flavor to the town. A nice place to live, raise your kids, sail your boat, catch the train—the last stop on the Port Washington Line out of Pennsylvania Station.

Sitting snugly, if not smugly, on a peninsula giving the community a distinct physical identity, I had assumed that Port Washington was a political entity, albeit within the Township of North Hempstead, just as the township was a part of Nassau County. I had in fact looked forward to living in a community of about 35,000 persons, which was the population of Port Washington, for I had recently read a study that concluded that the optimum size of a political entity to encourage citizen participation was 30,000 to 50,000 residents. It also stated that a common, contiguous geographic location not bisected or trisected by expressways or bodies of water, would enhance the political structure as it relates to residents and the governmental structure in its delivery of services.

Besides its physical identity, Port Washington, it seemed upon brief, casual observation before we moved there, had a number of other aspects favorable to self-government. There were three (now two) weekly newspapers, a few landmarks giving the area a sense of history, a new, imposing library, a distinguished volunteer fire department, a winning high school football team, a variety of active if not overactive organizations and a solid, somewhat stolid, school system. It was the type of town, one would think, where the old New England concept of town hall democracy has the best chance of survival; where citizens can still feel close to a government structure; where a person's voice can be heard in the decision-making process; where home rule is something more than a politician's slogan.

But like other dots on the maps of suburban counties across the country, Port Washington is not a political entity. It is an oppressed colony, as it was in 1775, when the local farmers declared their sympathies for a revolution, protesting that they had no voice in government. What I learned that fall evening in 1968 and in subsequent weeks reviewing draft portions of the proposed master plan and local history was that politically the situation had not changed very much in nearly 200 years. Port Washington was, and is, a political morass, confusing residents, defying logic and mapmakers while discouraging citizens to take part in the democratic process which home rule is supposedly protecting. My quick appointment to the Citizens Advisory Committee, therefore, I suspect, was not because of my minor reputation as a planner and urban administrator, but because I was a live body that showed some interest. It also could have been Mrs. Freund's revenge for some of the presumptuous remarks I had made after a few drinks the night I met her. Whatever the reason, it was apparent to me that the committee did not represent Port Washington, because no one really did, at least not through any publicly recognizable structure.

The Port Washington peninsula is gerrymandered into four incorporated villages, Sands Point, Manorhaven, Port Washington North, and Baxter Estates, parts of two others (Flower Hill and Plandome Manor), and about 2 square miles of unincorporated areas. Compounding the jurisdictional confusion are seven special districts: school, water, garbage and ashes, parking, police, sewers, and fire, along with a lighting district and overlapping fire districts, each with its own taxing powers and none with coterminous lines. In addition, the Village of Sands Point maintains its own water supply and police department. The Nassau County Police Department serves Flower Hill, Plandome Manor, Manorhaven, and parts of the unincorporated area, while the Port Washington police patrol Baxter Estates, Port Washington North, and the rest of the unincorporated areas. There is also a duplication of services in the villages, which as a rule are empowered to enact ordinances, levy taxes, control zoning, and maintain streets. These powers in the unincorporated areas, in which about half of Port Washington's population resides, are exercised by the Town of North Hempstead in what passes as the county's government structure.

North Hempstead is one of three townships, along with Hempstead and Oyster Bay, and two cities, Glen Cove and Long Beach, that make up Nassau County. Within the townships there are a total of 64 incorporated villages, counting Port Washington's 4 and 2 halves, and 280 special districts. Nassau's sister county, Suffolk, has 10 townships, 28 villages, and 527 special districts. Scattered about the Island like poor relatives are approximately 100 unincorporated, castrated communities gerrymandered in between villages.

The effect on residents can be disorienting. Describing how her family lives, Leona Baum, mother of two teen-aged boys, reported, "We live in East Meadow. I work in Garden City. My husband works in Syosset. We shop for clothes in Hempstead. My husband's Pythias Lodge meets in Great Neck. Our temple is in Merrick. The children's doctor is in Westbury. And we pay our parking tickets in Mineola."

Above this confusion, and sometimes adding to it, are the county governments of Nassau and Suffolk—together they comprise all of Long Island outside of New York City. The counties perform a number of services, principally health, welfare, recreation, and police, except when localities have established their own special service districts, such as police in some sections of Port Washington, or parks and recreation, in Great Neck. The only real planning powers the counties have are their control over county roads and their force of argument, which they support by piling studies upon studies, reports upon reports, plans upon plans, debating the Island's problems of housing, transportation, taxes, planning, natural resources, and pollution. Almost all of the studies, reports, and plans have recommended in one form or another accommodations by the villages and towns. For the most part the recommendations have been received respectfully— probably because no one really thinks they will ever be implemented—and then piled neatly in the corners of the village and town halls to gather dust.

Commenting on the 500-odd separate agencies in his county, former Suffolk County Executive H. Lee Dennison observed in frustration that "each is more or less as independent as a hog on ice, jealous of home-rule prerogatives, indifferent to neighbors, poised for instant rejection of intrusion or change, often callous to any contribution to the health, safety or well being of the County of Suffolk as such."

In his farewell address to the county legislators in 1971 after serving 12 years as executive, Dennison noted that as much as 20 percent of the total county expenditures could be saved each year by consolidating 10 towns into 5 and establishment of a county-wide taxing district for everything from schools to garbage collection. He added:

"It boils down to just how much the local taxpayer is willing to pay to support local pride, prejudice and politics. Because of a failure in town administration we have neon nightmares of strip development and unplanned, unrelated, conglomerate, wasteful, speculative boom-town growth."

Reaction to the proposed consolidations were predictable. "It would take a civil war to accomplish," said John V. Klein, the incoming County Executive. "It is for the birds," said Evans K. Griffing, then the eminence grise of the county's East End.

To liken Long Island, and most suburban counties across the country, to the Balkans at the turn of the century would be a gross understatement. Because of overlapping jurisdictions, aggravated by unequal tax burdens, suburban communities have been unable to work together in metropolitan areas to map and carry out rational land-use plans. The communities remain little islands, each zealously guarding in particular their zoning powers as if they were divine rights. But while they may not be divine rights, they are in fact Constitutional rights. Under the Constitution, jurisdiction over land use was left to the states. They in turn delegated it largely to localities, however and on what level the localities happened to have been incorporated. The result is that there are presently no less than 65,000 separate governmental entities in the United States with the power to determine their own land use. These entities, which include the four and two halves of villages controlling approximately 3 square miles of the Port Washington peninsula and the Town of North Hempstead controlling the other 2 square miles, have been, to say the least, reluctant to relinquish their now historic prerogatives to higher levels of government, despite the many and various arguments, especially in these days of ecological concerns, for rational and regional land use. Long Island is not the exception. It is the rule.

In California, as Los Angeles sprawled south during the 1960s, the population of Orange County doubled to 1.4 million, prompting the county's 25 municipalities and 133 self-governing districts to scramble to annex every piece of taxable land in sight. Little or no consideration was given to the siting or relationship of residential, industrial, or commercial developments. The result is a crazy-quilt pattern of roads, services, and boundaries, creating a garish tangle and a host of problems.

A similar confused state exists in Santa Clara County, south of San Francisco. Its Balkanized suburbanization is one of the sadder cases, if only because the county had been one of the most attractive regions in the United States. It is also one of the more prophetic and well-documented cases.

Before the 1950s the county, also known as Santa Clara Valley or, now, Metropolitan San Jose, was primarily a farming area, comprising 1,305 square miles of fertile soil, bordered by the university town of Palo Alto to the north, the redwood forests of the coast ranges to the west, San Francisco Bay to the east, and the garlic fields and vineyards of Gilroy to the south.

"Then, slowly at first, the new suburbanites (from San Francisco, 30 miles north) began pushing down," wrote William H.

Whyte, Jr. in *The Exploding Metropolis,* "and as the easy-to-develop sites in San Mateo County to the northwest were filled up, speculative builders began moving in on the valley floor. The pickings were excellent, the orchards had to be cut down, but the flat land was easy to bulldoze, and the farmers, dazzled by the prices offered—$3,000 to $4,000 an acre then—began selling off parcels quite readily.

"The builders had no stringent zoning rules to contend with in the farm areas, and while FHA loan requirements made them follow tight specifications for the houses themselves, they were not required to provide for park areas or school sites. And most didn't. For services, the developments looked to the nearest incorporated town, and with what to the farmers seemed infamous vigor, the towns began 'strip-annexing' down county roads so that they could take in the subdivisions, send out the sewer lines, and, presumably, draw back a good tax return.

"Retribution came fast. To their dismay, the farmers found that the tax assessor was raising the value of their land. The millage was going up too; the new families were mostly young people with lots of children to educate and not much money to do it with. Because of the checkered pattern of development, the land that remained was becoming more difficult to farm effectively. Much of the natural ground cover had been replaced by the roofs and pavements of the intervening subdivisions, and the storm runoff spilled onto the farmland. Worse yet, the suburbanites felt *they* were the injured parties; they didn't like to be wakened by tractors early in the morning, and they objected vigorously to the use of sprays and smudge pots. Meanwhile, the water table of the valley was going down.

"And the place looked like hell."

Whyte made his observations in 1957, and *The Exploding Metropolis* was published in 1958. It created a stir in public planning circles and even in some government committees. But the rape of the valley continued almost unabated, digesting an estimated 5,000 acres of orchard and open space a year, while Metro San Jose became even more politically convoluted. Picking up on Whyte's observations, Jack B. Fraser, a former reporter for *The San Jose Mercury and News,* made the following telling comments in an article 12 years later in the magazine *City:*

"Today, living in San Jose and the 14 other cities of the Santa Clara Valley offers a version of the rat race seemingly highly desirable to many persons, but crammed with postponed crisis.

Water, ribbons of highway concrete (perhaps $500 million worth), and capital have been imported at a dizzying pace to serve population and industrial spillover from San Francisco and Oakland. Growth has been greatly magnified by the valley's concentration of electronics, aerospace, and research industries, and incomes and expectations for most have spiraled.

"Miles of car lots, discount department stores, franchised takeout parlors line former rural roads, and signs blare the latest subdivisions. Gone is the Alameda of fine mansions, San Jose's Victorian city hall with its endless steps, the first state capitol, many of the vestiges of the past, the links of colors and sentiment that help build civic awareness.

"Driving through this remarkable valley it is impossible to gain a sense of place. Cities run together. . . . A stupefying phalanx of some 250 separate taxing, police, school and service districts confront the residents. At election time, city hall switchboards are swamped with persons trying to find out where they live so they can vote. The city of San Jose is conurbated in such fashion that one can drive in and out of it almost endlessly although headed in one direction. . . ."

The suburban sprawl that is politically defined as the "city" of San Jose lies like a crazy patchwork of 135 square miles and some 500,000 residents in the heart of the Santa Clara Valley, having grown like Topsy since 1950 when it was a sleepy county seat of 17 square miles and 95,000 residents. Since Whyte and Fraser made their observations, San Jose has tried to revitalize its center and give the sprawl a focal point, but at best the effort has only checked the deterioration of the "downtown."

The haphazard growth of the region continues, with each taxing district in desperate competition for the ratables generated by each new industrial and commercial development. Planning is a secondary consideration, left to the numerous citizens' committees and consultants trying to establish some sort of regional priorities to guide the valley communities. Each time there seems to be an agreement, some developer comes along with a "sweetened" proposal and plays the 15 valley municipalities off against each other to get zoning concessions, supposedly bringing the "winner" a tax boost. (See Chapter 13, Taxes, Schools, and Taxes.)

"The speculators and developers have raped a beautiful valley in 30 years and it will take 50 to put it back together," said Alden Campen, one of the valley's more outspoken citizens. Other citizens active in planning efforts think Campen is an optimist. The repeated frustrations have taken their toll. Alienation and anomie have set in.

In a survey by the Center for the Study of Responsive Law, it was found that only 60 percent of the eligible voters of Santa Clara County were registered and that only 20 percent of those registered voted in local elections. The same survey further disclosed that most of those few who voted were ignorant of the local government structure. Only 12 percent knew the county had a Board of Supervisors; only 26 percent knew the form of government the city had and the name of one of the elected officials, and only 5 percent could name their school district and at least one school official.

The Balkanized suburbanization of the Santa Clara Valley is a particularly sharp and ominous example, but its pattern is not an exception among the nation's 230 metropolitan areas. In almost every area there is a continuing battle going on to establish regional goals to guide the present haphazard growth, but local governments have balked for both political and economic reasons. The federal government entered the conflict in the sixties by recognizing metropolitan agencies or councils as a conduit for applications by local governments for various federal financial assistance. However, the agencies have few real powers, particularly zoning, and most of them have been content to act at best as advisory bodies. Their reports and recommendations continue to pile up in the town halls, while in the back rooms of the halls the real decisions on land use are being made. (The few exceptions, notably the Metropolitan Council of the Twin Cities of Minneapolis and St. Paul, are discussed in Chapter 13, along with the economic rationale for resistance.)

As noted by the Task Force on Land Use and Urban Growth in its report, *The Use of Land,* standing in the way of reform is "a long American tradition of localism in land-use control, dating at least to the issuance of the Standard State Zoning Enabling Act of 1924, an act which most states copied and which viewed land-use controls as a matter of local rather than state control." The act was the spur to the formation of the thousands of local governments now dominating and dividing metropolitan America. The accepted number for the New York region is 1,467 (from which was taken the title of the book *1400 Governments,* a study of the area's political economy by Robert C. Wood). Chicago's metropolitan area has 1,113 local governments. The maze that is the Philadelphia region covers parts of 3 states and includes 9 counties, 10 cities, 132 boroughs, and 190 townships. The list continues and so do the problems of land use, while in most communities an apathetic majority bears silent witness to the havoc.

Land use, of course, was the heart of the matter that the dozen volunteer members of the Port Washington Citizens Advisory Committee on the Master Plan were supposed to be concerning themselves with in the fall of 1968. Returning to the next meeting of the committee in October, I raised the question of whether the consultants could include the incorporated villages on the peninsula into the plan.

"Port Washington is a jigsaw," I said. "Until we have all the pieces before us, I don't see how we can have a true picture of the peninsula for us to base our review on. In its present form, the plan is like a plan of a house that leaves out the center hallway, a couple of bedrooms, a bathroom, and the kitchen."

"The incorporated villages are not part of our contract," replied the professional planner hired by the town.

"But how could you as a planner, acting in good conscience, draw up a plan with such obvious holes in it? It doesn't make sense."

"The incorporated villages are not part of our contract," repeated the planner.

"But at least you might have gathered some relevant data about the villages, as that data might affect the plan, without having to submit a specific plan for the villages," I argued. "For instance, how many building lots are in the villages, and if they were developed what would be the impact on the unincorporated areas, the schools, the traffic, the water supply?"

Silence. A faint blush passed over the face of the planner. He was embarrassed. And surprisingly, so were most of the dozen other members of the committee. As I was to learn, I had broken the golden rule of suburbia—amiability.

As related to me later by Mrs. Freund and Mrs. Edward Porco, another member, until my arrival the committee had been a pleasant monthly gathering of representatives of various local organizations to hear a monologue by the planner. No one had challenged the findings in the draft report or the methodology of the consultant, but instead dutifully took notes to report back supposedly to their organizations. My peppering of the planner with questions had introduced a disturbing tone to the proceedings. In suburbia it seems one attempts to be amiable at all costs, including integrity and honesty. The very worst thing one can do in a social situation, and those meetings of volunteers, as most meetings, were indeed social, is to embarrass someone. Whether the planner, or the chairman, or another member, might be misleading the group, or irrelevant, or even lying, was secondary to maintaining a pleasant ambiance to the gathering.

By accepting the invitation to the committee I had put my foot in the door. It now appeared after my second meeting I had put my foot in my mouth. I was to be viewed with suspicion by the committee and those on it reporting back to a cautious, concerned town board. As it turned out, they had every reason to be suspicious.

4

Planning and Politics

The monthly meetings of the Port Washington Citizens Advisory Committee on the Master Plan became even more embarrassing through the winter of 1968 and in the spring of 1969. I had concluded that since the committee really did not want to get up on its hind legs and bray about the obvious deficiencies of the plan, I might as well try to expose the planning consultant as inadequate to the task. I continued to press the consultant for more data and to question the few recommendations in the plan. I was aided and abetted by Mrs. Freund and Mrs. Porco, both representing the local chapter of the League of Women Voters, who had picked up the adversary spirit quickly after recognizing that the prior meetings had been a charade. However, the balance of the committee began to quake, though of course maintaining a pleasant ambiance.

To my advantage, I had witnessed and participated in the past in similar conflicts; as an active and minority member of the East Harlem Planning Board for four years, as a sympathetic reporter covering the tactics and battles of Jane Jacobs in Greenwich Village in New York City and Saul Alinsky in upstate New York, among others, and while representing the State of New Jersey as its development consultant in various town, city, and county planning efforts. I was well-versed in the semantics of studies, allowing me to challenge the plan and its planners with confidence. Pricked, the consultant planning firm rose to the occasion and substituted for its smooth, controlled, and experienced representative a young, confused assistant, who compounded the problems of presentation of the plan by being a severe stutterer. Attendance fell and the committee floundered, just as I suspect the planning consultants and the town fathers had hoped it would.

The League contingent and I remained undaunted. It had been the Port Washington Chapter of the League in 1959 that had urged the town to initiate a master plan. The League had published that year what can best be described as a "white paper" on local land-use abuses. Its title, *Patchwork or Paradise: A Call to Action,* set the urgent tone. "This is an appeal to all residents of the Port Washington and Manhasset communities who are concerned with the drastic, continuing changes in our suburban area, and who hope to preserve our pattern of living," the League declared. "Year by year the contrast with urban conditions becomes less apparent—evidence that our present methods of planning and zoning are obsolete and ineffectual. . . . Now is the time for action! Tomorrow may be too late!"

The town, however, was in no hurry, for with no master plan, no town planning board and not one planner on the staff, the shape of the town during the boom building years of the fifties was directed by the political whims of the town board and the town's Board of Zoning and Appeals. The boards were very much closed corporations, working closely with the vested interests of the town and county's Republican organization. (There had been no Democrats on the board since 1917.) The word was that if you were a speculator or a builder and needed a zoning change for a subdivision or some land abuse, you just hired at a healthy fee a local Republican lawyer. A campaign contribution would also be welcomed, whether there was a campaign or not. The result was that the town was very much a patchwork of zoning variances and uncoordinated and unfocused growth, typical of what was happening in suburban areas across the country.

The League's *Call For Action* was at the time very much a lone voice, for these were the years, the fifties and early sixties, when almost everyone viewed growth as good. Ecology was still a word that most persons had to look up in the dictionary. Discussions and debates over such concepts as "planned unit development," "cluster housing," "open space bonuses," "scenic easements," and "landmarks preservation" were limited to the monthly, seasonal, annual, and perennial workshops, clinics, conferences, and seminars of good-government study groups, foundations, academia, and similar tax exempt and generally powerless institutions—at least powerless when confronted by the backroom politics of local town and zoning boards.

Most of the time the boards easily put down good-government group efforts in support of rational land use by joining with special interests and waving a red flag. Master planning smacked of "socialism," and the reputations of some well-intentioned residents were smeared at local hearings by thinly veiled red-baiting. The motto of America's suburbs was well stated in the inscription on a wall of the meeting hall of the County Supervisors of Los Angeles: "THIS COUNTY IS FOUNDED ON FREE ENTERPRISE. CHERISH AND PRESERVE IT." As the various land scandals in suburbia have taught us, the motive of many of the public officials was not patriotism, but greed.

The dollar value of land is nothing except what use you can put it to. An acre of land for farming purposes might be worth, depending on one's crop, $500 to $1,000. If you could put one house on the acre its worth can be increased to, say, $10,000. If you can put two houses on it, the value could be $18,000. But if there is a market for a high-density use and the land is zoned appropriately, its value could be increased to $100,000 an acre. The power to zone therefore is the power to make money.

Almost every suburban community has its story of some person or persons in public office joining with, or aiding, special interests and speculators to make a killing, or some local real estate operator or builder who always just seems to know ahead of everybody else where the new Interstate Highway is going and where the exit will be. The farmer who sold the land to the operator or builder a month or so before the public announcement of the exit certainly did not know. It is therefore not a coincidence that the operator or builder always is ready to take a golden page or two in the local political journal or a table or two at $100 a seat at the perennial political banquet, or allow the incumbent office holders to put up signs on his property during election time. That the official is a silent partner or has his brother or brother-in-law in the law firm representing the operator or builder also is not a coincidence. And just who does handle the insurance in the townships?

The web of nefarious relationships is unfortunately endemic to politics, as illustrated by the Watergate, ITT, milk and wheat scandals, among others, of the Nixon administration. But before joining that infamous administration, many members of it cut their teeth in local politics: John Ehrlichman as a zoning lawyer in the suburbs of Seattle; Spiro Agnew as a County Executive in Maryland; and John Mitchell as a New York bond lawyer serving a host of special districts and counties in suburbia. The problem on the local level is that these webs generally have been hidden by the confused state of suburban government. For many years the few residents aware of the questionable relationships of their local officials and the workings of local government in suburbia accepted the status quo with a shrug or, worse, with a wink. Only occasionally, and with great effort, were the webs exposed and government reformed, at least for a time. As we shall explore in later chapters, there has been a growing awareness recently in the public, prompted by what can best be described in many cases as a territorial imperative—the protection of their property and the status quo that they think insures it.

However, this awareness of land use, for whatever reason—altruistic, environmental, economic, social and racial prejudice, aesthetic—has come too late for many communities that have been shaped and misshaped by the greed of special interests working in most instances with local politicians. What happened in Santa Clara County in California already has been described, but a more depressing example is Los Angeles County, considered by many the epitome of suburban sprawl.

The county itself is an amorphous mass of, at last count, 77 "cities," including the City of Los Angeles, and numerous unincorporated areas that seem to be held together by a mesh of crowded freeways. The "cities," suburbs, communities, neighborhoods, areas—call them what you will—are, to be sure, diverse. They range from "downtown" high-density residential developments in the city itself, to 5-acre zoning way out in the San Fernando Valley to the east and Rolling Hills to the west. There are sparsely settled mountain communities such as Rustic Canyon and highly developed mountain communities such as Mandeville Canyon. There are retirement "cities" and there are strictly industrial "cities." But while there are attractive, if not exclusive, comfortable communities with distinct identities preserved through careful zoning, such as Bel Air, Fremont Place, Hollywood Hills, and Holmby Hills, the growth of the county has been chaotic.

Driving off the freeways and onto the secondary roads through various communities a depressing scene unfolds of strip commercial zoning—gas stations, taco stands, discount stores, used car lots—cutting into residential areas. A gas station next to a single-family home. An industrial complex backing up to a tract development and a school. Backyards pushing up against a freeway. It is sprawl, unfocused and unplanned. The communities, if that is what they are, have grown formlessly, allowing blight and decay to set in. Not only is the air of Los Angeles County polluted, the irritating yellow smog from the freeways shrouding the autopolis, but so is the landscape.

It was not always so. When my wife's grandmother, Lillian McKay Paxton, "came over the mountains" from Oklahoma into the San Fernando Valley in the northern area of the Los Angeles basin in 1918, it "was like a garden." The Paxtons built a house in a grove of eucalyptus trees next to a grape orchard on the western slope of the Verdugo Mountains, and then over the years watched with sadness as the speculators sliced up the farms into tract developments laid out on an unimaginative grid pattern planned by compliant local politicians. Down went the eucalyptus trees and grape arbors and up went row upon row of neat stucco houses that is Glendale today. Now 85 years old, "Grandma the Great," as she is called by my children, sits in a rocking chair on her porch—believed to be the only front porch left in the valley —and wonders why "they" just could not have curved the road here and there and left a few of the trees in front of her homestead and the little hills and dales that made the area so charming. Because "they" could not have squeezed the last buildable square foot out of the land, Sam the planner tells her.

Grandmother Paxton's perspective of "they" is a limited one. "They" were first the politicians—to be specific, the mayor—who tried to buy her house in the twenties before the speculators moved in. The mayor's persistent efforts made her suspicious that "they" knew what plans the speculators had for that section of the valley and what values the property would have after "they" re-zoned it for the speculators. Then "they" were the builders themselves, following on the heels of the politicians and speculators and bidding on the homesteads being auctioned off in the thirties for nonpayment of taxes raised in reassessments by the politicians for "improvements." "They" also were the banks foreclosing the mortgages—and then turning around and offering new mortgages on the land to the builders. She survived because of her resolve not to be pressured by "they," and the little frame farmhouse remains today, a quaint landmark of sorts tucked into a monotonous subdivision.

We were offered a more dramatic glimpse of "they" manipulating land in the Los Angeles basin in the movie "Chinatown." The time frame was the thirties, when the value of land was contingent upon the availability of water. How the land was acquired

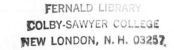

and how the water would be brought to it (by incorporating the area in a water district) was a strong subplot to a chilling detective story of murder, incest, and political corruption. In the fifties and sixties the value of land in the county was contingent upon the freeways. And how the routes of the freeways were selected and how the land was used and abused by an alliance of politicians and special interests explains in large part the chaotic sprawl that is Los Angeles today, and perhaps other suburbs tomorrow.

This nefarious alliance and what it did in one section of Los Angeles County, the San Gabriel Valley, was documented in a piercing study entitled *Backroom Politics*, by Bill and Nancy Boyarsky, which painted a depressing picture of the sprawl in the valley stretching along the San Bernardino Freeway. "All development in the Valley went on as if land and air were something that could be wasted," they observed. "It is an inhospitable, inhuman formless place—without character, identity, or beauty."

Focusing in on one large development in the valley, called Diamond Bar, the Boyarskys traced its history from 1840 when it was a cattle and sheep grazing range called Rancho Los Nogales, through its purchase in 1943 by William Bartholomae for $850,000, his sale in 1956 to the Transamerica Corporation for $10 million, to its development as a "model community" by the corporation in the sixties. They noted that the development of Diamond Bar was based on a zoning plan drawn up by the corporation and approved by the County Board of Supervisors. And they added that Transamerica over the years continued to initiate zoning changes to meet its own economic objectives, with little concern for their aesthetic and environmental consequences, to say nothing of the corporation's original promises to the homeowners who had settled in the "model community." The changes were not minor. Instead of building single-family homes, as Transamerica had first planned in its initial zoning application, it now wanted to construct high-rise apartments and a commercial complex. This would have the effect not only of completely changing the low-rise residential nature of the community, but would also reap for Transamerica a much greater profit. Despite some local protests, Transamerica was able to obtain the needed changes thanks to its friends on the Regional Planning Commission and County Board of Supervisors, principally its late supervisor, Frank Bonelli.

Why Supervisor Bonelli looked so favorably on Transamerica's zoning applications, ignoring local protests and rational planning principles, is explained by the Boyarskys in their investigation of Bonelli's campaign records. They had a difficult time combing the records, because they are kept only four years after an official's term of office has expired. In addition, campaign laws in the late sixties and early seventies were looser, and it took the Boyarskys much reading between the lines to get a clear picture. Nevertheless, the records did show that the general manager of the Transamerica subsidiary developing Diamond Bar was a campaign contributor. In addition, the records raised other questions. The Boyarskys found that in 1966, after an easy reelection campaign, Bonelli's "slush" fund was left with a $24,131.55 balance. Four years later the fund had a balance of $95,000, with no record where the extra $70,000 came from. The Boyarskys concluded that "it is reasonable to presume that Transamerica gave him some of it, along with the usual list of supporters—the land developers, contractors and real estate firms in his district."

To add a footnote, when Bonelli died in the early seventies he left an estate of more than $1 million, though his public salary had never been more than $35,000 a year. Part of the inheritance was $118,405.25 from his political "slush" fund, which he described in his will as "gifts to me." "His personal fortune and how he got it are unimportant," contend the Boyarskys. "His real legacy was the condition in which he left the San Gabriel Valley."

The condition of the San Gabriel Valley, sprawling and ugly, might be an extreme example of the results of special interest domination in suburbia, the mixing of planning and politics, but it is not an exception. Usually the abuses are not so blatant as the rezonings of Diamond Bar, just little spot rezonings here and there that nibble away at the character and fabric of communities, like what happened in Wayne, New Jersey, a town 20 miles west of New York City. With the population of the township increasing from 12,000 in 1950 to 49,000 in 1970, farmland and rambling neighborhoods gave way to tract residential developments and shopping centers. To be sure, growth was considered natural and was welcomed. The problem in Wayne, as in other suburban communities, was that the growth was unplanned, dictated by greed, and not by any rational land-use principles that attempt to integrate growth into the existing community character and environment. With the value of an acre of land in Wayne rising from $700 in 1950 to as much as $90,000 by the early seventies, little thought was given to planning, and much to profit.

According to Harry J. Butler, a former mayor of Wayne, the real profits were not made by the farmers who originally owned the land, but by "the land speculators and real estate operators." Butler, a Democrat, spent most of his time in office, according to *The New York Times*, denouncing the profitable relationship between politics, land speculation, and zoning. Most of the persons he accused were Republicans. One case Butler cited as an example of the relationship he felt was destroying the township involved three municipal officials who passed upon the rezoning of 2 residential acres to allow the construction of a private medical center. It was estimated that the rezoning increased the value of the acreage by $80,000. It was Butler's contention that without a zoning variance the same medical center could have been built in a "business-professional" zone only 1,000 feet down the same road without the need for a zoning variance. If that was done the residential zone in which the 2 acres were located would not have been compromised or invaded and, of course, there would not have been an $80,000 rezoning windfall. According to Butler, the three municipal officials turned out to be the principals of the corporation owning the land.

Similar conflicts of interest and windfalls have occurred all too often on Long Island, particularly in Suffolk County where vast areas have undergone rapid change from open land to residential, commercial, and industrial development. One such area was the Town of Islip, a 102-square-mile municipality on the Island's South Shore. The town has grown from a population of 60,000 in 1946 to more than 300,000 by 1976, with most of the growth occurring in the boom years of the sixties. It was during these years that the Long Island newspaper, *Newsday,* revealed in a stunning series of articles that five men who held official positions with the town or the local Republican party stood to make about $5 million as a result of land and zoning deals in Islip.

The manipulations of the men, and many of their friends, were made through a score of dummy corporations, or corporations in which they or their wives held hidden interests. The business, personal, and political relationships were tied in a Gordian knot, of which the only consistent strand was one that led before the town board for zoning changes, condemnations, road widenings, and a variety of other governmental actions that ultimately meant substantial profit to the landowners. *Newsday's* unraveling of the knot brought it a well-deserved Pulitzer Prize.

The deals uncovered were many and complex, but typical was

the story of how Donald J. Kuss, as an Islip Town Councilman and town consultant in charge of the development of a local public airport, MacArthur, parlayed an initial zero cash investment into a personal fortune of nearly $1 million in real estate holdings and "fees." He accomplished most of this by having his partners in land speculation put up the money, while all he put up were promissory notes, on which he never paid interest. But as *Newsday* reported, Kuss was helpful in other ways to his coinvestors.

It all started for Kuss, a former tree surgeon, with a hidden interest in a piece of land that was downzoned for a gas station by the Islip Town Board, of which Kuss was a member. It was clear in *Newsday's* story at the time that Kuss was made a partner, for no cash consideration, so the corporation could get the downzoning. This was a windfall in itself, for the land was on the major roadway leading into MacArthur Airport, whose expansion plans were known to Kuss. But Kuss sweetened the deal by voting at the same town board meeting to approve a moratorium on all future gas station downzonings on the roadway, thus making his rezoned property even more valuable. With this advantage in hand, Kuss's partners were able to conclude a very favorable lease of the property to an oil company. Now using the oil company lease as collateral, Kuss and his partners purchased for $75,000, 15 acres of land at the main entrance to the airport. His partners then put up the needed cash to go with a mortgage to build on the land a glistening 4-story office building, worth about $1.5 million. Kuss's share was the usual 25 percent.

As the office building was going up, Kuss, meanwhile, was hard at work for the town channeling federal, state and town funds into and around the airport, to add and extend runways, improve the terminal facilities and to build highways. Kuss was successful, attracting Allegheny and Mohawk Airlines to provide service at the field, and making MacArthur the ninth busiest general airport in the nation, which of course increased the value of his secret holdings.

Kuss also was successful in other ventures, joining with his partners again to purchase 35 more acres for $157,000, right outside the airport. And again he made no cash investment for his 25 percent share, according to *Newsday.* But he did help the corporation, this time by introducing resolutions as a member of the Islip Town Board to get the town to install fire hydrants and water mains along various stretches of the property—as part of the MacArthur Airport Fire Defense System. Thus, he and his partners would not have the expense of building water mains to bring water to the property. With the improvements and with the airport continuing to expand, it was estimated that the value of the land doubled within a few years, which would put Kuss's profit at at least $75,000.

Kuss also was busy elsewhere in the town, buying and selling. *Newsday* reported that Kuss had another 10-acre parcel of land that he sold to one of Suffolk's largest home builders at $50,000 more than the going price for surrounding land. The paper added that the sale came just one month after Kuss had pushed a zoning change for the builder through the town board. In another deal cited by the paper, Kuss, in a hidden partnership with an Islip lawyer, bought a large tract of land with a total investment of $2,400, and then sold it 16 months later at a $99,000 profit to another Long Island builder who occasionally had zoning changes before the town board.

Newsday also noted that Kuss, while a member of the town board, operated a large mortgage placement firm, masked by a corporate name, getting as high as 1 percent on all mortgages that he placed with banks. Many of the mortgages he placed came from builders doing business in the Town of Islip, and subject to its rules and decisions. In addition, Kuss had a variety of other questionable business relationships with other Islip officials, Republican party members, party contributors and even with the paper's former Suffolk Editor. It was *Newsday* itself that disclosed that the editor, the late Kirk Price, and his wife, Margo, a real estate broker, had made a profit of $33,000 on a cash investment of $50 in a sale of a parcel of land involving a syndicate of which Kuss was a secret member. *Newsday* said that Price knew Kuss was a partner in the syndicate, but that Price never informed the paper's management of his dealings. Price died two months before the paper started its investigation.

As *Newsday* noted in its articles, throughout his tenure as town councilman, and later as town airport consultant, Kuss was being paid by the town to plan and promote the airport and to encourage industry to develop the land around it. In an interview, Kuss said he did not think that there was any violation of ethics in taking money from the town to plan and promote the development of land in which he had a private financial interest. He said that he had not publicly disclosed his interest in the land around the airport "because some people might draw the wrong connotations."

"I concede that this may be a gray area," he added. "But I would do the same thing again. I put far more time and effort into MacArthur than most Councilmen have put into their jobs. The success of MacArthur proves this. Should I be precluded from the investment possibilities of the ordinary citizen?"

The question was answered by the town board, which fired him as its $15,000 a year airport consultant, and by a grand jury, which indicted him on a charge of bribery. Kuss was later convicted and sentenced to one year in the Suffolk County Jail. The other town and party officials exposed by *Newsday* also were disgraced, by firings and indictments, but the corruption in Suffolk County continued, just as it is continuing in various forms in other counties across the country.

Because corruption in suburbia has been so prevalent and pernicious, especially to the political process, we shall examine it further in the later chapters on politics. We also shall cite other examples, where appropriate, for the mixture of planning and politics is such a pervasive motive in suburbia that it is part of almost every action. Land and its control remain both the major battle and battleground in suburbia, with corruption and resulting scandals considered another method of warfare of special and vested interests. The public in many cases is just the innocent bystander—and usually the ultimate victim.

There was no land scandal, at least none that the public knew about, when the Port Washington Chapter of the League of Women Voters was pressing the Town of North Hempstead for a master plan in the early sixties, and therefore there was no real public outcry for rational land use as defined by a plan instead of politics. It just was not an issue then that people could get excited about, as they do in these times of environmental and, for some, racial and socioeconomic concerns. The town therefore continued to ignore the pleas of the League, until 1966, when it applied to the Federal Department of Housing and Urban Development for a grant to initiate an urban renewal program. To be sure, the program the town had in mind was a modest and typical one: to clean up a pocket of deteriorated stores and homes in an unincorporated area of the community of Roslyn. The area, known as Roslyn Heights, not only was unsightly and threatening neighboring land values, but it also housed many of the community's blacks, the domestics and dishwashers, among others, providing cheap and convenient labor for the stores and services in the town, as they had for generations. (Despite protestations by the town to the contrary, it seemed to me when I later reviewed a copy of the Urban Renewal Plan that it was a typical "Negro Removal Project," bulldozing the few houses, albeit deteriorated, available to the blacks at modest rentals in the area with promise in the vague future of new subsidized housing. A sensitive rehabilitation program and some new modest housing could have done the job, without major relocation and demolition.)

The urban renewal program was viewed correctly by the town as an opportunity for it to fatten its bureaucracy and patronage with federal dollars, while eliminating some physical blight and some blacks. It seemed like a surefire program, certain to please the clubhouse interests as well as friendly contractors. However, to qualify for the federal urban renewal funds, the town had to file something known as the Workable Program for Community Improvement, which in turn required the town to have or be preparing a master plan. So seven years after the League's *Call For Action,* the town finally responded—out of necessity. It awarded a contract to the firm of Community Housing and Planning Associates to draft a town plan, for which the board was roundly praised in the local press as responsible and far-sighted.

To the dismay of the League, however, the firm soon had fallen behind in its contracted schedule to produce the plan. It was apparent to Mrs. Freund, Mrs. Porco, and me that the firm was marching to a very deliberate beat of the drum of the town board. We urged the League to once again apply pressure on the town. Picking up our recommendations for a more thorough review, the Port Chapter appealed to the Town Supervisor, Robert C. Meade, for the convening of a town-wide Committee on the Plan representing all the communities. We wanted to accelerate the plan review process by bringing together representatives of the various committees that were presently each reviewing the plan in their respective communities. We were worried that the plan review process being conducted by the consultants was probably further frustrating and fractionalizing the town. If there were a few other live bodies kicking in the other communities, we wanted to know them, and hoped that maybe together we could better review the plan, try to get some satisfaction out of the consultant and, finally, prompt the town to act.

The Supervisor, an amiable lawyer, agreed, for good and expedient reasons. There was the fear within the town board that the League might complain to the Federal Department of Housing and Urban Development that the town was stalling on the plan promised in its Workable Program, thus prompting the department to withhold funds that were fattening the town payroll. In addition, it was an election year for the town board, and the master plan was becoming an issue. Meade could now defer the issue with a statement that the plan was above politics and under review by a bipartisan citizens committee.

Out of the 20 citizens eventually selected by Meade for the committee, Port Washington wangled 5, far in excess of its proportional share (15 percent) of the town's population. Port Washington, it seems, was making the most noise. Those appointed from Port were Mrs. Freund, who was the wife of a prominent surgeon and the daughter of a long-time Republican who served as commissioner of parks in Great Neck; Mrs. Porco, who was an aide to a local Republican benefactor and the wife of one of the leaders of the Port Washington Republican Club; Mrs. Dorothy Donovan, a venerable Sands Point resident and wife of Hedley Donovan, a close associate of Henry Luce at Time, Inc.; Mrs. Roberta Glassman, a stalwart in the League of Women Voters and also a Republican; and myself.

I had not expected to be appointed, for in addition to having served with some notoriety on the Port Washington Committee, I had unfortunately rung some wrong doorbells on behalf of the national and state Democratic slates in the last (1968) election. Being a recent resident and, of all things, a Democrat in a community that was almost two-to-one Republican was like hanging a bell around one's neck. My doorbell pushing and stamp licking during two weeks in the fall gave me a deeper coloration as a "liberal" and the recognition of a weak, somewhat insipid local Democratic organization, which appointed me a county committeeman. When in the spring I was proposed to the town board by the League to serve on the Citizens Advisory Committee, it was politely suggested that I resign as a Democratic committeeman, though they were kind enough to say that I could at least remain a registered Democrat. Weighing how I could best serve my new community, I did not hesitate to submit my resignation to the party.

5
Home Rule and Other Hoaxes

During the lull between the disbanding of the Port Washington Citizens Advisory Committee on the Master Plan and the convening of the newly appointed members of the Town Advisory Committee, I wandered out of curiosity into the monthly meeting of the Trustees of the Village of Baxter Estates, the incorporated village whose name was taken from the Baxter Homestead, which we now owned and were attempting to restore. The village for the most part was a pleasant, hilly enclave of approximately 250 homes on about half a square mile, through which ran a brook that fed a pond serving wild ducks in the spring, summer and fall, and ice skaters in the winter. The village was run very much like a club by five trustees, most of whom lived in the more expensive homes tucked away on the curving streets winding their way up the hills. Our house was at the foot of the hills, next to the duck pond and a heavily traveled county highway, Shore Road, on the edge of the village facing Manhasset Bay. The traffic and the more modest homes there made it a less desirable neighborhood.

In keeping with the tone of the village, the trustees were cordial enough when I made my appearance at the village hall, a meeting room attached to a small, nondescript one-story brick bank on Shore Road, two blocks north of our house. The trustees met on the first Tuesday of each month, before an audience of usually just two or three residents. That night there were eight persons, presumably residents, sitting in folding chairs, in addition to the five trustees, the village attorney, clerk, and secretary, who sat around a table in front of the hall. All was pleasant and routine (the reading into the record of resident complaints of unleashed dogs, a proposal by someone to build a swimming pool in his backyard), until a person in the audience, who identified himself as a traffic engineer for the county, rose to present perfunctorily, to my surprise, a proposal to straighten and widen Shore Road.

Highways are the honey pots of public works. With various federal and state funds subsidizing up to 90 percent of the total bill, local governments with a nod to local contractors are perpetually dispatching highway engineers to survey road conditions and take traffic counts. Budget battles over such public facilities as schools, libraries, community centers, recreation facilities, and parks may rage endlessly, as local governments debate proposals, but there is usually no hesitation to spend the same, if not more, public moneys on roads, albeit out of a different pot of funds.

The proposal for the four-lane Shore Road was just one part of a general plan by the county to "upgrade" roadways in the area, and a relatively modest one. It called for the addition of a few feet and a new curb to the west, away from our house on the east, cutting into the Baxter Estates' "beach" fronting on the polluted Manhasset Bay. A few feet would also be taken from a vacant piece of land owned by the Port Washington Sewer District to the south. The plan would eliminate a curve in front of our house and allow an extra south lane for cars to make a left turn into Central Drive, in effect creating at that point a five-lane highway. The curve and the present awkward left turn were cited as causes of various accidents in the past, according to the traffic engineer in his dry presentation to a nodding Board of Trustees.

The proposal seemed reasonable, but I questioned whether widening the road would encourage speeding, as it usually does, and just result in more serious accidents. Neither the trustees, nor the engineer thought so, adding to ease my apprehension that the widening would have the effect of moving the "active" traffic a few feet further from my property. I thanked them for the gesture, but suggested that perhaps they also consider moving the curb further away from my property to create a wider sidewalk for pedestrians. This was rejected.

"Who walks there anyway?" asked a trustee. Before I could comment that my family and others do, he answered his own question. "Everybody drives."

"If we cleaned up and improved the beach and put a few benches there, maybe we could create something that could attract pedestrians," I commented.

The trustees ignored my remark, approved the plan, and moved on to a discussion of a proposed parking lot on the west side of Shore Road, diagonally south across from our house. Just as in the plan for the road widening, it was the first I had heard of the proposal. It seemed that some of the merchants on lower Main Street, which Shore Road intersects two short blocks south of our house, had been complaining of a continuing drop in business, which they attributed to the difficulty customers had finding parking spaces. The only spaces available were curbside, so the merchants proposed that the vacant lot on Shore Road owned by the Sewer District be converted to a parking lot. The Sewer District had agreed, and now the matter was before the Baxter Estates Board of Trustees.

After hearing three persons in the audience, who identified themselves as merchants or owners of commercial property on lower Main Street, speak strongly in favor of the plan, the trustees seemed ready to vote their approval when one of the members asked me what I thought of the plan, since the lot would be diagonally across the street from my house. I answered that I sympathized with the problems of the merchants, but was not sure whether a parking lot in the proposed location would be the best solution.

"What do you suggest?" asked the trustee.

"Well, I just learned of the plan tonight," I replied, "and really would need some time to look it and the situation over before I made a suggestion, if any. If you would table the proposal this evening, I could get something to you at your next meeting, next month."

There was an audible groan from the merchants, which was ignored by the trustees. It was apparent that some of the trustees looked upon the merchants with a little disdain, for the merchants had pressed hard for the parking lot—and that was just not the way the trustees preferred to conduct the business of the village. They did not like pressure from anyone, but especially not from local businessmen who were not very high up the community social ladder.

"I don't see where one month will make a difference," said the trustee. Given the clubby ambi nce of the board, the others agreed in a consensus and the proposal was tabled. "We look forward to your report," said the mayor.

The problem now was to produce the report, and I immediately thought of enlisting the aid of a Mrs. Catherine Morrison, a part-time landscape architect whom I had met a couple of months earlier at a meeting of a few residents interested in forming a local committee to concern itself with a new issue—the environment. Mrs. Morrison, a pert, quick-witted woman in her mid-30s, was then recycling herself, attending graduate school for a master's degree in city planning. We had talked at length about the potential of the lower Main Street area, and I thought now was an opportunity for us to get a forum to air some ideas. She agreed to help.

After spending a few weekends walking around the lower Main Street area, we concluded that to use the proposed site for a parking lot would be a shame. Not only would it be difficult for drivers to get in and out of it without creating a real traffic hazard on Shore Road, it also seemed that the land, which fronted on a picturesque, albeit polluted, Manhasset Bay, could be put to better use. Waterfront property, we felt, was just too valuable to be wasted on parking alone. We thought that ideally it should be developed for some sort of housing, preferably for senior citizens, for which there was a definite need in town. Being near stores, public transportation and parks, the site was almost perfect. It also could help local businesses, by putting in the area 50 to 100 potential new customers, especially senior citizens who would probably prefer to shop in the immediate neighborhood. One of the stores hurting most (and later closed) was a drug store that adjoined the lot. A senior-citizens project would have been a boon to it.

Mrs. Morrison and I recognized, however, that to put together a reasonable proposal, especially for housing, would take time, which we did not have. In addition, a housing development, even one for senior citizens, was (is) one of the most emotional issues in suburbia (as we shall explore in later chapters), and before anyone would even suggest such a project, substantial support from all the "good-government" groups and religious institutions would have to be organized to withstand the usual violent reaction. We therefore decided to be politic, and hint in our report of a better, long-range use of the property, while in the interim it could be used as a temporary, small parking lot. We also proposed that a gas station and adjoining parking lot at the northeast corner of Shore and Main, which we understood was up for sale, be considered as a site for a permanent parking lot landscaped with some sitting areas. I wrote a report in typical planning prose, while Mrs. Morrison drafted an attractive plan for graphic display.

It was a vain attempt. The trustees, to be sure, were courteous, even amiable in keeping with the Golden Rule of Suburbia, but neither the report nor the plan impressed them. It was apparent that they had made up their minds beforehand, probably in the comfort and confidence of the living room of one of the members "on the hill," and now were just going through the motions of a hearing. There were a few questions, including a contentious one from a person in the audience raising the specter of "high-rise" housing as the "better, long-range use" hinted in our plan. That was enough for the trustees to issue a quick, polite "thank you," to Mrs. Morrison and myself, and approve without comment the parking lot as proposed by the merchants. As the trustees took up the next item on the agenda, Mrs. Morrison and I quietly collected the reports, rolled up the plans, and left.

It would be four years before I would again take an active role in an issue before the village trustees, and then, happily, before a more receptive board. I felt the board at the time was content, more or less, to concern itself with road conditions and garbage collection, while the larger issues of "planning" and "environment" were resolved on the town level. The village board was indeed parochial, protecting the prerogatives and the status quo, exercising home rule within the most limited definition.

While the Trustees of Baxter Estates plodded along reacting to the minor incursions into their domain, such as the road widening and the proposal for a parking lot, the Trustees of North Hills, another village in the Town of North Hempstead, were quietly taking another view of home rule, much to their personal advantage. What happened, and is happening, in North Hills puts into sharp focus some of the financial, environmental, and political implications of home rule as a planning vehicle of a privileged few.

A remnant of the "good old" Gold Coast days, the village lies about five miles south of the Port Washington peninsula, tucked behind the shopping centers of Northern Boulevard and stretching toward and along the Long Island Expressway and Northern State Parkway. It was very much a green sanctuary, enclosing 1,757 acres for 318 residents (the 1970 population) and 3 sprawling, exclusive country clubs. Zoning had been established for minimum 2-acre plots, but most of the houses and mansions were on much larger parcels. These included the estates of William S. Paley, Chairman of the Board of the Columbia Broadcasting System, Mrs. Joan Whitney Payson, owner of the New York Mets and the Greentree Stables, and J. Peter Grace, President of W. R. Grace and Co., the international conglomerate founded on the Grace Shipping Line fortune.

Other owners of estates in North Hills included Mrs. Payson's son-in-law, Vincent deRoulet, a former State Racing Commissioner and Ambassador to Jamaica, as well as a wealthy marketing and investment businessman; Henry M. Minton, the Chairman of Church & Dwight Co., makers of Arm and Hammer Baking Soda and Borax, a director of Home Life Insurance Co. and Allied Chemical & Dye Corp., and a trustee of the Williamsburgh Savings Bank; Joseph A. Martino, the former President and Board Chairman of the National Lead Company, and a board member of the Port of New York Authority; and Francis J. Sorg, head of Newsrad, Inc., a communication equipment manufacturing firm.

The village was incorporated in 1929, and since then run very much like a club by a five-member Board of Trustees. They convened many of their meetings by telephone, meeting irregularly at one another's homes, and even in the Manhattan offices of one of its members. The scheduling and siting of the meetings did not encourage, to say the least, other residents to attend, and certainly did not encourage any local newspapers to take an interest. In effect, the nearly 3 square miles of North Hills was a fiefdom of five privileged persons, protecting their personal interests under the guise of home rule, which supposedly is the foundation of participatory democracy. In the case of North Hills it was the foundation of greed.

Apparently prompted by public discussions of the Town of North Hempstead in 1966 concerning the need of a town master plan to qualify for federal urban renewal funds, as discussed in the last chapter, the village trustees quietly began debating among themselves the need for their own comprehensive master plan. The trustees at the time were deRoulet, who was mayor, Grace, Martino, Minton, and Sorg, all noted above. There was a fear among the trustees that the town might presumptuously undertake a plan that would include the villages, as was later recommended by me (and rejected by the town). So on September 16, 1966 Martino presented a resolution, seconded by Minton, that authorized a comprehensive land study. Nothing much was done in the town during the next two years but talk, and nothing much was done in the village. But when the town finally pressed the firm of Community Housing and Planning Associates to expedite its drafting of the master plan, the village acted, hiring the firm.

While the firm took its good time fulfilling its contract with the town, as we have noted, it dashed off in less than a year a plan for North Hills, calling for, among other things, the eradication of all 2-acre zoning. The trustees were reported pleased with the plan, but some residents were not, including the village planning board, which had not been consulted. Normally, this would not have deterred the trustees from acting, but one of the residents voicing opposition was William S. Paley, one of the largest land-owners in the village. As was his style, Paley hired his own planner, who worked with Community Housing and Planning Associates over the next nine months to come up with a new plan, incorporating, of course, Paley's suggestions. While Paley was able to have some input, the local planning board was still kept out in the cold, according to Norman Lau Kee, then a member.

"The trustees frankly were in this for personal gain," observed Kee years later. "They just wanted to make sure their piece of the pie was protected, and the fewer residents putting their finger into it the better. Mr. Paley, of course, was the exception, because he had clout. Even though he was not a trustee, he was a member of the 'club.' "

The new plan, made public in the spring of 1970, in effect called for the end of North Hills as a bastion for estates, recommending zoning changes to allow extensive and intensive residential, retail, and office development. Village Mayor deRoulet told *Newsday* when the plan was announced that he wished North Hills could remain the way it is, "but I don't think there's any way."

"North Hills was a marvelous sanctuary of gracious living," he said. "But things change: progress, the erosion of rural living, more people, more traffic, more service stations, more schools."

He and Village Attorney John Cleary declared that the rezoning was necessary because of "pressures" on the village, which included increasing school and county taxes, increasing traffic, and the increasing interest of real estate developers. They added that many of the property owners feared that their land would be condemned by the county or the state for recreation, roads, or even for subsidized housing projects. They noted that the Long Island State Park Commission had recently condemned land in the Grace family holdings and that of four other property owners for the widening of a section of the Northern State Parkway. With these "pressures" on the property owners, they decided to move first so the residents could at least profit from the "inevitable" intensified use of the land.

"What the trustees and the residents are saying," said Cleary, "is that 'We don't want to afford all this wide-open space—we don't want it enough any longer'; the others, the smaller land owners, say they can't afford such large lots and want to sell off. So you start to develop it to get out of it. . . . Within 10 or 15 years it will result in the loss of all these estates, and probably the golf and country clubs."

The plan was opposed by only a few residents, such as Mr. and Mrs. George Lewis, who lived in a converted carriage house right out of the pages of *Homes and Gardens.* "We're just crushed about this," Mrs. Lewis, a landscape artist, told *Newsday.* "I've lived on Long Island since I was 12 years old, and I've been looking for a place like this all my life." Asked whether the increased land value would ease her move, Mrs. Lewis replied: "The money isn't important. Money is only a means to an end, but we've found that end here."

Other residents also did not like the plan, but not because of what it would do to the village. They disliked it because the rezonings did not benefit them as much as it did the trustees themselves. "Almost everyone wanted a nicer piece of the pie," observed Kee. "They recognized that it really was hopeless to fight the trustees, so they just tried to angle for a better deal for themselves. Toward the end, almost everybody got on the bandwagon. It was a good deal."

Exactly how much the village residents and, especially, the trustees profited by the rezoning can only be estimated, but the estimates are spectacular. The plan called for the immediate rezoning of about 8 acres for garden apartments for up to 10 units per acre. The acreage at the time of the rezoning was owned by Trustee Minton and his wife, and had a value of about $200,000, according to county assessors. The rezoning pushed the value to about $1 million. Similar potential windfalls accrued to Mayor deRoulet and Trustees Martino and Grace, who also owned land that was to be rezoned—by themselves—from the existing 2-acre minimum residential lot for a single-family dwelling to multifamily units. In addition, Grace and his wife owned the bulk of the land proposed for the more lucrative commercial use, the rezoning of which would increase its value from an estimated $7 million to potentially as much as $70 million—a possible windfall profit of approximately one thousand percent.

"A bonanza," commented Horace Z. Kramer, who was then the Vice-Chairman of the Nassau County Board of Assessors. Kramer estimated that under the 2-acre zoning, land in North Hills was worth about $20,000 an acre. Zoned for multiple dwellings, the same land was worth between $120,000 and $200,000 per acre. Zoned commercially, he added, it was worth between $150,000 and $200,000 an acre.

Questions were raised whether the trustees might be in conflict of interest by approving a rezoning plan from which they would profit. The New York State Code of Ethics prohibits a village board member from voting on matters in which he or his family has an interest, though officials of the State Attorney General's Office said at the time that they did not know if the provisions covered a complete rezoning of a village. The trustees and the village attorney maintained that there was no conflict, noting that the village had no code of ethics covering the matter, as did the town and county. A suggestion that those trustees affected by the rezoning not vote on the matter was rejected by Trustee Sorg as "a ridiculous concept." He added that Trustee Grace, "as a person very much affected by rezoning . . . has a right to be involved in the decision-making process." The concept of home rule as exercised by the village trustees apparently was viewed as a private trust, rather than a public trust. The rezoning was approved.

In addition to the question of ethics, the plan also raised the problem of the effects of drastic zoning changes within the legal boundaries of a village upon the surrounding communities and the Town of North Hempstead. It was clear that with the rezoning of North Hills the ecology and character of the entire region would be affected. The population of North Hills now had the potential to increase from its present 318 to approximately 16,000, or more, with a tremendous effect on neighboring schools, roads, parks, the water table, and town services. The proposed retail and office districts would also generate a host of demands, especially on the road system.

A shudder went through the adjoining villages, which in turn pressed the town to take legal action against North Hills to reverse the rezoning. For four years the town battled the village in the courts, only to have the state Supreme Court rule in favor of the village's prerogative to zone as it pleases. That ruling was recently upheld (December 1974) in the Appellate Division of the State Supreme Court, where the town sought to prevent a developer, Rainer E. Gut, from building 23 townhouses on a 5.6-acre plot he owns in North Hills. Watching in the wings were two other developers, who already had received permission from the North Hills Village Board to construct a total of nearly 500 luxury condominium units, the construction of which would increase the population of North Hills eightfold. Other developers were expected to follow quickly in the wake of the court's decision. The transfiguration of North Hills has begun—all in the good name of home rule, and all at a good profit to its defenders.

Since the trustees held office as a public trust, and their decisions as trustees meant windfall profits, it would have seemed reasonable that those profits and others from rezonings should accrue to the public, not to the landowners and speculators, to be used to pay for the capital improvements and services needed to accommodate the new population to be generated by the rezonings in North Hills. This concept of a "public windfall" growing out of public decisions concerning zoning was one I later proposed to the town's Citizens Advisory Committee on the Master Plan and to the town Planning Board. (Though the concept was rejected, and my reputation as a fuzzy liberal strengthened, I still like the idea.)

I have followed the North Hills controversy over the years because it was just this situation—an independent village going its own way in a Balkanized town—over which I had expressed my concern when I first reviewed the draft of the town master plan in the earlier meetings of the Citizens Committee in Port Washington. I did not know at the time that the same consultant firm also was drafting the North Hills plan, nor did their representative volunteer that information. The first North Hills plan still had not been announced when Mrs. Freund, Mrs. Porco, Mrs. Glassman, and I began attending the restructured town committee in the spring of 1969, where I again suggested, among other things, the inclusion of the town's 31 villages in the plan.

Despite the attempts of the chairman of the committee, Gilbert Tilles, an engaging real estate developer from Great Neck, the meetings seemed to bog down. Requests for information or explanations for certain recommendations were noted by the consultant and the town's representative, but not answered. Various members of the committee quickly became frustrated, and attendance dropped. By the fall only about a dozen members at the most were attending the meetings regularly. Issues were being reviewed affecting communities whose representatives were not present. And I was becoming more and more agitated, especially in light of the proposed North Hills rezoning, of which we were finally informed.

Though the town in time took another position on home rule in the North Hills case, because of the consequences of the village's rezoning plan on surrounding communities, the theme voiced over and over again by the town's representative at the meetings was that home rule was inviolate, and that the villages be left alone. The town's representative, Donal Mahoney, a deputy supervisor, was certainly a pleasant participant, with a ready smile and some wit, but his complacent attitude to the consultants and his occasionally obsequious manner to the committee members reinforced my opinion that the town really did not want anything to come out of the group. The committee, it seemed to me, was just a bone the town board had thrown to the "good-government" groups, such as the League of Women Voters, to satisfy a federal requirement under the Urban Renewal Program. If the committee disbanded by default, however, I felt any hope to open the doors to the political backrooms of town hall where the real "planning" was being conducted would be lost. I therefore persevered.

Even if the committee was not accomplishing a thorough review of the plan as we hoped, its presence and persistence, I felt, did prompt the town board to appoint a Planning Board, if only to be ready to counter any possible "irresponsible" actions we might take. The town also hired for the first time in its history a professional planner, albeit on a part-time basis, to assist the newly formed board in its review of the master plan. Though I viewed the actions of the town as positive signs, most of the members of the committee saw it as an undercutting of the committee. As a result, attendance fell off further. Concerned that the committee might just fall by the wayside, as so many similar committees had in the past out of frustration, I decided to stir up some debate and, hopefully, inject some new bodies and life into the committee.

My first thought was to voice my concerns to the local papers. As a former newspaper reporter I had at the time a modicum of faith that the papers might see the plan as a story, especially in light of the controversy over North Hills and *Newsday*'s continuing probing of townships on the Island. I was dissuaded from this approach by Mrs. Freund and Mrs. Porco, who suggested that in fairness to the other members of the committee I first present my opinions and recommendations to them. I took their advice, and at the next meeting circulated a memorandum declaring that "the town at present is a patchwork of zoning variances and uncoordinated growth, at best ignoring its assets and, at worst, abusing and destroying them." I added that a master plan could help correct these ills, but that the proposed master plan did not. After noting a number of its deficiencies, I suggested that the consultants be dropped and the CAC restructured to work with a new planning consultant and the town's recently appointed Planning Board to come up with a new draft of an expanded plan.

I cannot report that the committee received my memorandum enthusiastically. Though there was some agreement as to the failures of the master plan as I had stated them, there was more concern that my memorandum make its way to the local papers. The feeling was that the problems should be kept in the town "family," and dealt with there, for if they became public they would just be used as ammunition by community groups that were sure to be opposed to any master plan, good or bad, that came out of the committee.

I reluctantly agreed not to make the memorandum public, for the moment. I added that I was not concerned that "they," whoever "they" were, would use the memorandum to oppose the master plan, for I would oppose it too if it did not meet my minimum standards, which included, among other things, the inclusion of the villages and the consolidation of the special districts. In addition, I wanted some assurances that the town was sincere in attempting to put together a reasonable master plan.

What everyone did agree on was that the committee be enlarged, as I had recommended. Deputy Supervisor Mahoney said he would take up the matter with Supervisor Meade, and start sending out feelers to various organizations in communities whose representatives were no longer attending the meetings to consider proposing more conscientious volunteers. He added that he would also try to get some residents from communities not now represented on the committee to attend. As for the need for a new draft of a master plan to be directed by the recently retained part-time town planner, in cooperation with our committee and the Planning Board, Mahoney hedged, saying that he would discuss it with both the Supervisor and the members of the Planning Board.

Though the town as expected continued to drag its feet, I never did make my memorandum public. What I did do after a month of vacillation was write an article for the weekend supplement of *Newsday,* in hopes that it would stir some local debate. Taking off my community volunteer hat and putting on my journalist's hat allowed me to confront Supervisor Meade for one, and also expound on some of my observations and prejudices garnered in my 16 months as a presumptuous resident of the town.

The article was not on the master plan in particular, which I knew would turn off readers, but on how I thought home rule was failing Port Washington. I wanted the article to be a challenge. Entitled "Will the Real Port Washington Stand Up?", it described, as I did in Chapter 3, the jumble of jurisdictions in the Port Washington area, and then with some license declared that:

... when the polite rhetoric of the workshops and meetings of the League of Women Voters, the chamber of commerce and civic associations in Port Washington is carefully considered, the summary is the same: home rule is not working; there is taxation without representation; participatory democracy in suburbia is a sham.

So far no Port Washington organization has taken it upon itself to make a blunt public statement that the system is failing, as I as an urban critic would make. But organizations are expressing increasing "concern" over the Balkanization of the community and some individuals are saying out loud that perhaps some changes are needed . . .

. . . Change comes slowly to settled, secure suburban communities like Port Washington, but change is in the air. And as problems press down on the population, the concept of home rule just might take on a new look.

In addition to allowing me to vent my feelings, the article did touch some responsive chords, and I received a number of friendly and congratulatory telephone calls. I also received, as I have through the years in Port, some crank calls, and even a threatening call. I did not hear from Meade or Mahoney, though it was apparent in the months and years ahead that I had destroyed what little credibility I had left with the town power structure. It did not bother me, for I clearly saw myself in an advocacy role. The town was not going to do anything about the problems I had articulated unless it was pushed. And so I pushed.

6

Frustration and Failure

There had been three attempts in the past by residents of Port Washington to incorporate the community as a political entity, and by so doing declare its independence from the Town of North Hempstead. The first attempt was in 1912 by the Port Washington Board of Trade, then an active organization of local businessmen. With the coming of the commuter railroad and a subsequent boom in real estate, the community was rapidly expanding. However, there were no police, water, garbage, or sewer districts, and the community, for the most part, then as now, had to depend on the whims of the Town of North Hempstead and the County of Nassau for services. By incorporating the community into a village, the Board of Trade hoped Port Washington could better meet its increasing needs by serving itself.

However, politics got in the way, as always. The board was dominated by Republicans while the town was controlled by the Democrats. The issue of what form of government could better serve the community became secondary to the issue of who should have the political power that comes with the delivery of public services. A special election to decide whether Port Washington should be incorporated was scheduled, and a bitter campaign ensued, in effect splitting the community. The election was held on July 10, 1912, in the Protection Engine Company firehouse, with 377 ballots cast. The vote, announced by North Hempstead Supervisor Philip J. Christ, was 184 for incorporation and 193 against. Following the failure, the three settlements at the northern tip of the peninsula, Barker's Point, Sands Point, and Mott's Point, voted to consolidate as the Village of Sands Point.

The next attempt to incorporate Port Washington (now less Sands Point) came in 1930, and was again sponsored by the business community, with the Chamber of Commerce taking the lead. This time the movement was to incorporate the community as a city. The Town of North Hempstead again felt threatened, though the Republicans now held control. With the chamber issuing calls for political action, the local paper, the *News,* gave the effort much publicity, undoubtedly cognizant of how its major advertisers felt. But while the community debated the issue, three small areas on and about Manhasset Isle adjacent to Sands Point quietly incorporated themselves that summer into a village known as Manorhaven.

As reported by Ernest Simon, the *News'* venerable associate editor and Port's unofficial historian, the incorporation of Manorhaven "startled residents of other sections of Port and stirred up fear among the Chamber of Commerce that Port would soon divide into several small villages." The chamber quickly formed a City Charter Committee, which drew up a proposed charter and submitted it to the state legislature, along with a bill that would allow the community to hold a referendum on the issue. Two chartered buses carried forty residents in favor of the bill to Albany on the day of the hearing, March 17, 1931.

Despite strong statements in favor of incorporation by the Port representatives, backed by supporters in the hearing room waving placards stating "We Want the Charter," the legislative committee did not report out the bill, in effect rejecting it. According to Simon, "it was widely thought at the time that (it) was killed because leaders in Albany were of the opinion that 'Long Island cities always go Democratic.'" The legislature was then Republican.

Recognizing that there was now little hope for incorporation as a city, the Charter Committee turned its efforts toward incorporating the community as a village. New maps were drawn and signatures gathered for a petition to hold a "village" referendum. However, two residents outside the proposed village boundaries filed objections, including a charge that several signers were not residents of the proposed village. A long court battle followed, during which much of the enthusiasm for the village waned. Meanwhile, sections of the community started to go their own ways. Rumors that the Village of Manorhaven was planning to annex the new developments of Baxter Estates and the area that is now known as Port Washington North prompted both areas to organize and form their own villages. The area of Flower Hill

straddling Port Washington, Manhasset, and Roslyn also incorporated itself as a village, leaving now about half the peninsula,
including the commercial center, gerrymandered and unincorporated. The result was the political fragmentation of the peninsula, killing whatever chance there was for a governmental entity
of Port Washington and creating for the decades to come the
frustrations I was then expressing to the Citizens Committee and
in the local papers.

One of the many Port Washington residents to confide to me
similar frustrations was Michael F. Teitler, a loquacious lawyer
long involved in local good-government efforts. Teitler has had
many mantles of local leadership passed to him over the years,
and in the spring of 1970 he was asked to assume the presidency
of the Greater Port Washington Civic Council, a faltering confederation of the peninsula's villages, neighborhood associations,
and similar groups. The council had a long history of frustrations,
among them trying to get quorums. Teitler recognized that for the
council to come alive and have some impact it needed an issue,
and perhaps that issue could be the call for a unified political
entity of Port Washington. But Teitler was not as presumptuous
as I was, and he decided to approach the issue cautiously, as was
his style. With the help of William V. Hickson, an executive of the
Long Island Lighting Company, and some other advertising and
marketing research professionals in town, Teitler drafted a very
sophisticated questionnaire that he hoped could give the council
some guidance as to the real concerns of residents.

The questionnaires were distributed in the late spring through
the representatives on the council and through every major civic
group on the peninsula. The response was excellent, with 1,018
families of the peninsula's estimated 8,000 returning the ques-

SURVEY OF THE CONCERNS OF THE RESIDENTS OF PORT
WASHINGTON

Proposal	Attitude Index	Approve Strongly	Approve	Neutral	Disapprove	Disapprove Strongly
Discourage through traffic	60	56.7	18.5	12.6	4.9	3.9
Improved appearance of Port Washington Boulevard and Main Street	53	43.4	29.3	15.3	4.7	2.6

Proposal	Attitude Index	Approve Strongly	Approve	Neutral	Disapprove	Disapprove Strongly
Teenage center	46	35.8	37.1	12.3	7.1	4.9
Neighborhood parks and playgrounds	41	34.5	36.4	11.7	8.1	7.4
Parking for shoppers	38	21.9	45.9	18.2	6.1	4.2
Local Port Washington government	35	29.9	28.2	22.6	7.1	5.1
Local bus service	32	24.4	35.3	23.3	7.9	6.3
More complete police coverage	29	18.6	35.9	30.6	7.3	4.2
More local employment	28	15.6	38.1	30.6	5.5	4.4
Commuter parking	27	20.4	36.6	23.6	9.1	6.8
Housing for retired persons	21	20.2	33.5	22.6	11.2	10.6
More street lights	21	19.3	29.6	28.6	12.1	7.1
Better garbage service	21	18.7	23.3	39.4	8.9	5.3
Public beaches and mooring areas	19	25.2	28.5	15.6	15.6	13.1
Encourage light manufacturing	13	20.4	32.2	13.6	14.4	16.1
Housing for young married or single persons	2	13.2	25.1	26.6	15.9	16.0
More local shops and services	2	8.9	25.2	33.6	17.8	10.3
Additional school facilities	2	16.5	21.4	23.8	18.0	16.1
Large parks	0	19.0	18.9	17.2	22.9	18.3
Housing for low income persons	–5	14.6	24.8	16.2	16.3	25.2

Proposal	Attitude Index	Approve Strongly	Approve	Neutral	Disapprove	Disapprove Strongly
Encourage Industry to locate in area	-7	16.7	22.1	12.0	21.3	24.7
Local employee housing	-10	8.5	19.6	28.2	20.5	19.3
Additional traffic lights	-12	10.7	14.6	29.9	20.3	20.8
Build sidewalks where none exist now	-19	12.1	12.6	22.0	24.4	26.4
Better roads for through traffic	-25	13.0	13.9	14.8	20.2	35.5
Shopping centers	-27	6.9	14.6	18.4	30.5	26.5

Results of a questionnaire prepared, distributed, and tabulated by
The Greater Port Washington Civic Council, Inc.—September 1, 1970
Total replies: 1,018
Index factors: 2, 1, 0, -1, -2

tionnaires. The questionnaires were then processed as a community service by the Publisher's Clearing House, which put the responses onto punch cards, and by the Long Island Lighting Company, which ran the cards through its data processing computers. In addition to a summary of all responses, the replies were analyzed by areas, families with and without children, commuters by train and car, local employees and retired individuals, among the major categories. It was the most thorough study of attitudes ever conducted in Port Washington. Bearing in mind my prejudices, Teitler asked me to analyze the survey, and prepare for him a memorandum he could circulate to council members. I *tried* to be as objective as possible.

Noting that four of the six items with the highest attitude index concerned the community's image and control of that image, I declared that it was "apparent to me ... that the residents of Port Washington are seeking a community identity." After analyzing the entire list of items, I repeated my theme of "community" and suggested that the council take steps "in uniting Port Washington to meet its needs."

It would be a pleasure to report that the Civic Council seized upon my memorandum and began a concerted effort to unify Port Washington to meet the needs indicated by residents in the survey. The *Port Washington News* did give the survey and my memorandum front page prominence, backing up the story with a sympathetic editorial, but the council could not arrive at a consensus of what exactly should be its role. Despite his good intentions, Teitler just could not give the council a focus. After attending a couple of frustrating meetings, I gave up hope that the council would do anything, and so apparently did a few other members. The council eventually disbanded. However, some of the concerns about the community's appearance expressed in the survey were picked up as a charge by the more active Residents For a More Beautiful Port Washington.

It was too bad the council did not choose to act then, for a few months later the whole problem of the jumble of jurisdictions that is Port Washington surfaced over a simple but emotional local issue—the need for a traffic light to help shepherd children between an elementary school and a library across one of the busiest streets in town, Main Street. The new, modern and expensive Port Washington Library had recently opened with much deserved fanfare across from the Main Street Elementary School, and parents, myself included, were concerned over reports of children in near accidents attempting to cross the street. There already had been in a few short months a couple of minor accidents involving cars trying to pull out of the library parking lot onto Main Street, and many of us were worried that it was just a matter of time before there was going to be a serious or fatal accident.

As I was to write later in an article in *Harper's Magazine* recounting the efforts of the parents, "presumably, the installation of a traffic light, on a street between a library and a school, would have presented an opportunity for participatory democracy in its simplest form. But a closer look at Port Washington reveals the contradiction that goes under the misnomer of home rule, and puts into dismal perspective the growing alienation and anonymity in suburbia."

The group of parents leading the effort for the installation of the light soon learned, as I had, that the school on the south side of the street was located in an unincorporated area of Port Washington, therefore controlled by the township. The library on the north side was located in the Village of Baxter Estates. The street itself was a county road, but located in and patrolled by the Port Washington Police District, which is independent of the village, town, and county. Traffic lights on the county road, however, are the responsibility of the county. But parking on the street falls under the jurisdiction of the town. As a result, the parents' request for the traffic light, made through the library board of trustees, ended up being passed from one jurisdiction to another. Finally, the county in December turned down the request (basing its rejection on outdated traffic statistics gathered for the most part before the library was opened), and recommended that the police district propose to the town the elimination of parking on a section of the street, on the spurious theory that speeding drivers and anxious children would have a better view of each other.

Since the recommendation for the parking ordinance required a hearing by the town board, the parents at last were given the rare opportunity to confront openly a political entity. The hearing, as all board hearings, was scheduled at town hall in Manhasset on a weekday morning, when most commuter husbands and some wives are at work 20 miles away in Manhattan. The parents tried to get an evening hearing, but the request was refused by Supervisor Michael J. Tully, Jr., who had recently been appointed to the town's chief executive position following Meade's elevation to the state supreme court, as we all had expected would happen in time. Tully had been a town councilman, and his vacated seat had been filled by Jerome Weinstein, a Sands Point resident and a strong financial supporter of the local Republican party. The hearing on January 19, 1971, was Weinstein's first day as councilman.

Despite the scheduling, nearly a dozen commuters, including myself, took the morning off from work to appear with another dozen parents at the hearing. Filling the front rows, we each stepped forward in turn to attack the ordinance and urge instead the installation of the traffic light. The only speaker in favor of the ordinance was Chief James Rankin of the Port Police District, who was somewhat stunned by the turnout and the repeated questions from the audience demanding current traffic data.

Ordinarily a 15 minute routine affair, the hearing went on for an hour. The board declared that it had no jurisdiction over the installation of traffic lights and that the only matter before it was a parking ordinance. The speakers for the parents' group replied that the board was the political entity closest to the problem and, jurisdictional questions notwithstanding, the parents would hold the board members responsible for the installation of the traffic light.

"Let us not delude ourselves that a simple matter of just a traffic light is involved," I declared in a prepared statement before the board. "The concept of home rule and the viability of town government is being questioned. If the town cannot serve its immediate constituency on a matter of a traffic light, one wonders what it can act on."

Urging the board to reject the parking ordinance and instead petition the county to install the light, I concluded that "the credibility of the town board, as a viable political body sensitive to the needs of its constituency and created and perpetuated in the interest of that constituency, is at stake."

"I guess you're telling us to put up, or shut up," commented Supervisor Tully.

"You said it," I replied.

At this point, Councilman Weinstein uttered his first words as the newly appointed honorable member of the board:

"Let's reserve decision on this matter, coupled with meaningful action. We will not throw this under the rug."

Two months later at a quiet meeting of the board the parking ordinance was approved. We had expected as much, and in anticipation had collected 1,700 signatures on petitions for the traffic light, which were submitted along with Councilman Weinstein's favorable recommendation to the county. This apparently was enough for the county to have second thoughts, and it promised a light. Still, it took a year before the county installed it, and when it did, it was not the usual red and green, stop and go light, but one that just flashed yellow. Three years later the library and parents are still writing letters to the county for a "real" traffic light.

In my subsequent article for *Harper's*, I described the town board's inaction on the traffic light as typical. "The board seems to encourage the local state of political apathy, depending on entrenched hacks and knee-jerk Republicans to turn out the winning vote," I wrote. "It has discouraged any attempt to consolidate villages, unincorporated areas and districts, which could define a political identity (for Port Washington) and possibly set up the machinery for political change. The strength of the board derives from the continued Balkanized state of the township."

It was a familiar refrain, but this time I added a new thought, growing out of my frustration over the past year with the Citizens Committee on the Master Plan and the lack of any significant concern over the abuses of home rule:

"As long as the problems don't become crises, no one expects any significant change in the present distorted concept of home rule. A few parents might become angry over the need for a traffic light; a few more conservationists might express concern over pollution; a petition might be circulated to get housing for some senior citizens, and there is growing protest against the constantly increasing taxes. But while North Shore suburbanites may be unhappy with the status quo, they are fearful of change —particularly the effort and hard feelings that would have to be borne and bared to bring it about.

"The Port Washington parents pushing for the traffic light were constantly reminded by spouses and friends not to become abrasive, to keep their efforts amiable—even if it meant defeat. The majority of suburban residents, certainly those in Port Washington, are indeed silent, seemingly content to be governed by a political system that is suited, at best, to the problems and conditions of a generation ago. The politicians and political scientists connue to swear unswerving allegiance to home rule, filling the newspapers with their rhetoric. It reads well, but the reality is that at the end of the commuter line, the newspapers—and their stories on home rule—will be discarded, to be collected by a scavenger, sold, and recycled."

I also might have included in the scavenger's pile the Report of the Citizens Advisory Committee on the Master Plan, for after two years of meetings we had finally come up with a document, only to have it filed away in a dusty corner of town hall by Supervisor Tully—and from the town's point of view for very good reason.

As the meeting had worn on toward the eventual drafting of the report, the "good-government" members had persevered, including myself, the indomitable Mrs. Freund, Mrs. Glassman, Mrs. Porco, and a few other converts, including Mrs. Dorothy Donovan of Sands Point, Roy Anderes of Manhasset, Benjamin Jenkins of Great Neck, and the chairman himself, Gilbert Tilles. In the end we were in a clear majority, and the resulting report reflected it. With the cover letter and recommendations drafted for the most part by Mrs. Freund and myself, the committee urged, among other things, that the town board "examine the reorganization, realignment and consolidation of the villages and unincorporated areas to effect more meaningful units of government and to encourage community identity and participation." I had pushed hard for its inclusion and I had won, but, as we shall see, it was a Pyrrhic victory.

The report also called upon the town board to "examine the consolidation of special districts to effect economies," "aggressively pursue and acquire land for a land bank," and establish a planning department that would aid in preparing a new master plan that would "take into consideration the incorporated villages and actively include them in the planning process."

If that was not controversial enough, the report also stated that one of the major goals of the town should be to "provide adequate housing and jobs, with an emphasis on meeting the immediate needs for housing of senior citizens, the economically disadvantaged and young marrieds." So that there be no misunderstanding, the report demanded "that the Town Board recognize that it has a social and economic responsibility to provide adequate housing" and that it "seek means to inform the public of the advantages and necessity of multifamily housing."

The report in effect was, in the context of the current climate in suburbia, a planner's fantasy. It also was a piece of political dynamite that if brought before the bumbling town board members for discussion could easily explode in their faces. The one member who understood its import was Supervisor Tully, and he acted quickly to defuse it by simply accepting the report with a polite thank-you, and dismissing the committee. There was no public discussion, except for a couple of garbled stories in the local paper in which I was misquoted and attacked by another member of the committee, Mrs. Marilyn Koplik of Roslyn, who had attended only a few meetings and none when the draft of the report had been discussed. Tully, meanwhile, declared that now that the Citizens Committee had executed its responsibility, the town would move ahead with the assistance of the newly appointed planning board to produce an acceptable plan.

The board's action, or nonaction, as it were, was summed up in a *Newsday* article. Though it annoyed me at the time, the article, written with some license by Andrew Mollison, was an appropriate obituary for the committee:

Manhasset—Like Quintus Fabius Maximus, the Roman general who kept Hannibal from conquering Italy by delaying every confrontation as long as possible, North Hempstead's town board muted a citizens' rebellion against a proposed town master plan in March, 1969, by appointing a broad-based study committee.

The town has since formed a five-man planning board, with a part-time consultant, to work closely with the town board to draw up a new master plan. A first draft of the new plan, designed as a basis for public discussion, had been originally expected last June. It is now due in late May, according to planning board chairman Arthur Pierce.

Lo and behold, three weeks ago the 2-year-old study committee submitted its report—on the old plan. The 21-page report criticized 14 aspects of the discarded plan and made 18 recommendations, ranging from forming a landmark commission and a fully staffed planning department to developing cluster zoning and industrial park ordinances.

For 20 days the report sat in a town hall in-basket. This week, copies were distributed to the town board members. Yesterday, without the fanfare and briefings that mark the release of a major document, the report was made available to the press.

"It's certainly a constructive input," Pierce observed politely. "We're trying to get as much input as we can." A spokesman said that Supervisor Michael J. Tully, Jr. "hopes the planning board will take it into consideration, along with the bicounty master plan, some recent village traffic studies, and the Metropolitan Transportation Authority's plans for North Hempstead."

Quintus Fabius Maximus, also known as Cunctator ("the delayer"), of whom Marcus Tullius Cicero (known to Latin students as Tully) said, "By delaying, he preserved the state," died in 203 B.C. But his spirit can be said to live on.

It was obvious that the town was not really going to do anything except go through some motions. There would be no master plan and the town would continue to be developed in piecemeal fashion, at the whim of a politically motivated town board and Town Board of Zoning and Appeals, for the most part behind closed doors in the back rooms of town hall, just the way they had always operated. The two frustrating years that I and others had put in reviewing the proposed plan and finally producing what we thought was a conscientious report was in the end just an exercise in futility. The status quo continued.

One month after the report was submitted, on March 21, 1971, and the committee dismissed, on April 5, 1971, I filed an *amicus* brief in support of an appeal by F. Arnold Daum of Port Washington to reverse a state supreme court decision allowing 163 acres in the so-called sand pits area of the peninsula to be developed for an industrial complex. Daum, a senior partner in the Wall Street law firm of Cahill, Gordon, Sonnett, Reindel & Ohl, owned a large piece of property adjoining the 163 acres, which the town, in 1968, had rezoned from residential to industrial use. Daum's suit before the supreme court had been based upon the fact that state law requires that zoning be in accordance with a comprehensive or master plan, which of course the town had been dawdling over.

It was Daum's contention that there should be no major rezonings, such as was done in the sand pits, until the town produced and approved a master plan. "It is wrong to take the last big open space in Nassau County (the entire sand pits area covered about 1,200 acres) and develop it a little here and a little there," he said. Daum added he was taking the town to court to force it to come up with a master plan. "It's for the benefit of the community," he said, "and that's why we're doing it."

Also joining me in the *amicus* brief was Mrs. Dorothy Donovan and the local chapter of the League of Women Voters. The appeal was in due time, unfortunately, turned down. However, the suit and appeals did delay the development of that portion of the sand pits for no less than four years, frustrating the town and allowing other community groups, principally concerned with environmental issues, valuable time to become involved. We may not have succeeded in forcing the town to adopt sound and rational planning principles, but we had put a bell around *its* neck.

7

Plans and More Plans

North Hempstead was not alone in its reluctance to act on a master plan that, no matter how lacking, was sure to stir up controversy. Almost every municipality that has attempted to map some sort of comprehensive plan has come under fire: from the "liberals" or "elitists," depending on one's point of view, who may want more low- and moderate-income housing; from "radicals," usually home during semester breaks or doing an independent-study project, who think the whole proposal is a facade for a conspiracy of special interests; from the "conservatives" who are concerned with the "character" of the area and keeping the taxes down; from the environmentalists who see a threat in most construction projects, public and private; from the builders who, of course, want to keep building and therefore eating; from the local merchants who want more customers, parking lots and roads, without any increases in competitors or in the tax rate; from realtors who want to make sure the buying and selling of property will continue forever; and from other interest groups and individuals, all with legitimate concerns, at least from their own perspective.

As a result, public hearings are unique events, with many bordering on mass hysteria. I have seen at hearings mature professionals transformed into raving demagogues, liberal politicians into fascists, modest laymen into nitpicking self-appointed experts and loving mothers into shrews. I have heard at hearings clergymen curse, atheists call on God with conviction, and more threats than I care to remember. School auditoriums built and maintained with hard-to-come-by taxpayers' dollars have been wrecked, not by vandals or juvenile delinquents, but by law-abiding parents out of anger when confronted simply by multicolored charts and maps of a plan presented "for discussion purposes only." I have witnessed at hearings bloody fights and, despite my bulk, have been pushed and shoved and had my clothes ripped. To stand before a packed auditorium and sense the fear of an audience over a particular plan turn into hate is a frightening feeling.

Most of the master plans of communities across the country were initiated in the sixties when municipalities could pay for their preparation by tapping the generous allocations provided under Section 701 of the Housing and Urban Development Act. Though the act was passed in 1954, it was not until the early sixties and the Kennedy administration that substantial funds were made available to encourage communities to apply. The incentive to communities was further heightened during the salad days of the Johnson administration and its Great Society programs, which favored the more aggressive and imaginative municipalities with a gush of federal funds.

As the town board recognized in North Hempstead, master plans were a prerequisite for federal and state funds not only for urban renewal, but also for such projects as water and solid-waste disposal programs, open-space grants, some anti-poverty allocations and mass-transit demonstrations, to name a few. It was a nice way to supplement a budget. Planning was viewed as a stick, but the funds were certainly a compensating carrot.

The temptations also were too great for even the more conservative communities that dominated suburbia. On Long Island, no less than 60 municipalities, including villages, towns, and counties, authorized the drafting of master, or comprehensive, plans in the late sixties. As could be expected, the results were varied.

The plans ranged from a 6-page, double-spaced report for the Village of Saddle Rock in the Great Neck peninsula that cost $700, to the 25 volumes of documentation that supported the Nassau-Suffolk Regional Planning Board's Comprehensive Development Plan for Long Island, which took five years to draft and cost an estimated $1.5 million. Prepared by the firm of Raymond and May in 1965, the Saddle Rock plan reported that the village, with its 261 single-family homes, was "sound and of the highest quality." It concluded by declaring that "few, if any, changes can be expected in the foreseeable future. For this reason, and because of the village's location outside the mainstream of regional activity, the plan contains no recommendations for any changes."

In contrast, the so-called Bi-County Plan, with its 25 volumes and scores of multicolored pull-out maps, was one of the most thorough and impressive planning documents I had ever read. It clearly stated and substantiated the Island's problems, then recommended both broad guidelines and specific actions to achieve its planning goals, within the legal constraints of county government, which has no real zoning powers.

"Nassau and Suffolk Counties possess a unique combination of assets—almost 1,000 miles of shorefront; woods, fields, ponds, clean air and waters; moderately priced housing, good schools and community services; and accessibility to New York City. Today, these attributes, which have attracted more than two and one-half million residents, are threatened." With that as the introduction, the plan went on to note on the Island the increasing pollution, overcrowded beaches and parks, a frustrating transportation system, urban sprawl wasting open land, the declining old downtown areas, dispersed employment and services, and the lack of decent housing for minority groups, the young, the aged, and the large moderate-income families. The essence of the plan's recommendations were three concepts: *corridors* of transportation and employment down the center of the Island; *centers* of commercial, industrial, and institutional activity spaced along the corridors; and *clusters* of new housing and neighborhoods to absorb a recommended 400,000 new residential units, of which it noted 128,500 should be apartments, including 76,000 to be publicly assisted.

The mere mention of subsidized housing in the Bi-County Plan and the scores of other plans that have been dutifully prepared by conscientious consultants and concerned citizens is enough to relegate them, or at least their housing recommendations, to the dusty back shelves of village and town halls. Only about half of the 60-odd plans drafted for Long Island communities have been formally adopted by governmental boards or commissions. And even for the many that have been adopted, implementation has been sporadic.

In attempting to come up with some sort of plan to guide the inevitable development of its land that would be acceptable to the body politic, one community on Long Island directed a planning consultant to draft no less than nine alternative plans for one of its last parcels of almost vacant land. In the introduction to its report, the consultant firm, Raymond, Parish & Pine, Inc., noted that the land, 627 acres in the Town of Oyster Bay, was "one of the few contiguous places still available for development anywhere in Nassau County outside the North Shore villages. This area can be said to be self-contained and suitable for almost any type of development which may be deemed appropriate . . ." The plans ranged from recommending homes on 2-acre lots to relatively high density apartment and office clusters. Most of the plans called for a mixture of 1-family homes, apartments, office buildings and the preservation of some open space. The planners said they were trying to strike a balance between the school tax burdens of residential development and the traffic load of commercial zoning, while, of course, retaining the best natural features of the land, which included the prestigious Meadowbrook Country Club. The result was that instead of having 1 group for a plan and another against, there were 10 groups, 1 for each of the 9 plans and 1 group against any plan.

The plan eventually accepted after a year of heated discussions was the most conservative, restricting building to single-family homes on 2-acre lots for most of the area. Nevertheless, two developers persisted and submitted proposals to the town board for approximately 1,700 luxury condominium apartments, on about 170 acres they owned that was zoned for 85 units. In addition, the owners of a third smaller parcel went to court to challenge the 2-acre zoning. As a "sweetener" one of the developers said he would donate 25 acres of his property for a community park, if his proposal was accepted. The board rejected the offer and instead proposed that the town buy the 25 acres, and build its own park at a cost calculated at about $100 annually for the average Jericho homeowner. The board's proposal further split the community. The debates continue.

What the community seems firm on, however, is its resolve to fight any court challenges of the master plan. The fear is that once a parcel is downzoned for whatever reasons, the master plan will collapse. "It's what we call a domino theory," said Councilman Kenneth Diamond of Jericho. The owners of the land and developers contend that the plan deprives them, among other things, of their property rights. "In this instance," observed a local planner, "it is the greed of developers versus the fear of homeowners, not an uncommon situation. If the community had selected a more reasonable plan recognizing that property owners have some rights, it would not end up in court in a winner-take-all situation. They're simply using a master plan to build a wall around their community."

Still, good-government groups and the few dedicated public servants continue to push for the implementation of plans; for it had been shown that plans could make a difference in the quality of life and the tax rate of a community, as well as reaping some federal grants. One example often cited is the comparison of two neighboring communities in central Suffolk County, Commack and Hauppauge. Faced with the relentless encroachment of suburban sprawl moving eastward on the Island, Commack debated various plans, but did not act. Hauppauge did, due in large part to the volunteer efforts of Lee E. Koppelman, a resident and a planner who in time went on to become the driving force behind the Nassau-Suffolk Regional Planning Board.

As a result of its inaction, Commack grew at the whims of real estate developers, who spread their subdivisions across vacant farmland with little respect for the terrain and the ecology. Commercial development followed along the highways, creating unsightly shopping strips and traffic hazards. Squeezed out in the sprawl were adequate tracts for industry, which would have eased the tax burden on the homeowners, who were soon hit by staggering increases to pay for needed services and schools. In addition, no land was set aside for schools, let alone public facilities, parks, and recreation. When the community eventually "had" to buy land for such things as schools, it was forced to pay exorbitant prices to piece together a minimal site to meet state standards. Meanwhile, the taxpayers screamed. The result was unfocused sprawl and squandered natural assets, similar in many ways to what happened a few years earlier in the Santa Clara Valley outside of San Francisco. Commack had not learned from the mistakes of other communities.

In contrast, Hauppauge's development was guided by a master plan adopted in 1960 and later adapted to changing conditions, as a plan should be able to be. The plan called for, among other things, relatively high and diverse residential zoning requirements, the concentration of commerce so as to avoid strip commercial zones along the highways, large tracts near major transportation routes to attract industry, the preservation of substantial acreage for parks, recreation and open space, and the advance acquisition of school sites, which turned out to be a financial coup. (Hauppauge paid on the average $3,000 per acre when it purchased in advance 10 school sites. Commack a few years later was paying for its school sites $15,000 to $25,000 an acre—for less desirable land.) The balanced mix of residential, commercial, and recreational uses in Hauppauge has resulted in a much more attractive community with more extensive and better located facilities—and a tax rate that runs about two-thirds of Commack's. The differences in the communities also have been reflected in land values. Hauppauge is more desirable, and therefore property values are higher. And yet originally the communities were quite similar in their physical qualities. What made the difference in time was Hauppauge's master plan.

It should be noted, however, that Hauppauge fortunately adopted its plan before the growing concerns and contradictions over such sensitive issues as subsidized housing and the environment emerged in the early seventies. Whether its master plan would have had a chance to prove its worth in the volatile climate of today is questionable.

It has become evident in the community debates on Long Island and across the country over the many and varied plans drafted in the late sixties and early seventies that the key to their "success" is how restrictive they are in dealing with growth. A general equation has emerged that indicates that the more a plan limits growth through various recommendations for environmental standards and exclusionary zoning, the better its chances are for acceptance.

Even neighborhoods in the inner cities that traditionally were open and "liberal," welcoming change as a sign of constant renewal and vitality, are now building walls, under the guise of "creative" planning. In New York City in 1974, the chairman of the City Planning Commission, John Zuccotti, espoused a "new" concept called "neighborhood plans," which were special zoning districts that would retain the character of distinctive communities. For some observers it was hard to define the common planning threads that were woven into the special districts, until you looked closely at the varied plans to note what they did *not* contain: public housing, junior or senior high schools, methadone clinics, welfare offices, sewer treatment plants, garbage truck depots, or any other necessary but controversial projects. The concept was hailed by *The New York Times* as imaginative. It certainly was.

But it is suburbia where the conflicts over growth and the various plans to deal with it are greatest, for it is in suburbia where the pressure of growth has been strongest. For many who have been involved in rational planning efforts the situation is a conundrum.

When good-government groups and individuals such as myself

pushed for the development of comprehensive and master plans in the sixties, it was viewed by many as just a liberal exercise and therefore something to be spurned. The efforts were attacked as "socialistic" by conservatives, who in the spirit of capitalism supported a laissez-faire land policy. They were usually backed by real estate speculators and builders, whose motivations were clearly economic. Our motivation, immodestly, was pride and concern. We simply wanted to make sense out of how our communities were growing. We were concerned that development was occurring helter-skelter, with little thought to the ecology and economy of the areas, and no thought to their relationship to the regions and their needs for balanced growth, including housing. When it became clear that for a variety of reasons, but mainly federal aid, some sort of plans would have to be drafted, other groups became involved. Their motivations were less altruistic and more out of self-interest: keep the taxes down and keep out "undesirables," especially ones with children. The conflicts were many as communities strove for compromises. Then came the ecology movement.

With a concerted assist by the media, the ecology movement thrust itself into the consciousness of suburbia in the early seventies. To be sure, many of the issues raised by the various and growing associations, groups, lobbies, and individuals are quite valid and absolutely critical to the welfare of suburbia, the nation, and indeed the world. However, the immediate effect of the movement on various planning efforts was to give a new momentum and respectability to "conservatives." They embraced the movement and turned its valid concerns into strong, declarative arguments to simply pull up the gangplanks to their communities and stop all growth, especially housing. The master plans became critical weapons in the arsenal of a strange alliance of conservationists and conservatives—many of the very same conservatives who attacked the master plan process a few years prior as "socialistic."

The problem for those in favor of balanced growth, including suburbia's "fair share" of subsidized housing, is that some of the environmental arguments are legitimate concerns. The water supply is limited in many communities, especially on Long Island. Garbage-disposal and sewer-treatment problems plague almost every town, while the prospect of capital expenditures for new facilities to handle the problems staggers the already overburdened taxpayer. Open space is constantly being threatened, as are ecological landmarks, such as shorelines, salt marshes, ponds and streams, mature woods and vistas, if there are any left. The list goes on and on, and causes any concerned planner or responsible citizen to pause before strongly advocating any growth, no matter how "balanced" or "controlled." It is much easier for the planner and the citizen to use one of the many environmental arguments to rationalize an exclusionary plan.

Plans in more and more communities actually have become in effect no plans, but rather a compendium of controls implementing a "slow-growth" or "stop-growth" policy. According to a survey conducted in 1974 by the Federal Department of Housing and Urban Development, some 226 municipalities had imposed moratoriums on building permits, water or sewer connections, rezonings, subdividing, or just about any permit that was necessary to allow construction. There is no figure for the total of all communities, villages, townships, and counties in addition to cities, that have imposed moratoriums, but estimates run into the thousands. The Federal Environmental Protection Agency reported in 1974 that 200 communities in Ohio, Illinois, and Florida alone had sewer-hookup moratoriums and that 30 communities (of the 112) in the Passaic River basin of New Jersey had building moratoriums based on one environmental concern or other. While some communities have not imposed moratoriums per se, they have imposed very strict requirements that almost have the same effect. It is estimated that the requirements for new sewer connections in the Washington, D.C., suburbs of Montgomery and Prince Georges counties in Maryland and Fairfax in Virginia have caused a 50 percent dropoff in construction in the region.

The most common tool used by communities to thwart growth has been their zoning power, within and without the guidelines of a comprehensive or master plan. The power is exercised in many and imaginative and devious ways, including large-lot zoning that makes building sites too expensive for most homes; restrictions on height and building setbacks that make it almost impossible to construct anything on some parcels, or simply just changing the designation of buildable land to protected open space. Other devices include a variety of special levies on developers, such as steep building and sewer permit fees and the donation of a portion of their land for community facilities. The basis of these powers date back a half century to 1926, when, in a legal landmark, the United States Supreme Court upheld zoning as a valid exercise of a community's "police powers," or authority to act for the general welfare. Given this power, and given the ecological, economic, and racial pressures of the times, more and more communities are acting to put a lid on their populations, and in one case even attempted to eliminate a portion of the existing population.

Among the hundreds of communities that have adopted zoning plans that in effect place limits on their population are Salem and Eugene, Oregon; Boca Raton, Florida; Ann Arbor, Michigan; and Livermore, San Jose, and Palo Alto, California. Palo Alto did it with a flourish, zoning no less than 10 square miles of undeveloped land into 10-acre parcels. Gray's Harbor County in Washington was a little more flexible, prohibiting construction of single-family houses on less than 5- to 10-acre parcels, except within the boundaries of incorporated towns. St. Petersburg, Florida also adopted a restrictive plan with a population lid on it, only after an earlier ordinance, requiring the last 25,000 people who had settled there to move out, was rescinded as unconstitutional and impractical.

More typical and expeditious, however, have been suburban communities just rejecting rezoning applications by developers. Almost every day in newspapers across the country there appear reports of communities rejecting proposed housing developments: a 1,300-unit complex in Oyster Bay, Long Island; a 4,200-unit "new town" in Loudoun County, Virginia, outside of Washington, D. C.; subdivisions near Boston, San Francisco, Denver, Chicago, and San Diego; "planned-unit" projects bordering Atlanta, Dallas, and St. Louis. This list grows and grows. "Giving tools like this (zoning) to suburban governments is like giving the atom bomb to Libya," observed Fred Bosselman, a Chicago lawyer and land-use specialist.

The result is that what happened in the suburbs of Washington, D.C.—a dramatic dropoff in construction—is happening in many other suburban areas across the country, according to the National Association of Home Builders. To be sure, the faltering economy of the mid-seventies has been a factor, but the association insists, and sales and rental figures back them up, that there is a steady and increasing demand for residential development in suburbia at all price levels. And building is booming where it is allowed. "While the crucial questions of financing, energy conservation, and land and labor costs continue to plague the building industry," commented Ray Lehmkuhl, President of the Pacific Coast Builders Conference, "the overriding obstacles to providing adequate shelter for our citizens continue to be restrictive land use policies."

"Past growth rates may have been too fast," said Duane L. Searles, an attorney for the National Association, "but if they've slowed down, we'll have a severe housing shortage. Growth control hinders builders and increases the costs of housing."

What the various controls have done is to shunt growth to the less sophisticated, exclusionary, or fearful communities, or communities where politicians feel they can, with enough "support" of the developers, put down objections. The shifting of this growth based on purely the political consideration of whether it will be accepted and not in consideration of its economic, social, or ecological impact on a particular community has created havoc in the attempts to rationalize regional land use. "We simply cannot expect to resolve the problems associated with growth on a case-by-case community basis," Russell E. Train, Administrator of the Federal Environmental Protection Agency, told Gladwin Hill, the respected environmental correspondent for *The New York Times*. "The patterns of development that result from this approach must inevitably be both socially unfair and environmentally unsound."

What the various controls also have done is to make the buildable land scarcer and the prices higher, in effect pricing a larger and larger portion of the population out of the housing market. The exclusionary policies of residents couched in expedient ecological terms prompted some observers to redefine an environmentalist as a person who bought his house or cabin last year. Earl I. Finkler, a planner and former senior research associate of the American Society of Planning Officials, put it more bluntly: "This (the moratoriums) is really a policy of the haves—the ecological and economic haves—to keep out the have nots."

As indicated by the quote, the efforts of communities across the country, particularly in suburbia, to take growth control actions have touched off a clash among environmental, economic, social, racial, and political interests. The results have been the inevitable court cases, with growth advocates for a variety of reasons attempting to knock out restrictive zoning and building ordinances, while no-growth advocates attempt to defend the ordinances and block proposed developments. Communities generally are arguing that growth must be controlled to protect their general welfare, and the way they control it is by more restrictive zoning and building codes. That is their right under the 1926

Supreme Court ruling, according to community or home rule advocates.

Meanwhile, civil rights advocates, aided in some instances by the real estate and construction industries (a new and ironic alliance), are arguing that the no- or slow-growth policies of communities are denying the constitutional right of any person of any creed or color to move and settle where he wants. (Actually, the right is not mentioned per se in the Constitution, but in its precursor, the Articles of Confederation. However, the Supreme Court has repeatedly ruled that the right is an inferential part of the Constitution.)

Most of the arguments by such civil rights groups as the Suburban Action Institute have attacked the exclusionary policies of communities as blatantly discriminatory, economically as well as racially. Suits have challenged almost every aspect of the zoning and building codes of communities, including their right to in effect ban multifamily housing, limits on the number of bedrooms allowed per unit (a favorite of hard-pressed suburban school districts), minimum floor space requirements, certain bans on trailer homes, height and setback (from the road) requirements, and, of course, arbitrary large-lot zoning.

The problem for the courts is that there are no legal precedents on what "reasonable" restrictions a community can impose on its growth, nor are there any guidelines or criteria on what constitutes an economically, environmentally, and socially balanced community, on which the courts could base a judgment. As noted previously, there are an estimated 20,000 suburban communities and 65,000 legal entities controlling land use in the United States, and no two entities' problems or proposed remedies are alike. In addition, rarely do the cases come before the same court, and if they do, there are always slight, but meaningful deviations of law. "So unlike other areas of law where precedents become guidelines, community planning rulings often do not apply beyond the original cases," concluded Gladwin Hill in a *New York Times* article on conflicting court decisions concerning community growth controls. "It's a legal labyrinth," commented Dr. Arnold W. Reitze, Jr. of the George Washington University Law School.

Among the contradictory court decisions often cited are the "landmark" cases of Concord Township, Pennsylvania; Ramapo Township in New York; the exurb of Petaluma, north of San Francisco; Belle Terre, Long Island; and Mount Laurel, New Jersey. The Concord case was first, when in 1970 to the dismay of home-rule advocates the Pennsylvania Supreme Court toppled a local decision by the township to reject a housing subdivision in an effort to limit in-migration (Appeal of Kit-Mar Builders, Inc.). In its decision, the court declared: "It is not for any given township to say who may or may not live within its confines, while disregarding the interests of the entire area. If Concord Township is successful in unnaturally limiting its population growth through the use of exclusive zoning regulations, the people who would normally live there will inevitably have to live in another community, and the requirement that they do is not a decision that Concord Township should alone be able to make."

However, the decision did not deter other townships across the country from continuing their efforts to limit their populations. Ramapo, a Rockland County suburb of New York City, had grown from 38,000 to 78,000 persons between 1960 and 1970, and the town was worried. "Land was being gobbled up haphazardly," an official there recalled. "Some of the most beautiful parts of the town were being hewn away." In reaction, the town adopted a unique 18-year so-called delayed-growth model, which called for the phased development of such service facilities as waterlines and sewers, thus in effect rationing building permits. Any developers wanting to build had to show by their plans that they would not excessively burden public services. Only when they demonstrated by a complicated proximity point-score system that their plans were in phase with the town's plan were they allowed to build. The effect, of course, was to limit growth. Developers appealed the ordinance *(Golden v. The Planning Board of the Town of Ramapo)*. Ramapo lost its first court test, but appealed to the state's highest court, the New York Court of Appeals. The court ruled in favor of the town:

"Far from being exclusionary, the present amendments (to the local zoning code) merely seek by the implementation of sequential development and timed growth, to provide a balanced, cohesive community. . . . Ramapo asks not that it be left alone, but only that it be allowed to prevent the kind of deterioration that has transformed well-ordered and thriving residential communities into blighted ghettos . . ."

When in November, 1972, the United States Supreme Court, in turn, refused to review the decision for lack of what it called a "substantial Federal question," home-rule advocates, environmentalists, and many planners cheered. Ramapo soon became a model for other communities. One community acutely aware of the Ramapo "landmark" decision was Petaluma, a 100-year old farming center that was being engulfed in the suburbanization of the San Francisco Bay Area.

Petaluma had grown from 14,000 people in 1960 to 25,000 in 1970 and 30,000 by the end of 1971, prompting the town's public works department to issue a dire warning that the sewage system could handle only one more year of growth at the current rate. In addition, the town's consumption of water had caught up with its availability, schools were on double session and park land was being threatened. Reacting to the increasing concerns of residents, an ordinance similar in some ways to Ramapo's was instituted in August, 1972, "rationing" growth in the town for the next 5 years to 500 residential units a year. The ordinance was ratified by voters in June, 1973, by a 4 to 1 majority.

However, in January, 1974, the United States District Court of San Francisco ruled that the Petaluma plan was unwarranted and unconstitutional, an infringement of people's right to travel, immigrate, and settle. Echoing the decision of the Pennsylvania Supreme Court in the Concord Township case, Judge Lloyd H. Burke enjoined Petaluma from implementing any policy "which may have the effect, the intent directly or indirectly, of placing any numerical limitation, whether definite or approximate, upon the number of persons permitted to enter the City of Petaluma in order to establish residence."

Attorneys for Petaluma argued that given the community's overburdened water, sewer, and school systems, the court's decision would have the effect of forcing the residents to vote for expensive bond issues. In reply, Judge Burke declared that "neither Petaluma City officials, nor the local electorate may use their power to disapprove bonds at the polls as a weapon to define or destroy fundamental constitutional rights" of others. Regional planners, civil rights advocates and the real estate and construction industries cheered the decision. "Petaluma is really an effort by people living there to pull up the ladder and say, 'no more people, or if they do come, they should be like us,'" declared Martin E. Sloane, an attorney with the National Committee Against Discrimination in Housing. The committee had supported the appeal to the district court by the National Association of Home Builders, the Associated Building Industry of Northern California, and members of the construction industry.

The decision was immediately appealed by Petaluma, backed by legal briefs filed by the National League of Cities, the Sierra

Club, the Natural Resources Defense Council, and the Environmental Defense Fund. The case escalated to become a major test of whether a community could determine its own future needs, without regard for larger, common regional problems, in particular the need for decent housing. The decision by a three-member federal appeals court in August, 1975, was unanimous and unequivocal: "We conclude . . . that the concept of public welfare is sufficiently broad to uphold Petaluma's desire to preserve its small-town character, its open spaces and low density of population to grow at an orderly and deliberate pace."

Writing for the appellate court, Judge Herbert Y. C. Choy declared that "the concept of public welfare is, in fact, broader than the right to travel," which had been cited in the Concord Township case and in the decision of the district court. Judge Choy acknowledged that municipalities were not isolated and their decisions inevitably affected a broader community, but Petaluma had a right to use, "in its own self interest," the police powers of zoning "lawfully delegated to it by the state."

Judge Choy added that "the Federal court is not a super zoning board," and if municipalities in fact were abusing their powers by not serving the broader social needs of a region or state, then it was a matter for the state legislatures to deal with. He concluded that "the Federal court should not be called on to mark the point at which legitimate local interests are outweighed by legitimate regional interests."

Nevertheless, the new alliance of civil rights groups and real estate and construction interests seem determined to appeal the issue, though there is a question of whether the case involves a "substantial" federal qustion. "We're going to the Supreme Court," declared Gordon Blackley, executive vice-president of the Associated Building Industry of Northern California. "We regard it as the most critical land-use planning issue in the country."

The Supreme Court did rule in April, 1974, on a local ordinance of the Village of Belle Terre, Long Island, which limited land use to single-family dwellings, specifying, in addition, that the unit occupancy be limited to two persons "not related by blood, adoption or marriage." The intent of the ordinance was to stop "group" or commune occupancy of the units, a common practice of many single persons attracted to the shore community during the summer vacation months. The court upheld the ordinance. While the ruling did not involve population restrictions directly, it did emphasize environmental considerations and, according to lawyers, appeared to give communities a firm directive to control their future growth. Whether this ruling will be applied to the Petaluma case or whether the Supreme Court will even entertain the case remains to be decided.

One of the most unequivocal decisions against local zoning that excludes by various ordinances housing for low- and moderate-income families was handed down in March, 1975, by the New Jersey Supreme Court. Not only did the court strike down exclusionary zoning, but it required communities to enact an affirmative action plan to attract low- and moderate-income families. "We conclude that every such municipality must, by its land-use regulations, presumptively make realistically possible an appropriate variety in choice of housing," declared the court. "More specifically, presumptively it cannot foreclose the opportunity of the classes of people mentioned for low- and moderate-income housing, and its regulations must affirmatively afford that opportunity, at least to the extent of the municipality's fair share of the present and prospective need."

The opinion basically upheld a lower court decision invalidating the zoning laws of Mount Laurel Township in Burlington County, a suburb of Philadelphia, on the ground it excluded housing for all but the affluent. The suit was brought by the Camden Regional Legal Services, Inc., a federal antipoverty agency, in cooperation with the local chapter of the National Association for the Advancement of Colored People and other plaintiffs, who charged that the township's zoning ordinances were abusing state constitutional guarantees of equal protection and due process. Specifically, they contended that the zoning, which in some areas prohibited apartments and mandated large, expensive lots, had the effect of keeping the community economically segregated. And since many low- and moderate-income persons are black, it also kept the community racially segregated.

In its decision, the court noted that local zoning is generally based on the broad power to protect the "general welfare," and that communities use this as a rationale to draft ordinances to preserve the character of neighborhoods, protect the area's ecology and, most important, to maintain a high tax base to provide schools and local services. "The conclusion is irresistible that Mount Laurel permits only such middle- and upper-income housing as it believes will have sufficient taxable value to come close to paying its own governmental way," the court said.

"It is plain beyond dispute that proper provisions for adequate housing of all categories of people is certainly an absolute essential in promotion of the general welfare required in all land-use regulations," the court continued. "It has to follow that, broadly speaking, the presumptive obligation arises for each such municipality affirmatively to plan and provide, by its land-use regulations, the reasonable opportunity for an appropriate variety in choice of housing, including, of course, low-income and moderate-cost housing. . . . Negatively, it may not adopt regulations or policies which thwart or preclude that opportunity."

The township said it would appeal to the United States Supreme Court, but there is doubt whether there is involved a substantial federal question. There is no question, however, that the decision will affect New Jersey, where several other similar zoning cases are pending, in Middlesex, Bergen, Somerset, and Morris Counties. Planners and politicians expect that eventually the state will have to step into the zoning vacuum created by the court and establish regional land-use and housing plans, which undoubtedly will explode the home-rule issue for the better across New Jersey.

The United States Supreme Court a few months later did rule in a parallel case that parties living outside a community had no legal standing to challenge that community's zoning practices. The Court's 5 to 4 decision rejected the plea of a group of inner-city residents of Rochester, New York, who charged that the zoning pattern of the nearby affluent suburb of Penfield deliberately priced houses out of the economic range of the poor and minority groups. The city residents were joined in their challenge by the Rochester Home Builders Association and a county housing council.

Writing for the majority, Associate Justice Lewis F. Powell declared that the courts had to impose "prudential limitations" on who could challenge a town's zoning ordinances, noting that the complainants were not subject to the ordinances and had never attempted to get an exception to the ordinances so they could move there. "Their inability to reside in Penfield is the consequence of the economics of the area housing market, rather than of respondents' (Penfield zoning board) assertedly illegal acts." In a sharply worded dissent, Associate Justice William J. Brennan, Jr., accused the majority of exhibiting "an indefensible hostility to the claim on the merits . . . which tosses out of the court almost every conceivable kind of plaintiff who could be injured by the activity claimed to be unconstitutional." In a separate dissent,

Associate Justice Douglas called for a trial on the charge that zoning had been used "to foist an un-American community model, on the people of this area."

Despite the ruling in the Penfield case, the Mount Laurel decision is expected to stand, for that decision was decided on the basis of the New Jersey constitution and its general welfare provisions regarding due process of law and equal protection. Simply stated, the Mount Laurel case was a state affair, as was the Ramapo, New York, case and, according to lawyers, involved no federal questions.

In a variation on the Penfield decision, the United States Court of Appeals ruled, also in June, 1975, that nonresidents *do* have legal standing if they challenge federal grants to a community allegedly practising zoning discrimination. The decision came in a case brought by several black residents of Westchester County, who, with the aid of the Suburban Action Institute, filed suit to enjoin payments to the Town of New Castle, New York of a $385,-000 Department of Housing and Urban Development grant for the construction of a $2.1 million sewer system and a $52,000 grant toward the purchase of a park. The blacks, who were not residents of New Castle, said the town's "discriminatory land practices" prevented them from moving there.

The basis of their case *(Evans v. Lynn)* was not the alleged zoning discrimination, however, but the failure of the federal government in approving the grants to take "affirmative" action required of it under the 1964 Civil Rights Act. Writing for the 2 to 1 majority, Judge James L. Oakes declared that the impact of federal grants may "increase the disparity between living styles by supporting 'white enclaves' while diverting funds which otherwise would have been used to alleviate ghettoization." The court did not rule on the merits of the complaint, only that the nonresidents have the right to make the complaint.

There are numerous other cases in courts, high and low, involving legal battles over various forms of growth restrictions, and more can be expected as the battle over land control continues. Almost all the cases have dealt with legal questions of exclusionary policies and environmental considerations. An interesting exception was another case involving New Castle, New York, in which a group of builders sued to have the town's zoning ordinance declared unconstitutional on the ground that it deprived them of the right of "lawfully carrying on their trade" by prohibiting the construction of multifamily housing. The plaintiffs, the

Builders Institute of Westchester and Putnam Counties, Inc., and the Builders Council of Suburban New York, Inc., charged that the zoning action by the town infringed on their property rights guaranteed by the Fifth Amendment, and deprived them without due process of law of their right to conduct their occupation. The courts in time upheld the town's ordinance, but the case raised some interesting questions concerning property rights that are yet to be resolved.

"It's very clear that we are in the midst of probably the most radical change in our concept of private property rights that we have ever seen in this country," declared James Rouse, the developer of the "new town" of Columbia, Maryland. "The notion that a developer has a right to develop because he owns a piece of land, and the public must let him, is rapidly changing."

"I'm one of the largest landholders in Westchester," declared Robert Weinberg. "Within a half hour of here (the suburban city of White Plains), I've got 500 to 600 acres I can't do anything with because of zoning. It's all zoned for one house an acre to keep out anyone earning less than $25,000. All they want here is the status quo—a guy wants to walk his dog in my woods; he thinks they're his woods. Citizens have an absolute right over zoning. We just can't run with local little hometown rule. Every idiot can come down to the town hall and have his say and the guys up front tremble because they're afraid they won't be reelected."

"It's the politics of the territorial imperative, the protection of their property," explained John F. English, a Nassau lawyer and former county Democratic Chairman. "That means opposing new housing and new people, anything that might change the status quo." But, of course, the status quo is constantly changing, as more people and businesses move to and grow in suburbia. The situation was summarized clearly in the task force report sponsored by the Rockefeller Brothers Fund, *The Use of Land: A Citizens' Policy Guide to Urban Growth:*

To those who think the solution to development excesses in the past lies in policies aimed at no growth or markedly slowed growth in the near future, the statistics bear little comfort. Although the Census Bureau projects a slowed population increase, buried in the data is a legacy of past population increases that will keep us growing for decades. Whether we welcome or fight it, development is going to continue during the rest of this century . . .

The case for more development is not based simply on demography or projections of economic growth. There is also an ideal involved, that of respecting the free choices of Americans to move in search of a better job or a better life. Mobility has been a traditional road to opportunity in America. Wholesale growth restrictions, imposed by many communities, could block that road for the many who still want to travel it.

The desirability and the inevitability of a measure of development must be faced in any responsible effort to achieve better quality in urban growth. No growth is simply not a viable option for the country in the remainder of this century. Stop growth here and it will pop up there; slow it down there and it will speed up somewhere else, because people are not going to go away . . .

The challenge, if not the responsibility, of communities, therefore, is how to plan both to accommodate and control the growth consistent with the new ecological awareness, while respecting the rights of citizens who live or want to live in their community. A master plan is the logical vehicle. But the problem the conflicting court cases and conflicting interests raise for suburban communities at present is that if they choose to attempt any planning, particularly a master plan, they must move cautiously. But how cautiously?

When the Bi-County Plan for Long Island was unveiled in 1971, the three concepts stressed were *corridors* of transportation, *centers* of commerce, industry, and institutions, and *clusters* of new housing, as previously noted. In December, 1974, Suffolk County's largest township, Brookhaven, published a draft of its new master plan. In addition to following in part the Bi-County Plan's suggestions to stress corridors, centers, and clusters, the Brookhaven plan included and emphasized a fourth "c," *conservation.* Discussing the $250,000 plan for the 326-square-mile township, which extends across the Island from the Sound on the north to the Atlantic Ocean on the south, Edith Litt, the project manager for the planning firm of Raymond, Parish and Pine, Inc., declared that some of the main concerns as the plan evolved were environmental factors.

What the plan lacked, and why many believe it was generally received favorably by the public, was no clear statement on the need for housing, in particular subsidized housing. While the plan was quite detailed in recommending the preservation and acquisition of park lands, wetlands, waterfront, and open space and examining such ecological considerations as water supply and sewer capacities, it did not contain any proposals for the elimination of substandard dwellings and the construction of needed subsidized housing.

"We're not satisfied," declared Ernest Boyd of the Brookhaven Housing Coalition. "The median income for Brookhaven residents is $11,143. At that level, most people can't afford to buy or rent at the level of housing now." Janet Hansen, director of Suffolk Housing Services, an agency of a coalition of local ministries, was more blunt: "The whole idea of making a master plan with no housing is insane, a waste of time."

The protests, however, were decidedly in the minority. Politicians, public groups, and newspapers for the most part praised the plan, especially its "sensitive" recognition of the town's fragile ecology and the need for centralized corridors for the development of commerce and industry (and the tax income they will bring). The consultants apparently had learned the lesson of political expediency in proposing plans for suburbia: stress the environment, tickle the tax base, and avoid at all costs housing, especially subsidized housing. No one had to say it at public hearings anymore, for it was clearly understood: subsidized housing meant more of "them," and one of the major reasons people moved to suburbia was to get away from "them."

8

"Them"

As far back as anyone can remember there have been some blacks in Port Washington. Local history has it that blacks were spirited into the area by the underground railroad in the 1850s, coming ashore at night off ships where they had hidden deep in the hulls behind cotton bales being transported from the Southern planta- tions to Northern mills. Jobs were found for them as farmhands; then, after the Civil War, as laborers in the sandpits, and at the turn of the century as servants in the Sands Point estates. And there were always the menial jobs in the mills, stores, and on construction sites. If they did not live in the servants' quarters on the estates, or in the backrooms of the stores, they settled in a cluster of modest frame houses and shacks in a dank dell just off the approach to Sands Point, about halfway between the estates to the north and Main Street and the stores to the south. There they lived as second-class citizens, out of the mainstream of com- munity life. While Port Washington grew, the Harbor Road neighborhood remained a relatively stable pocket of poverty, with its no more than 150 black families rarely venturing out beyond a 3-square-block area, except for the children to go to school, the parents to go to work, as domestics, servants, and laborers, and a few adventurous men to fish in the bay at dusk and on Sundays. For all intents and purposes, the black community of Port Wash- ington for the first half of the century only showed itself in the census.

In 1950 the local chapter of the League of Women Voters, after some debate, turned its talents toward a survey of housing conditions in Port Washington. The League's action, which caused some murmurs of protest from the real estate community, was prompted in part by a national housing "crisis" being given a play by the media and the recent passage of the progressive Federal Housing Act of 1949. In addition, the local chapter had pressed hard in the late forties for the Town of North Hempstead to establish a housing authority, and had supported approval of the authority's first project, a 102-unit development known as Pond Hill in the Great Neck-Manhasset area. It was now looking for a second site, and the Harbor Road area seemed a likely choice.

The League's survey supported the choice, for it had found as expected that many of the houses in the area were substandard, with some lacking indoor plumbing and electricity. The report of the conditions shocked some local residents, for they had always thought of the Harbor Road ghetto as a "good" ghetto, which is to say, an invisible ghetto, something that could be kept out of sight and mind. The report helped rally support of a proposal to clear some shacks on Harbor Road and have the authority build a 66-unit project of attached, 2-story garden apartments. There was some opposition from the real estate community and from Harry F. Guggenheim, the publisher of *Newsday,* a portion of whose vast Sands Point estate was diagonally across the road from the project site.

As an inducement to the authority, Guggenheim proposed that he donate the cost of the purchase of an alternative site for the project. Faced with the prospect of having to look for a site outside the ghetto area and thus face almost certain white resident reaction, or incurring the wrath of Guggenheim, who was well known for his wrath, the authority chose to stick with the Harbor Road site, no matter how much it would cost them. The project was eventually approved without much rancor, and built and occupied in 1951 without incident, a very uncommon script for subsidized housing in suburbia. "Being on Harbor Road and in an area that already was a ghetto, it didn't frighten or threaten anyone," recalled a Port resident. "Nobody was moving next door to anyone. You could drive right by the project every day and never know it was there."

As an invisible ghetto, the Harbor Road cluster was similar to other "established" black neighborhoods in other suburban areas that existed then—and that still exist today in many communities. In the Town of North Hempstead, in addition to the Harbor Road area, blacks also had settled around the railroad station in Roslyn, in New Cassel, Westbury, along Steamboat Road bordering Kings Point, and in a section of Great Neck and Manhasset border known as Spinney Hill. Each ghetto has a long history as a source of cheap labor serving the growing affluence surrounding it. Somehow the affluence never rubs off.

In many ways the ghettos I found in North Hempstead were like the ghetto I was surprised to find in Princeton. The ghetto there, a few square blocks west of Nassau Square, the pleasant, pseudocolonial center of town, had been a part of the history of Princeton for about 150 years, ever since a few students from the South had established a tradition of sorts that upon graduation they would free their "house" slaves they had brought with them to wait upon them while at college. Many of the freed slaves stayed on in the town to work as servants and laborers at the university, while importing their families and friends and forming households to establish their own community. In time, however, it was a community that some whites and real estate interests in Princeton felt the town could do without. When I was a resident there, blacks were attempting to fight to save their neighborhood and "community." Increasing rents and substantial offers from real estate brokers were prompting many who had lived in the area for generations to move, usually to the burgeoning black ghettos of nearby Trenton.

The erosion of the black community in Princeton has been slow and subtle, left to the whims of a private real estate market buoyed by unwitting young white professionals just looking for an apartment or a house in an attractive town and in walking distance of the university and its amenities. The erosion has not been as subtle in other suburban areas.

Baltimore County is the 600-square-mile ring around Baltimore, Maryland, and one of the fastest growing suburban counties in the country. Fed by whites escaping the city of Baltimore, subdivisions have spread further and further into the countryside, engulfing a number of small black communities, vestiges of the county's rural past. But unlike Princeton, which left the erosion of its black community to the marketplace, Baltimore County gave its black residents a little push by the use of its zoning powers. According to a report of the United States Commission on Civil Rights, the county's unwritten policy was effectuated in two stages: "First, the displacement (by zoning actions) of the poor rural or semirural black population enclaves that were often found in what have become today's suburbs; then the zoning of land to be developed in such fashion as to discourage the construction of housing within the price range of low-income groups."

To be sure, some of the housing for blacks has been lost to decay, code enforcement, and fires; some to highway expansion, and some to the marketplace, as blacks sold to real estate developers. However, the commission reported that a "significant factor in the demolition of many black-occupied homes" in the county has been the "nonresidential zoning of black residential areas." The report continued: "New construction or even additions to or renovations of existing structures may be prohibited and, as the existing homes fall into disrepair, they are often vacated and demolished. Other homeowners, surrounded by decaying houses or by industrial uses, are prompted to move out."

As an example, the commission cited the recent history of a working-class suburb called Turner's Station, which sits at the southeastern tip of the county overlooking the Back River estuary and the steel mills at Sparrow's Point. The community was established during World War II specifically for blacks brought in from the rural areas of the state and from parts of the South to work in the mills. By 1960, the community had a total of about 6,000 persons, mostly blacks, who resided in a segregated neighborhood. However, with the construction of an interstate highway through the community and its location on the estuary, land in the area became particularly attractive to industry. Under strong pressure from real estate interests and with the hope of increased tax ratables, the county approved the rezoning of the black residential area to industrial use. Most of the black homes were torn down and replaced by factories, while the few remaining homes just decayed. The effect was to destroy the black community. The small white community of Turner's Station was more fortunate. Though it also had been built at the same time the black homes were built and also was located in an industrial area, its residential zoning, in contrast to the black pockets, was actually strengthened, and thus avoided destruction.

Black residents of a community called Sandy Bottom in the suburban boom town of Towson suffered a similar fate at the hands of Baltimore County. Towson is the heart of the county, and as such has been since the early sixties (when Spiro T. Agnew was County Executive) under constant real estate pressure for new and expanded shopping centers, office buildings, and, indeed, even high rise apartment buildings. Unfortunately, Sandy Bottom lay in the path of progress. Despite its relatively stable population, decent, solid housing stock and a history dating back to the Civil War, the whole area was rezoned commercial. In a short time real estate developers moved in and the black community was completely wiped out. It is no wonder that while the population of the county has doubled and doubled again in the decades since World War II, the percentage of its black population has steadily declined (from 6.7 percent in 1950 to less than 3 percent in 1970).

In addition to zoning, local, state, and federal highway programs also have provided suburban governments an effective tool to squeeze, squelch, and in some cases destroy black residential areas (as the programs have done in cities). Town boards have been known to encourage the mapping of freeways through and around black areas, to create a new form of ghetto walls; no longer is the slum "on the other side of the tracks," but on the other side of the expressway. With the tacit cooperation of highway administrators, roads also have been planned by localities to have the effect of substantially decimating black neighborhoods, usually forcing the residents to relocate in central cities. Hampered by little political muscle and less community sympathy, the black neighborhoods offer the least resistance to the "highwaymen" and their supporters, usually real estate interests desperate to get the roadways and the suburbanite shoppers who travel on them downtown. That blacks have to be displaced for the economic lifegiving suburban roadways cannot be viewed with sadness by the typical suburban politician, knowing in his heart how his constituency "really" feels.

That is the feeling one gets in the suburban city of Pasadena, which sprawls beside the San Gabriel Mountains in the Los Angeles Basin. For years the bloom on the rose of the home of the Rose Bowl has been fading under a cloud of smog. Its millionaires, who lived in stately mansions along Orange Grove Boulevard and had given the city a reputation of exclusivity, have long since moved away or died. The famed opera house and playhouse they supported also are long gone. And for the last decade the aspiring white middle class that replaced the wealthy in the fifties also has been leaving, pulled by the cleaner air of suburbs beyond the valley and pushed by the aspiring lower-middle class, mostly minorities, moving in. Once the most fashionable residential address in Los Angeles County, Pasadena is now the home of one of the largest ghettos in the West. About 40 percent of its population of approximately 112,000 is minority, mostly blacks, many of whom are moving up the ladder from the deeper decay of Los Angeles. Pasadena is not a poverty community, but it is not what it used to be, a bastion of white middle-class suburban values.

A few years ago the business community and political leadership became convinced that the only way to pump new life into the suburban city was to put some new freeways into its heart. If Pasadena became the hub of two new proposed freeways, planners were sure that industry and business would follow, thus building up the economic and tax base that would allow the faltering city government to make the improvements needed to stop the cycle of decay. It was a reasonable assumption, given the economic history of Southern California, which has been built around the freeway system. Only when the routes of the freeways were approved did the motives of the business and political interests come into question.

"They put the freeways where the resistance and the power was weakest, and now we have the biggest intersection in the world where a lot of black families used to live," said Don Wheeldin, an active black resident of Pasadena. It is estimated that the construction of the freeways displaced more than 4,000 residents, mostly black and Chicano families, many of whom were forced to return to the ghettos of Los Angeles they had recently escaped from. The impact of the freeways on the economic life of the city has not yet been measured, but we do know that the schools are now less crowded and fewer public services are needed. The businessmen and politicians are not weeping.

Supposedly created to aid the poor and minority groups, urban renewal programs also have been manipulated by many suburban governments to effectuate an unwritten policy to drive out blacks. It is for good reason that civil rights groups have aptly renamed urban renewal "Negro removal." The typical past abuse under the program (now renamed "community development" and hopefully reformed) was the bulldozing of black neighborhoods with the vague promise of new, subsidized development to house the families that had to be "temporarily" relocated. Somehow the housing was always delayed, and if and when it eventually was constructed, the former residents somehow could not be found. More often than not the proposed housing site was "redesignated" at the urgent request of merchants for a "temporary" parking lot, that eventually became permanent, or for a shopping center that town officials felt was desperately needed for the taxes it would generate.

In criticizing urban renewal programs as government actions that can force blacks out of their suburban neighborhoods and back into central city ghettos, the United States Commission on Civil Rights in its landmark (but ignored) report, *Equal Opportunity in Suburbia,* cited the case of the Elmwood Park section of Olivette, a suburban community outside of St. Louis. Located in an isolated neighborhood along the railroad tracks in the northern part of Olivette, Elmwood Park was the home in 1960 of about 30 families, 29 of them black. Then came urban renewal. The plan proposed in 1961 by Olivette and approved by the federal government was to create an industrial park in the Elmwood section to attract jobs for the black residents. It called for the residents to be first relocated to public housing in a neighboring area outside Olivette and within the city of St. Louis; their homes in Elmwood to be demolished for industrial redevelopment; and then for them to be relocated again near the new jobs. "Nine years later no relocation housing had been provided by Olivette," noted the report, "and as residents saw the inevitability of industrial redevelopment and residential displacement, they moved out, reducing the population of the area to five or six families. After pressure from HUD [the Federal Department of Housing and Urban Development], Olivette set aside land in the urban renewal area for 24 units of relocation housing, but as of May, 1971 none had been built." Meanwhile, the black neighborhood of Elmwood Park had all but disappeared.

In a footnote in its report published in July, 1974, the commission added: "It should be noted that responsibility for the delay in the construction of the 24 units is as much HUD's as Olivette's."

While some suburban communities will, if opportunities present themselves as they did in Baltimore County, take actions to erode their black neighborhoods, most communities are content to just try to contain "them." Since almost all black neighborhoods are unincorporated—a very conscious political decision of the dominating white power structures of the past—they are therefore at the political and racist whims of white planning boards and governing bodies. Using their powers, the boards and bodies have with imagination approved zoning and map changes that have had the effect of isolating the ghettos. The changes have included permitting shopping centers, commercial strips, "nonconforming" gas stations and industrial parks to create noxious no-man zones between white and black neighborhoods, with the black, of course, getting the worst of the pollution and traffic. Another tactic used to isolate black neighborhoods has been to discontinue street patterns from adjacent white neighborhoods, or simply just not keep up the roads so as to make them impassable. It seems blacks are always getting the short end of the public service stick.

As noted in a study conducted for the Commission on Civil Rights, "many black residential areas are characterized by unpaved streets and a generally low level of public improvements, while adjacent white residential areas often . . . are better served." Commented a planner: "There is no doubt about it, whether we are in the South, North, Midwest or anywhere in America, suburban governments consider blacks second-class citizens and their homes second-class neighborhoods. I guess the local politicians hope that if they ignore the blacks—don't pave their roads, don't give them any parks, or the like—they'll go away."

But they have not gone away. Indeed, most of the black ghettos of suburbia have persevered and, in some areas, have spread. The ghettos are most evident in the old, large towns of suburbia; Hempstead, Long Beach, Glen Cove, Freeport, among others, on Long Island; Hackensack, Perth Amboy, and Passaic in New Jersey; New Rochelle and Tarrytown in Westchester; Bridgeport in Connecticut; Compton, Long Beach, Pomona, Santa Ana, parts of San Jose, in California; Chester City, Darby, Ardmore, and Crestmont, outside of Philadelphia; East Cleveland; Kirkwood, over the Atlanta city line—the list is long and growing longer. Old age, blockbusting in some places and the stiff competition of the mushrooming shopping centers and new subdivisions off the interstates, expressways, and freeways have taken their toll in these and other relatively older suburban areas. Upwardly mobile whites and the commerce they supported have moved out and the blacks have moved in, desperate for housing near the jobs relocating in suburbia. The old towns are struggling to keep the grime off their facades, but the side and back streets are succumbing. Decay has set in. Many of the towns have become what planners now label as the "slurbs"—the slums of suburbia.

Less conspicuous, but no less insidious, are the "slurbs" isolated by expressways or tucked behind the commercial strips of gaudy gasoline stations, blaring bars, and discount stores that scream out their wares in neon every 50 feet on crowded highways. These "slurbs" are the suburban subdivisions that never made it. Constructed too cheaply and too quickly in the late forties and fifties, the houses are now literally falling apart, sold off or rented by white families to blacks, Hispanics, or Chicanos who, because of discrimination or little money, never had a choice. Despite their condition, the houses are still in demand, simply because there is no other place. On Long Island, a survey of the housing stock of Nassau and Suffolk Counties revealed that 36,000 units of the Island's 700,000 units were "dilapidated, deteriorating, or lacking some or all plumbing facilities," and that another 36,000 units were "substandard," bringing the total of deficient units to about 1 out of every 10.

It is not exactly the picture of suburbia most Americans have, thanks to the conscious effort of local governments and real estate interests to hide, contain, and, hopefully, destroy the slurbs. Honest efforts to improve the conditions for the predominately black residents of the slurbs have been attempted in some areas, but with little success. Wherever there is a proposal in a white-dominated community involving blacks, racism and greed replace amiability as the credo of suburbia.

Given the diversity of suburbia, there is no typical "slurb." But coming close to that dubious distinction is North Amityville, a 3-square-mile, flat unincorporated area in the Town of Babylon in Suffolk County, about 40 miles or a long hour's train ride east of Manhattan. Not by coincidence, it is bounded by four major roads, including the commercially encrusted Sunrise Highway on the south and the limited access and landscaped Southern State Parkway on the north. Turning off Sunrise Highway and its gas stations and discount stores onto the back roads of North Amityville is like driving off an interstate highway in the black belt of Alabama. Two-by-four timbers prop up sagging porches of faded homes patched with tar paper. Piles of uncollected garbage lie on the side of unpaved, rutted lanes. Junk cars rot on front lawns. A small brick store at an intersection is abandoned and gutted. Sidewalks are overgrown with weeds. Sign posts are bent and defaced.

But beyond a cluster of shacks there are a few, new attractive ranch and split-level homes, with well-kept lawns, a picture of middle-class suburbia. The rutted, unpaved road gives way to a newly surfaced street, but it leads into an empty field and ends. Remnants of cars lie rusting in the field, as if the field was the scene many years ago of an armored battle. A half a mile further is a decaying postwar development of small homes, then another small cluster of well-maintained landscaped homes, with a street leading to a main road and a large trailer camp. The census indicates that North Amityville contains about 11,000 persons, most of them black, and most of them poor. Exact figures are difficult to come by, say the planners, because many families are doubled up, and do not report it to the few survey takers brave enough and bothering to knock on the doors, out of fear of being evicted for housing code violations.

In the late 1960s the Nassau-Suffolk Regional Planning Board recommended in a controversial housing study of Long Island that North Amityville be singled out for special attention. Noting its "scattered and haphazard growth" and large tracts of open land, in particular a United States Army missile site and a seldom used airport, the board suggested that North Amityville could be transformed with a minimum of dislocation from an amorphous area into a coherent community. The prototype plan proposed a major remapping of streets and rezonings of the entire area, including the missile site and airport, to create a variety of housing types, including single-family homes, townhouse clusters, garden apartments, and a few high-rise apartments, the result of which would more than double the area's population to 25,000. Also proposed in the plan was a town center of commercial, cultural, and civic facilities, an education complex, some land for office and industrial development, and, of course, greatly expanded recreation areas linking the entire new community. As *Newsday* declared in an editorial, the plan was outstanding, "too good to be ignored."

It was certainly not ignored. With the exception of the then Democratic county executives, every elected politician and any politician who wanted to be elected within 30 miles of North Amityville attacked some aspect of the plan. Some did not like the idea of a "superagency" that would be needed to sponsor the development; others did not like the high-rises, or the zoning precedences to be established; or the suggested income mix of the housing, which included low-income units. The local community even had reservations. "Basically, the people aren't alien to the proposal's concept," said Marquette Floyd, board chairman of the Neighborhood Opportunity Center, "but the community wants to participate in the project. We need decent housing at a cost we can afford, but we are concerned and want to know where it is going to be placed."

While the community loudly debated the plan at heated open meetings, the legislators quietly killed it in their cool, closed sessions. Though no one of course publicly said it, it was apparent what concerned many of the politicians was that the plan if implemented would have doubled the *black* population of North Amityville. The increase of blacks undoubtedly would have a number of ramifications, not the least of which would be political. Some blacks at the time were coincidentally organizing a drive in North Amityville to form what would have been the first predominantly black incorporated village on Long Island. (Incorporation could have given the legal power to the community, and the blacks, to implement at least some components of the plan.) The blacks pressing for incorporation were charging that the Babylon town government was short-changing public services in North Amityville and permitting spot zonings, which were accelerating deterioration. To anyone who had toured North Amityville and contrasted it to the neighboring white communities, it did not seem like an unreasonable charge. Even the local councilman at the time, Richard DiNapoli, hedged his reply. "The town is not overlooking improvements in the area, at least not *consciously* [italics mine]," he told *Newsday.* "There has been no conscious effort to slight the community." The town supervisor could not be reached for comment.

The efforts by the blacks to incorporate North Amityville eventually failed, as have other efforts there to create a sense of community, or at least obtain some public services on par with neighboring white communities. It remains a second-class community, a "slurb," in contrast to the popular image of suburbia. And there the black residents will remain, until they can put enough money together to perhaps move up the suburban ladder to a black middle-class neighborhood or, if they have the constitution for it, into a white middle-class neighborhood.

Ten miles or so from North Amityville in the Town of Huntington is the community of South Greenlawn, which is considered to be the largest middle-income black area in the county. Here several thousand blacks live in an attractive neighborhood of ranch and colonial houses in the $50,000 or so bracket, though there are some more modest homes (which a few residents worry are deteriorating and will attract welfare families) and some more expensive homes, replete with backyard swimming pools. Many of the black residents moved to South Greenlawn from other, albeit low-income, ghettos on the Island, such as North Amityville, Huntington Station, Roosevelt, and New Cassel, as they moved up the economic ladder. Some had wanted to move into white areas, but found the real estate community conspiring to keep them in neighborhoods in which they feel "more comfortable."

"They don't take you to good areas, when you're black and want to move out of Huntington Station. They'll never take you to a predominantly white area," said a black woman who eventually settled resignedly in South Greenlawn. The problem of "steering" by real estate agents—showing white persons houses for sale only in white neighborhoods and showing black persons houses listed for sale only in predominantly black or changing neighborhoods —is of course a practice of most brokers, who contend that they are only acting in response to the discriminatory desires of homeowners or developers whom they represent as agents. Some are more frank, admitting that brokers actually encourage white desires for exclusivity. In testimony before a hearing of the United States Commission on Civil Rights, Malcolm Sherman, a broker from Maryland, declared that "it is really not the homeowner who is making that decision to keep that neighborhood all-white for his friends and neighbors, so much (as) the real estate broker who is in business and who still considers it economic suicide to make a sale to blacks in that all-white neighborhood."

The problem of a dual housing market—one for whites and one for blacks—confronted another resident of South Greenlawn, Michael Baldwin, when he tried to move away and further up the socioeconomic ladder. He had contacted a builder by phone, who had told him of two plots in a rather nice (white) section of Huntington. Baldwin made an appointment to see the land to determine whether he wanted to build a house. "You should have seen his face when he saw me for the first time and saw I was black. He said the deal on the two nice plots had fallen through and all he had to show me were in black areas in Huntington Station."

There also are some white families in South Greenlawn, and they too, oddly enough, experienced discrimination when attempting to move into the community. "A real estate man tried to discourage us from taking the house, saying the area was in danger of becoming integrated. We reported him to the state," said Mrs. Lesley Gershtoff. She added that they had moved to South Greenlawn because the houses were comparatively inexpensive and because the neighborhood was racially mixed. "Our children deserve a chance to find out what all people are all about." The attitude of Mrs. Gershtoff is unfortunately an exception, among blacks as well as among whites.

According to a study of attitudinal factors in the choice of housing, blacks, like whites, make their decision based on how convenient the house is to their job, its size, special features, and cost. Blacks were found to be "generally willing" to live in interracial communities "if necessary to find desirable housing," but were found to be "reluctant" to locate in practically all-white areas, because of the fear of racism. In testimony before the Civil Rights Commission, black witnesses described the hostility they and their children encountered when they moved to white suburbia. Their conclusions concerning integration were mixed. Mrs. Doris Stanley, a resident of Montgomery County, Maryland, said she liked "getting the services of the whites they perform for their own," particularly the quality of the schools, but did not know whether she would recommend the experience to other blacks.

"I would recommend that they be told ahead of time, don't fool yourself, it is hostile. But I feel that, you know, this whole country is hostile wherever you are. . . . So I would recommend that they would come out but they would need an awful lot of help. The suburbs are not open to them and are not welcoming them in, it is a fight." Mrs. Stanley concluded with the observation that "living in the suburbs is nice if you're white."

Putting Mrs. Stanley's comments in perspective, minority groups have never been welcome in suburbia. The blacks, Hispanics, and Chicanos, like the Jews, Irish, Italian, and other immigrant groups before them, are viewed by the majority as suspect, an alien force with contradictory life-styles that somehow will undermine the social fabric and property values of communities they settle in. It is important to keep in mind that the prevailing myth in suburbia is the Protestant Ethic, which, simply defined, is that an individual through hard work shall reap his reward—and that reward according to the ethic and embellished by advertising and the media is ownership of a single, detached house on a plot of landscaped ground in an economically, socially, and racially homogeneous community free of the turmoil of the evil city. There is little tolerance in the ethic for anyone or any group that may wander off. In general, conformity is the accepted mode of behavior in suburbia. That minority groups, subjected to the same media bombardment, might pursue the same ethic, and be just as concerned and protective of the social and property values of the communities they want to live in, is usually lost in the waves of fear that wash over "threatened" suburban communities.

The continued racial isolation in which most suburbanites live only enforces the stereotypes of minority groups, particularly of the blacks, generated by our history and perpetuated by the media. The general effect is the creation in the minds of many whites of a monolithic "them," which disregards individualism and variations, including economic class. It makes the individual black bigger than life—"see one, see them all"—which could explain the panic sometimes when one black family moves into a white neighborhood in suburbia. That one black family can, and has, touched off a mass migration of whites out of an established neighborhood is staggering, frightening, and absurd.

The fear among whites that property values in their neighborhood will decline if blacks move in has been reinforced not only by many brokers, but also by lending institutions. A common practice of banks is to "redline" a black or integrated neighborhood, making it very difficult for an applicant who wants to buy or improve a house in the area to get financing. In a survey by the Federal Home Loan Bank Board, 30 percent of the responding mortgage lenders admitted to disqualifying neighborhoods because of their residential composition. The effect often of denying financing in an integrated neighborhood is to touch off a vicious cycle of decay, usually speeding the exodus of those able to flee—and those are usually the whites. That was the fear of A. J. Wilson, director of the Human Relations Commission of University City, a suburb of St. Louis with a black population of 16 percent and growing. Charging that it had been "redlined," Wilson said that all in the suburb have had to suffer "many of the same forms of discrimination that black people have experienced for years. We have trouble getting developers to come in; we have trouble getting financing for development; we have trouble getting mortgages; we have some insurance companies starting to say: 'We are going to stop insuring.' "

The suburbs that appear to have been most often "redlined" are the older, so-called inner-ring suburbs, such as Oak Park, a leafy enclave for about 62,500 persons outside of Chicago. Despite its solid middle-class character enhanced by about two dozen architectural landmarks created by Frank Lloyd Wright, Oak Park is suffering "an almost total boycott of home improvement loans," according to community leaders. Paul Bloyd, chairman of the Oak Park Community Organization, noted that recently Oak Park's four savings and loan associations merged or branched out to newer suburbs, ignoring the community. He added that a study by his group indicated that the suburb's largest lender, Oak Park Federal, with assets of $240 million, made only $40,000 in conventional loans in Oak Park, while at the same time it made more than $1.5 million in loans in newer suburbs.

Some lenders admitted in the survey by the Federal Bank Board to "using the race of an applicant as a factor in determining whether he would be given the loan or in determining the terms under which the loan would be made." (Blacks I know responded to this disclosure with "what else is new?") It was only in 1973 that the Federal Bank Board specifically prohibited in its guidelines to lenders questions of race. But the history of the role of the federal government in combating housing discrimination has not been, for the most part, a very proud chapter. In particular, the Federal Housing Administration is considered to have played a primary role in establishing enduring segregated neighborhood patterns.

Created under the National Housing Act of 1937 to provide a system of home mortgages insurance, the FHA for nearly two decades recognized and accepted local restrictive covenants. "If a neighborhood is to retain stability," stated the agency's underwriting guidelines, "it is necessary that properties shall continue to be occupied by the same social and racial group." Another exponent of racial discrimination to preserve neighborhoods and therefore investments was the Federal Home Loan Bank Board, which provides assistance to the nation's principal mortgage finance institutions, the savings and loan associations. The active support of segregation policies by these two key federal institutions during the time of intense suburbanization, the late forties through the fifties, did much to reinforce local prejudices that are just now being chipped away at.

The official policies of the federal government in regard to discrimination have been, indeed, reversed, following the issuance in November, 1962, by President Kennedy of Executive Order 11063 (prohibiting discrimination in federally assisted housing), and the passage of the Civil Rights Act of 1964 (prohibiting discrimination in any federally assisted programs or activities), and the Civil Rights Act of 1968 (prohibiting discrimination in most housing; private, as well as public). We now have the legislative, administrative, and judicial mechanisms aimed at implementing a national policy of equal-housing opportunity. Though they may have created the necessary legal climate, the laws by themselves, however, will not desegregate suburbia. In fact, despite the laws, segregation in suburbia is actually becoming more pronounced.

Almost all indices in the last census, extrapolations to the present and projections into the future indicate an increasing racial separation, with white suburbia becoming more white and the central cities more black. Between 1960 and 1970 the suburban rings of our main metropolitan areas had a white population increase of 12.5 million and a black population increase of only 800,000, mostly in established ghetto areas. Some suburban areas as we have noted actually lost blacks. At the same time the central cities of these metropolitan areas lost about two million residents, mostly white, but their black populations increased by nearly three million. In New York City alone, the Bureau of the Census reported that the net migration of whites out of the city during the decade was 955,519—or 1 white out of 7. Meanwhile, the City's nonwhite population increased by 702,903.

Reviewing the statistics, the United States Commission on Civil Rights commented that "this picture of racial separation in metropolitan residential areas persists for two main reasons: past and present discrimination in the sale and rental of housing and because of the lower income of blacks and other minority members." But the commission also cited statistics to show that at every income level whites are more likely than blacks to live in suburbia. In 1970, 85.5 percent of black metropolitan families earning less than $4,000 lived in the central city, as compared with 46.4 percent of white families in the same income range. In the $4,000 to $10,000 income range, 82.5 percent of the black families and 41.6 percent of the white families lived in the central city. For families with an annual income of $10,000 or more, the central-city figures were 76.8 percent black and 30.9 percent white.

The commission did note that many white suburbanites bought their houses at a time when prices were significantly lower and discrimination against blacks was more blatant and pervasive. Now that discrimination is not practiced as frequently or as openly as it was before, and now that more blacks have incomes comparable to whites, the supply of inexpensive suburban housing that the whites had moved into years ago is just not there anymore. And as we shall explore in the next chapter, the inexpensive housing is not there not only because of market forces, but also because of local practices motivated by racial and economic concerns.

"This economic-racial exclusion may well be called the racism of the seventies," concluded the commission. "Coupled with vestiges of the more open racism of the past, it furnishes an explanation for the picture portrayed by the census figures, an image of a suburban 'white noose' encircling a black inner city."

With a black population of less than two percent, and most of that population living in the Harbor Road area and still invisible to many, Port Washington is very much a strand in the "white noose." Though most of the residents—my neighbors—would deny it, Port Washington is a racist community. To be fair, I have never known its racism to be virulent (but I'm not black). When residents on a rare occasion have had to face the issue of discrimination, it has been handled with none of the usual accompanying hysteria. Voices have been kept calm. Epithets and threats have not filled the air as they have in many suburban communities. But the very fact that Port Washington seldom has been confronted with the issue, or, worse, seldom has bothered to face the issue, is what makes it a racist community.

9

Rare Occasions

Audrey and Farrell Jones were not the first black couple to attempt to purchase a home outside the Harbor Road ghetto through a real estate broker in Port Washington. Other black couples were said to have made inquiries, but somehow, someway, never were able to reach a contract or, in most cases, never even got to see the houses listed. According to Mrs. Rosalie Jordan, the former owner of one of Port's most successful agencies, Town and Country Realty, local brokers had an "understanding" that if a black person appeared at an agency the broker on duty would somehow hint at the fact over the phone to the owner of the house on the market so they could make up an excuse why they could not show it. Brokers also were supposed to notify other agencies that a black was looking for a house in Port so they could take appropriate evasive steps. In one instance, a broker in the Mac-Crate Agency, upon seeing a black couple approach the office, simply locked herself into a bathroom and didn't answer the door.

The Joneses were lucky. They drove into Port Washington one bright spring day in 1964 and had the good fortune to select at random Town and Country Realty, where of all people, Mrs. Dwaine Walther, my mother-in-law, happened to be the sales agent on duty.

"I knew what the understanding was among the agencies," recalled Mrs. Walther, "but I'd be damned if I'd discriminate. I just handled them like any other prospective buyer. I did not give any signal to the owners of the houses the Joneses were interested in, but simply said I was bringing over a buyer. I was afraid someone would slam the door in our faces, but no one did. After looking at a number of houses, they finally selected one in the relatively new Soundview section of Port. They met the asking price, and went into contract with the owners, Regina and John Bauer. Then came some unpleasantness."

"Word must have gotten around quickly," said Mrs. Jordan, who worked on the sale with Mrs. Walther, "for soon after the contract was signed we started receiving hate mail and phone calls, warning us that if we sold the house we'd never sell another in Port. The Bauers also were getting pressured not to sell the house. In fact, neighbors on both sides of the Bauers put their houses up for sale. To calm fears in the neighborhood, the local rabbi held a meeting, which seemed to work. We, of course, had every intention of going through with the sale, and told that to the Joneses and Bauers."

Mrs. Jones recalled that Mrs. Jordan was indeed insistent as well as supportive. "Her resolve was helpful, for in fact we were nervous," said Mrs. Jones. Mrs. Jordan remembers it somewhat differently. "They were very calm, considering they were going to be the first to break the color barrier in the better sections of Port."

Also easing fears in the community was the fact that the Joneses, like most aspiring middle-class blacks, were a cut above the educational and vocational level of their white neighbors-to-be. Attractive and articulate, Farrell Jones was a graduate of Lincoln University and New York University Law School and Mrs. Jones a graduate of Hunter College. At the time, Jones was director of the Nassau County Human Rights Commission, which could explain why he remained calm during the period of heightening neighborhood anxiety just prior to the move-in. Concern was like a cloud over the closing, but the sale and move went without an incident. If anything, once the Joneses settled in, their neighbors were friendly almost to the point of being obsequious. It was not as easy for the next black couple who attempted a year later to move to Port Washington.

Adriana and John H. Powell, Jr., did not seek a house in the neighborhood already breached by the Joneses, but rather in the Beacon Hill section, an area that for many years was said to have a restrictive covenant. When the first Jewish family somehow moved into the neighborhood in the late fifties, the rumor was that there was an understanding that the family would not use the association's swimming beach on Hempstead Harbor. Powell, a graduate of Harvard Law, and his wife, a Radcliffe graduate, were not fazed—the year was 1965, not 1955, and civil rights was in vogue, or so they thought. They had been charmed by an attractive house on Beacon Drive and were willing to meet the asking price, and even pay a "color tax," as Mrs. Jordan called it, to get it. However, the neighborhood was even more determined not to see it sold to a black, and agreed to band together to match whatever price Powell offered and buy it themselves. Tension mounted, and in the end the owner backed down and Powell backed out. Beacon Hill would remain white, just as it is today.

Disappointed but still wanting to live in Port Washington, the Powells found another house, in the more modest Park section bordering Beacon Hill, only to be told by the owners that the house already had been sold. "It was a lie," commented Mrs. Jordan, "and the owner and the Powells knew it. I was furious, but the Powells didn't want to pursue any action." Finally, the Powells found a house and a willing seller in Port Washington Estates, an area that actually is more prestigious than the Park or Beacon Hill sections. It was apparent that residents there felt a little more secure. Aware of the problems the Powells had encountered, their new neighbors went out of their way to welcome them, and they soon became social fixtures in the community.

When the Powells moved to Washington, D. C., five years later, they rented their house to Bernard Purdy, the black jazz composer and musician, whose hobby it seems was not the care and feeding of the lawn. The property became an eyesore, and there were murmurs of resentment to the effect that the Powells had rented out the house in malice. The gossip disappeared when the Purdys moved out in the spring of 1972 and the Powells sold the house to Lynne and Lawrence Randolph, a white couple, albeit with a McGovern sticker on their car. As a footnote, the Randolphs tell the story that just before they moved in, they were vacationing on Shelter Island where Mrs. Randolph struck up a casual conversation on the beach with a young mother, who mentioned that she lived in Manhasset, a town that borders Port Washington.

"That's a coincidence," said Mrs. Randolph. "We're moving to Port Washington."

"Where?" asked the Manhasset matron.

"Port Washington Estates," replied Mrs. Randolph.

The woman raised her eyebrows and leaned toward Mrs. Randolph. "Do you know what," she said rhetorically in a confidential tone. "There's a black family living in the Estates."

"Yes," replied Mrs. Randolph. "We are buying their house."

With the Powells moving, the number of black homeowners in Port's upper-income neighborhoods was reduced to an estimated three. The latest estimate is six. The "integration" of the neighborhoods—if 6 black families out of 6,000 is integration—really did not stir up a broad reaction for, typically, the situations were kept relatively quiet. With the exception of the resistance in Beacon Hill, where residents had a perverted sense of tradition, Port Washington reacted well, certainly in comparison to the many suburban communities in which violence and vandalism have greeted blacks moving into white neighborhoods.

Where Port Washington really excelled itself, however, was in the rarest of suburban efforts, the community sponsoring of a subsidized-housing project and the dogged pursuit of the needed approvals, including a downzoning. The effort also illustrated how a small, but influential and determined, segment of the community could, when it wanted to, shame the majority into a position of at least not being actively opposed, and thus persevering. It was a rare occasion.

The idea for the project was generated in 1968 by the Port Washington Community Relations Council (CRC), a collection of local liberals, and the Port Washington Community Action Council (CAC), an innovative local antipoverty agency then thriving on federal aid. Along with the local chapter of the League of Women Voters, the CAC and the CRC at the time were harbingers of a sentiment in town, prompted by a mixture of genuine concern and some guilt, that the relatively affluent community (median family income then of about $17,000) should be doing more for the estimated 20 percent of its population earning less than $10,000 a year. To be sure, the groups and their friends were a minority, but a very activist minority, with its members supporting and serving the traditional town volunteer efforts. The community conservatives, also a minority, grumbled and wrote letters to the editor attacking various do-good activities, but they did not then attempt to challenge the leadership (as they did a few years later in the school board elections). Meanwhile, the majority, mostly the commuters, were usually oblivious to what struggles might be going on in town, content to ride the train back and forth to work five days a week so they could play tennis, golf, or sail on weekends and with a drink in their hand watch the sun go down over the bay.

In pursuing the idea of a federally subsidized moderate income housing project, the CAC and the CRC were reacting to the growing gap in the Port Washington real estate market between the rents at the Harbor Homes low-income project and private housing. The 66 units at the Homes were very much in demand, as were the 225 other low-income units in the entire Town of North Hempstead. The official waiting list was then 491 families, though the actual need was estimated by the Housing Authority at 2,100. In addition, there were few turnovers in the existing public projects, for alternative low- and moderate-income housing one step up the economic ladder for those who might want to move out of the projects was just not available. According to a survey at the time by the League of Women Voters, 32 families whose income exceeded the Housing Authority limits were paying extra rent so they could remain. The survey further disclosed that there were four wives in the Harbor Homes project who had quit jobs and at least one man who had turned down a promotion so their families would not be over-income and susceptible to eviction.

If moderate-income housing was available, reasoned the sponsors, then eligible families would be able to move out of Harbor Homes, creating vacancies for those who could not afford anything else. In addition, many other families not living in low-income housing were paying an exorbitant portion of their limited incomes for private housing, since nothing else was available. And without rent control, the demand was skyrocketing rents. The cost of housing also was found to be pushing out of Port Washington many people who worked there. The League survey noted that 20 years ago all the men on the local police force lived in Port, but now only 20 did of the roster of 43.

"Lack of housing is a big complaint among the men," reported the survey, citing the chief of police as its source. "It adds difficulty to recruiting and the efficiency of the force." Complaints also were registered by teachers and mailmen. It was noted that at one time almost all who worked in Port lived in Port, but now most lived outside, some as far away as Suffolk County, where the cost of housing was considerably less. "The community will in time become economically segregated," warned the League.

The housing effort was spurred on during the summer of 1968 by the availability of a vacant 4-plus acre site on Harbor Road, just a few blocks from Harbor Homes. The site, an old sand mine, seemed almost ideal, lending itself to a design of 88 attached garden apartments, many more than the CRC and the CAC had hoped for. "We had been just looking for a couple of building lots here and there for a few attached houses that could be constructed cheaply and sold at cost to moderate-income families," said Dr. Charles Beggs, a member of CRC, "but the Harbor Road site changed the whole picture." With the volunteered aid of Richard Rosen, a local architect, Harvey Cohen, a lawyer, Robert Bernhard, a prominent building contractor, and many others, a proposal was put together for a cooperative to be developed under the subsidized mortgage program, so-called Section 221 (d) (3), of the Federal Housing Act.

The immediate problem was to find $14,000 for an option on the land, and for this the groups turned to the North Shore Unitarian Society, which had been blessed 10 years ago by a bequest of mineral rights to an oil and gas field in Germany that was now yielding increasingly substantial royalties. Not only did the Society, known as the Plandome Church, agree to provide the funds, but it also agreed to become cosponsor of the project with the CAC.

The decision was a critical one, for along with the financial involvement of the church came the volunteer services of one of its more prominent members, Edward A. Lawrence. A wily chemical engineer and executive at Union Carbide, Lawrence understood well the political implications and the backlash such a project could have. To prepare for any reaction, he and his wife, Laurene (Lee), quietly lined up support with the aid of their friends for the project using their numerous social and volunteer organization associations. In addition, the nonprofit corporation that was formed, the Cow Bay Housing Development Fund Co., Inc., retained at Lawrence's suggestion Bertram Daiker as its lawyer. Daiker was a stalwart of the local Republican machine with an unusual record of successes in zoning cases before the Republican town board, and the project was going to need a downzoning. Also lending political clout to the proposal was the fact that the lawyer for the seller of the site was Vincent R. Balletta, then the Republican assemblyman for the area. In addition, there was the hint that construction of the project would probably go to local contractors, subcontractors, and workers.

"In my talks to various interests in town I consciously stressed the aspect of the project that I knew would appeal to them," said Lawrence, "whether it was jobs, political feathers in their cap, or just local pride. We also kept a low profile so as not to stir up the majority, who might start asking questions about things like tax abatement the project would need."

My involvement came two months after we moved to Port when

I accompanied my mother-in-law, Mrs. Walther, to a meeting of residents in the Harbor Hills section of Port, an unincorporated neighborhood of about 250 ranch and split-level homes, the northern-most block of which sat on a bluff over the proposed housing site. Word had finally filtered out that the housing company had taken an option on the site and was seeking a needed zoning change before the town board. With the hearing only a week or so away, a number of Harbor Hills residents were scurrying around trying to organize an opposition.

However, the Lawrences and their friends in the church, the CAC, CRC, and the League had done their work with the few contacts they had in the neighborhood. Where most suburban neighborhoods would be vociferously and unanimously opposed to a subsidized housing project for "them" on its border—the sand pit had been a convenient barrier between Harbor Hills and the Harbor Road ghetto—Harbor Hills was actually split, thanks to a few "liberals" there who had been bolstered by what amounted to the town's establishment. A meeting was called to air the issue, and among those invited was Mrs. Walther, who then was chairperson of the Human Resources Committee of the League. I had been discussing tactics with Lawrence, and decided to tag along with Mrs. Walther, wearing the cloak of the Citizens Advisory Committee on the Master Plan.

The opposition had hoped to use the meeting to fire up residents against the project and plot strategy. However, by a calm, protracted presentation of the need for moderate-income housing in the community by Mrs. Walther and the few liberals present, the meeting almost took on a rational tone. The opposition remained adamant, but they did not win over any new converts and they also had wasted an evening. Their plan to form a civic association and speak before the town board as a "community" and not as a collection of individuals had been dissipated, in large part by Mrs. Walther's calm demeanor.

The only tactic now left to the opposition, before turning to the courts, was to collect signatures on petitions opposing the project and try to turn out in force at the public hearing.

Stumbling into the railroad station on my way to work the morning of the public hearing, I found a commuter from Harbor Hills at a card table collecting signatures on a petition. The petition I noticed misrepresented the project as a low-income development of the town Housing Authority, which would bring "them" into the community. "And that's why we moved out here;

to get away from 'them,' " he was saying to a gaggle of commuters waiting on line to buy the morning *Times*. I interrupted him, pointed out that the project description on the petition was incorrect and suggested that he change it to "community-sponsored moderate-income development." He declined, and so I placed myself next to the table and proceeded to call attention to the error to anyone looking over the petition.

"That project is for Port Washington residents and is sponsored by the community," I said again and again, adding when I thought appropriate that it also was church-sponsored. If a person said he did not care and was going to sign anyway, I would try to lure him to a long debate, while blocking the table. The resulting scene disrupted the morning calm of the station, and prompted most of the commuters to avoid the apparent unpleasantness, and of course not even look at the petition. I missed three trains and stayed in the station until the Harbor Hills resident left, presumably to go to town hall with the few signatures he had collected.

At the hearing, the CRC, CAC, the League, and the church had orchestrated behind Daiker a strong presentation for the rezoning, overwhelming an opposition thin in both quantity and quality. But it was Dominic Badolato, a member of CAC and a resident of Manorhaven, the most blue-collar of Port's villages, who eased the unspoken fear among the opposition and the politicians that the project would just be a black extension of the black Harbor Homes. "My people want this housing; my people need this housing," he pleaded before the town board in an emotional voice that some of the audience said was tinged with a slight Italian accent, which was unusual for Dominic because he spoke perfect English. The rezoning was approved.

It was more than two years before construction could begin, however, because of lawsuits by a few Harbor Hills residents and the red tape of the FHA. "The only reason we persevered was because we had a steady supply of money (approximately $110,000) from the church to pay for lawyers and other incidentals," said Lawrence, sipping a beer in the den of his attractive Sands Point home, about two miles from the completed project, now called Cow Bay Green. "We were determined to see the project through, because we believed in it and because if we failed with all our resources, what hope would there be for others?"

Lawrence took another sip of beer and reflected further: "We also were lucky. The time was right; the climate in the community was conducive. That the project needed tax abatement was not an issue, as it certainly would be today [1975]. We built up a head of steam and coasted in under the wire, no thanks to the FHA. I guess we were an exception, and I'm glad for the 88 families now living in Cow Bay."

The success of Cow Bay Green was very much the exception. Three other efforts in the Town of North Hempstead in the next few years to obtain sites and zoning changes for low- and moderate-income housing projects were shouted down with a vengeance by local residents, each time shaking the politically sensitive town board. One of the victims, a willing victim some say, was the town supervisor himself, Robert C. Meade.

After winning reelection in the fall of 1969 by a comfortable 2-to-1 majority, Meade declared that there was a housing crisis in the town and he was going to try to do something about it. Considering Meade's previous neutral posture, his new stance came somewhat as a surprise. Agreeing with all the local chapters of the League of Women Voters that a tract of vacant land in an unincorporated section of New Hyde Park would be an excellent site for a low-income housing project, he voted in the spring of 1970 against an application to rezone the site from residential to commercial use. The site had been quietly identified by the town's Housing Authority for a project, but the owner and neighborhood residents got wind of the plan and had sought the zoning change, which would have the effect of blocking the housing. After a heated hearing, the town board overwhelmingly rejected Meade's appeal and voted 4-to-1 for the change, killing whatever hope there was for the housing, while, incidentally, giving the owner a windfall zoning profit.

The League appealed the decision. "We must ask what kind of town are we if we can allow more than 450 of our neighbors (the Housing Authority's waiting list) to live in housing without proper facilities for so many years when there is such widespread prosperity within the town, and then let a potentially good site for alleviating some of their housing difficulties be lost through this rezoning decision." The decision remained.

During the hearing, Meade was challenged by New Hyde Park residents that if he thought housing was needed so badly he should put it in his own backyard. A few weeks later he proposed just that, a 60-unit low-income project in the exclusive Village of Kings Point. The site, 3½-acres of vacant land owned by the Great Neck School District, was about three blocks from Meade's home.

If a threatened, conservative, Republican, middle-class community like New Hyde Park would not accept low-income housing, it was hoped that perhaps the more secure Kings Point would, certainly in view of its national reputation as a wellspring of financial support for liberal causes and Democratic politics. With a median family income then estimated at $35,000—almost three times that of New Hyde Park—the village was the site of pilgrimages by civil rights leaders to solicit funds for a variety of integration efforts, mostly in the South. Low-income housing in their village, it turned out, was another matter, confirming the equation for some liberals that the closer to one's home the results of one's actions may be, the more conservative one is and, conversely, the further from home the more liberal one is.

In explaining the Kings Point Civic Association's "unalterable opposition" to the proposal, Samuel Goldstein, one of its board members, declared: "We have a very selective village with 1-acre zoning and we want to keep this 1-family residential type community. We want to make it absolutely clear we are not against black people. It's very ticklish because opposition is sure to be interpreted as racist. I'm all for the blacks. I'd sell my house to one of them." In response to a reporter's question, Mr. Goldstein estimated the value of his house at about $125,000, and that was 1970 prices. The proposal did receive the support of 14 members of the Great Neck Association of Ministers, Priests, and Rabbis. There were few others, and the proposal soon died, as did Meade's political career.

Worried that his strong housing stand was becoming more than political rhetoric, and that it might damage the party in the next town and county elections, Meade was tapped by the Republicans for a seat on the state supreme court. With Meade "kicked upstairs," the local Republicans chose for the supervisor's job Town Councilman Michael J. Tully of New Hyde Park, an attractive, glib clubhouse politician. While Tully has talked about the need for housing in the town, especially before such groups as the League of Women Voters, nothing much has been initiated, which is actually just what most of the voters prefer. The politics of suburbia, as we shall explore in a later chapter, is the politics of the status quo.

Whether Meade knew that bucking the status quo would get him a coveted judgeship, out of the center ring of county politics, or whether he acted out of conscience can be debated. At the time he took his strong stand for subsidized housing there was a mounting concern over the Island's housing problem, at least among good-government groups and liberal politicians. With the "environment" not yet in vogue, county planners and consultants also were pushing hard for action, releasing a series of reports that indicated a need on Long Island of nearly 50,000 subsidized units. The then Democratic county executives of Nassau and Suffolk, Eugene H. Nickerson and H. Lee Dennison, used the reports to challenge the Republican-controlled towns to assume their "fair share" of the units needed. Addressing the town supervisors, Nickerson declared in a speech that "there is no excuse for a generally affluent suburban community, where 90 percent of the people enjoy good housing, to permit the other 10 percent to live in conditions which rival some of the worst slums in the nation."

In response, Meade had the town's own planning consultant, Harold T. Letson, estimate what constituted North Hempstead's "fair share." In a confidential report, dated July 22, 1970, Letson declared that "taking into consideration the 291 units of public housing presently in operation, and the 265 units programmed for Roslyn, there is a long range need in North Hempstead *including the villages* [Letson's emphasis] for 1,540 public-housing units." Six months later Meade was on the bench and the report was in the dead file. There has been little talk since of "fair share" on Long Island.

One of the few areas where a "fair-share" plan to disperse low- and moderate-income housing in the suburbs has worked is in metropolitan Dayton, known as the Miami (Ohio) Valley. The city of Dayton, the hub of the five-county valley, had been more or less economically and racially integrated up through the fifties. Then came the suburban explosion in the sixties, and the city of 250,000 residents began losing population while, of course, the suburbs grew and grew to over 600,000. And typically, it was the white population of means that moved out, leaving behind the poor and the black. The vicious cycle of decay that so many other cities have experienced set in. Abandoned white, middle-class neighborhoods soon became black ghettos. Following their middle-class clientele, businesses moved to new shopping centers in the suburbs. Pressed to find more tax ratables to support their growing school system and public services, suburban communities created industrial parks to lure jobs and industry out of the city. It did not take much of a sales job, for the owners and management already were living in suburbia. By 1970 a white noose had formed around the city, choking it racially and economically.

Blacks attempted to follow their jobs, but were effectively shut out of the private housing market by both costs and discrimination. There were a few attempts in the late sixties by nonprofit and private builders to develop sites for subsidized projects, but these efforts also were stopped. The projects had been supported by the Miami Valley Regional Planning Commission, a confederation of sorts of the elected officials of the 5 counties and 29 municipalities in the greater Dayton metropolitan area. "If the price is right," reported the commission at the time, "the utilities are not available. If the price and utilities are right, the zoning is wrong. If all are right, the neighbors do not want it."

After the rejections of the housing proposals in isolated suburban communities, the commission came up with a bold plan assigning a quota of subsidized units throughout the entire metropolitan area. Using a mathematical formula that took into account the amount of existing housing for low-income families, population density and other factors, the commission proposed a total of no less than 14,000 units in communities that previously had neither poor nor minority residents. As expected, residents in most of the communities exploded in vocal opposition. Dale F. Bertsch, the executive director of the commission, was subjected to numerous threats, and at one meeting as he attempted to explain the plan the microphone was snatched from his hand.

A typical reaction was that of the community of Oakwood, one of the wealthier areas in the valley, described by a local newspaper as "a compound" and "the local Brigadoon." Presented with the plan that assigned 637 units to be located in Oakwood, one resident responded that "you can't strengthen the poor by weakening the rich." Another declared that "the vast majority of the people can find homes if they're willing to work for a living." Despite the reaction, the Oakwood City Council endorsed the plan. And eventually so did almost every other community in the valley. At this writing, about half of the 14,000 units under the plan have been completed and occupied. In the opinion of government officials in the valley, most if not all of the units would have been completed had it not been for the moratorium on subsidized housing instituted by the Nixon administration in January, 1973.

Nevertheless, the fact that most communities in the valley voluntarily accepted the "fair-share" plan and that about 7,000 units were built must be regarded as remarkable, considering the strong and persistent opposition to such plans almost everywhere, under every rock, in suburbia. Three reasons have been cited why Miami Valley became an exception.

First, the plan had a very articulate spokesman in Bertsch, a calm, soft-spoken man who, with a dedicated staff, went into each community and patiently tried to reason with residents. It was stressed that by sprinkling small, "vest pocket" projects in every community, no one community would be picked on or "overrun." In addition, residents were reassured that the projects would not be monolithic eyesores, but rather attractively designed to blend in with the scale and tone of the neighborhoods.

There also were the moral arguments. Throughout the debates, Bertsch expressed the belief that all persons should have the option of living wherever they wanted to. "That's the American ethic," he is quoted as saying. As in Port Washington, the reasoned, ethical approach also had the support of the area's "establishment," which quietly and effectively worked behind the public stage to try to isolate the demagogues in opposition and to calm the majority.

A second factor in the success of the sale of the plan to the valley communities was the strong and constant support of the *Dayton Daily News*, in particular, its editor, James E. Fain. A protégé of the late Ralph McGill, the humanist Southern editor, Fain attacked "snob zoning" in the "white-on-white suburbs, those lily fields that encircle Dayton and other such urban centers." His columns were both educational and entertaining, a rare combination. When Oakwood was debating the plan, Fain wrote that "the opportunity to live in Oakwood is a burden that should be shared without regard to race, creed, color, religion, national origin or draft status." While he might have pricked the anger of the opposition, he also pricked the conscience of many. Debates in some communities were said to be almost rational.

But as we have learned, rationality and ethics rarely prevail in open debates over racial and economic integration proposals for suburbia. If anything prevails, it is usually fear and greed—and in the opinion of some observers that is actually what did prevail in the valley, and was the third and most critical factor why the plan was approved.

In addition to making planning recommendations for the growth of the region, the commission recently had been delegated authority to coordinate and review federal grants going into the area. The authority gave the commission the potential of a tremendous carrot to dangle before the communities as it brought its stick in the form of the "fair-share" plan to bear upon the rear of the communities. Most of the communities already were at the federal trough feeding upon a variety of grants—urban renewal, sewers, open space, and education, to name a few—using them as an important source of funds in the always delicate art of balancing the local budgets to keep down property taxes, the bane of suburbia.

Shortly before considering the "fair-share" plan, the incorporated suburb of Kettering, a white middle-class enclave of 70,000 persons south of Dayton, had an application to the federal Department of Housing and Urban Development for a $65,000 park grant rejected. The reason given was that Kettering, with an estimated black population of 20, had restrained its human relations commission from seeking housing for black families. The rejection sent a shiver of fear through officials in the valley that maybe, just maybe, the commission would reach an understanding with the federal government to use the grants as a weapon to force open communities. The officials were reminded that this strong arm tactic had been recommended repeatedly by George Romney, then the secretary of Housing and Urban Development. The feeling among the officials, therefore, was that maybe it would be better to go along with a reasonable voluntary "fair-share" plan in which all the communities had input through their representation on the commission and in which all would participate than have an arbitrary plan imposed on selected communities by federal bureaucrats.

Whatever the reason or reasons—the federal "threat," the commission's educational campaign, the support of the Dayton "establishment," or the proddings of Fain—the fact remains that most of the communities accepted the plan, projects were built, about 30,000 black and low- and moderate-income persons are now living in communities that had been denied to them, and the Miami Valley moved a little closer to the pluralistic ideal of America.

The Dayton plan has drawn much national attention, with scores of housing and planning officials making pilgirmages to the offices of the commission. Fain takes the praise with a typical grain of salt. "The interest so many people are showing in what we are trying to do here," he observes, "is more a reflection of tragic failures in the rest of the country than of any particular success in Dayton."

There have been attempts to implement a "fair-share" plan in a few other metropolitan regions. About 3,000 low- and moderate-income units were built in the suburbs of St. Paul and Minneapolis, under a plan adopted in 1972 by the Metropolitan Council of the Twin Cities. A plan for the suburbs of Washington, D. C., was announced in 1972 by the Metropolitan Washington Council of Governments, but so far nothing has been built. The reasons cited for the failure there were the federal housing moratorium, the recession and the ban on new sewer construction in Montgomery County, Maryland.

One of the more publicized failures was the attempt to sprinkle nine projects throughout Westchester County by the New York State Urban Development Corporation (UDC), which had the exceptional powers as a public benefit corporation to override local zoning and building codes. Unique in the nation until it fell on hard times, the UDC also could plan, finance, and construct low- and moderate-income housing. In fact, that specifically had been UDC's mandate, but up to 1972 it had not tread upon the hallowed ground of suburbia without invitation. The UDC plan called for about 100 units in each of nine communities; Greenburgh, Bedford, Lewisboro, Harrison, Cortlandt, Somers, Yorktown, North Castle, and New Castle. The towns exploded in opposition. "If we want New York City to move to New Castle, *we'll* tell you," said Stuart Greene, head of United Towns for Home Rule, a countywide organization formed to fight UDC and its plan.

The remark was among the milder in the debates that raged across the county at community meetings, cookouts, coffeeklatches, and cocktail parties. Unfortunately, it also spilled over into the political campaigns in the fall of 1972, prompting the UDC to declare a moratorium on the plan until after elections. It did not ease the tension. Nothing did until January, 1973, when the mentor of the UDC and then governor of the state, Nelson A. Rockefeller, requested the agency to withdraw the plan. But the opponents did not just want the plan killed, they wanted it buried with no hope of resurrection. Drumming up sympathy among suburban politicians across the state, they pressured the legislature to strip the UDC of its override powers in towns and villages. Whatever hope there was in New York State to implement a fair share housing plan that also could serve as a model for other states was now dead. The only hope was now the federal government, and that was not much hope at all.

10

The Rule of
Law and Mobs

The housing advocates in the Miami Valley were lucky. No one in the opposition really pressed the federal government on its implied intentions to use its grants as a weapon to open the suburbs. When the government was pressed a short time later in the suburbs of Detroit, it denied with some obfuscation any such intentions. However, the denial did not stop one community, Warren, from rejecting in an unprecedented referendum a $13 million federally assisted urban-renewal program out of fear that it would bring with it forced integration. The suburb's vociferous reaction to the somewhat confused and at times contradictory appeals by Secretary Romney of HUD, the state's former governor, also is said to have eventually led to his exasperation over the issue and his resignation. Warren was his Waterloo and the federal government's "Munich," as far as using its powers were concerned to integrate the suburbs.

"Despite disclaimers by Romney that 'forced integration' was not an objective of his Department, Warren became an ideological watershed both for advocates of open housing and for those who began to sense a threat to racially and economically exclusive residential sanctuaries," observed Simpson Lawson, the former executive editor of *City*. "Persisting speculation suggested, in essence, that HUD was developing strategy for implementing the assertions often made by Romney, and sometimes amplified by others in the Nixon administration, that every American is entitled to a decent home within reasonable distance of his job. No official disavowals could dislodge the belief that this meant a move to 'integrate the suburbs' and that Warren was the testing ground."

If so, a tougher community for the test could not have been selected. Warren has been described as the archtypical working-class suburb, high on flagwaving and low on blacks. According to the last census, its residents are of predominantly Polish descent, followed by Germans and Irish. Among its approximately 40,000 families are, officially, 28 black families, 20 of whom happened to be military transients in government housing when the census was taken. Thousands of blacks do commute to Warren each day —to work in the automotive plants there, and then commute back to Detroit. The story told in Warren is that the only way blacks will ever move there is feet first, to be buried in the Detroit Memorial Park, a sprawling 80-acre cemetery owned and operated by blacks since the twenties, 30 years before Warren was incorporated. The census also disclosed that Warren is a slight cut above the national median for income and jobs and a good cut above for housing, with most of its residents owning homes of relatively high value. To the casual observer, Warren presents the picture of a comfortable suburban community, a bastion of white middle America.

Eyeing the liberal federal grants being bestowed on some of its neighbors in the late sixties, Warren decided to get some for its own needs. Decay had set in in one of its older neighborhoods, McKinley, where many senior citizens lived on pensions and social security payments. A housing rehabilitation program was needed, if not some new, subsidized projects for the elderly. In addition, Warren was having a continuing problem with its drainage and sewerage. Severe thunderstorms would flood some sections. In fact, after a 90-minute, 5-inch downpour in July of 1967, whole neighborhoods had to be evacuated and the town was declared a disaster area for federal aid. It was now hoped that urban-renewal funds could be used to upgrade the sewer system.

As in the Town of North Hempstead and other suburban communities, urban renewal, then titled the Neighborhood Development Program (NDP), also was seen as a boost to the local budget. Warren had a particular problem because its city charter did not allow deficit spending and limited the property tax rate. As a result, the property taxes were low, but so were services and the financial ability of the municipality to initiate such capital improvement projects as new sewers and street repairs. Under NDP,

Warren could undertake the projects along with its housing programs and in effect get two dollars from the federal government for every dollar it spent, including some municipal salaries for persons assigned to various "development" programs. It was a pretty package and the Warren City Council endorsed it heartily.

One hitch in the negotiations between Warren and HUD was the request of the department's regional office that the suburb enact a fair housing ordinance and establish a human relations board to enforce it, consistent with the "affirmative action" provisions of the Civil Rights Act of 1968. When Warren balked, Romney reportedly told a delegation of its councilmen to have the "political courage like I did to get a fair housing ordinance passed in Birmingham (Mich.)." As Governor in 1967, Romney had fought hard for the ordinance in the Michigan city, which was next door to his home community of Bloomfield Hills. In light of the Civil Rights Act, however, the ordinance was now considered a relatively weak document, without the teeth the HUD regional office wanted. Warren copied the Birmingham ordinance word-for-word and approved it. The cackling among the councilmen could almost be heard in Washington. "Now let's see Mr. Romney duck this one," a councilman said at the time. "We'll force his hand; he can't talk his way out now." The council's ploy worked, and Warren's application was approved. A $3 million project got underway almost immediately, while plans were put into the works for projects totaling $10 million more.

The bombshell that eventually blew the $13 million program out of the waters of Warren and destroyed whatever resolve there was in HUD to achieve a modicum of integration through its programs came on July 21, 1970, in a copyrighted story in the *Detroit News,* headlined: U.S. PICKS WARREN AS PRIME TARGET IN MOVE TO INTEGRATE ALL SUBURBS.

The story announced that "the federal government intends to use its vast powers to force integration of America's white suburbs—and it is using the Detroit suburbs as a key starting point." Citing the "drawn-out struggle" between Warren and HUD, the story implied that Romney had selected the blue-collar suburb as an initial test to use federal funds to force integration. The "meat" of the story was based on a HUD memorandum on file in Washington, which the *News* somehow had gotten hold of and reproduced in full. It read:

Detroit suburbs present an unparalleled opportunity for the application of a fair housing strategy. Nowhere else in the Midwest, perhaps nowhere else in the country, is there a combination of a large central city with a substantial black population (more than 40 percent), surrounded by large white suburbs which may use HUD programs, and in which (suburbs) there is extensive black employment and a great deal of middle-income housing. This suggests racial rather than economic exclusion . . . it is proper for HUD to use its resources to (loosen) the "white noose" surrounding the central city.

Commenting on the memorandum, the *Detroit News* declared:

The memorandum sets the policy guidelines through which Romney, who is deeply committed to equal opportunity for all races, hopes to break down segregated housing patterns in the United States.
It tells the story of Warren.
It is also the story of Royal Oak, Hazel Park, Dearborn, Madison Heights, St. Clair Shores, Center Line, Southfield, Ferndale, Dearborn Heights and several other nearly all-white suburbs.
It is also the story of white suburbs everywhere.

The memorandum had been written by Edward M. Levin, a career civil servant in the HUD Chicago regional office, to Francis D. Fisher, the HUD regional administrator. As one of the officials reviewing the Warren urban renewal program, Levin knew the suburban community well. Only a few months prior he and Fisher had received a report from a HUD study team recommending rejection of Warren's application. Noting that 30 percent of the workers in the community's major plants were black and financially able to live near their jobs, as did their fellow white workers, the team wrote that "the pattern of housing and the composition of the work force leads us to reasonably presume that equal opportunity is not being provided relative to the benefits derived from federal programs."

Levin and Fisher also knew that Warren wanted and needed the NDP grant. Writing in *City* magazine, Martin V. B. Weston commented that the HUD officials therefore reasoned "they were in an excellent position to force improvements of the city's former performance with integrated housing. In addition, they figured they could count on the unqualified backing of Romney." Or so they thought.

The *News* ran six subsequent stories, quoting at length various HUD memorandums implying that Warren and other Detroit suburbs were to be the "principal starting place" for a nationwide campaign of "affirmative action" to enforce the Civil Rights Act of 1968. By the seventh day the Detroit suburbanites were foaming at the mouth, prompting Romney to hurry to Warren for an emergency meeting "to clear the air."

Holding copies of the *Detroit News* clenched in his left fist, Romney in shirtsleeves declared before an audience of area officials, local mayors, newsmen, and television cameras that "there is not now, nor will there be, a HUD policy mandating forced racial integration in the suburbs." He continued: "The department does encourage integration through voluntary action. And we have a statutory mandate to enforce a national policy of fair housing. But our role is not to prescribe quotas or numerical standards which a community must meet."

The statement apparently appeased most of the suburban politicians who had packed the meeting. However, it did not appease the angry crowds that had gathered outside, waving signs that read "Get Rid of The Dud at HUD" and "Romney is a HUD-ache." Some of the signs came down on the heads of policemen trying to contain the crowd. The mood was ugly, reminiscent of when a black automotive worker, Corado Bailey, and his white wife were greeted by riotous whites in 1967 as they moved into a Warren subdivision. While the Warren City Council, at the urging of Mayor Bates, voted 5 to 4 to continue with the urban renewal program and go through with the motions of appointing a fair-housing board, civic associations and neighborhood groups gathered 14,800 signatures in just eight days to put the urban renewal program on the November ballot as a referendum.

The issue was not urban renewal, of course, but racism. However, the tone of the arguments by some of the opposition was so blatant and ugly that many moderates were turned off and began leaning to the urban renewal proponents who were stressing the physical benefits the program would bring to Warren. Then came another bombshell from Washington.

Appearing before the Senate Select Committee on Equal Education Opportunity, Romney took his foot out of his mouth to declare that Warren "had an obvious policy of discrimination. . . . They're not going to get any money unless they comply with requirements to at least create a human relations council." Whether Romney had a change of heart or whether he was just clarifying Warren's obligation under the proposed HUD contract was beside the point at the moment. With the urban renewal issue about to go before the voters in Warren, he could not have picked a worse time to comment. Confusion erupted in the community, prompting Mayor Bates, who was a strong force behind the renewal proponents, to demand Romney publicly apologize to Warren. Despite reassurances from Romney that his earlier statement still stood, Bates under pressure from the opposition declared "if I detect any changes in policy, if I detect that HUD is attempting to force integration, then I will abolish HUD funds in Warren."

He did not have to. The voters did it for him. By a 26,471 to 19,906 count, they rejected the urban renewal program and repealed various ordinances created for its operation, the first community to do so in the nation.

The vote was recorded loud and clear in Washington, effectively dampening any enthusiasm in the federal government to use its grants as a tool to combat the obvious growing racial and economic segregation of suburbia. The *Detroit News* and other newspapers had in fact been correct in reporting internal debates within HUD over how to develop a coordinated strategy to open suburbia. A profusion of memoranda had been circulating that fall in the department recommending a variety of actions, including bonuses to communities that provide low-income housing, higher priorities for urban renewal to cooperating communities and, generally, a concerted effort by all branches of the government to come up with a regional approach to the problem. Writing in the *National Journal,* William Lilley, III, of the department's policy section, declared that HUD was "in the final planning stage of a full-scale effort to disperse largely black and poor populations of center-city ghettos into largely white and affluent suburbs." There was every indication at last that the issuance of a policy of affirmative action was imminent.

The Dayton so-called "fair-share" plan for the Miami Valley was referred to again and again in the memos and articles as an example of what could be accomplished if the federal government wanted to back local housing advocates in opening up white communities by applying a little financial pressure. *Newsweek* observed in a special report that while the education campaigns in the Miami Valley were impressive, the prevailing view was summed up by a resident who declared that "none of us wanted to have Washington cut off Dayton's allowance."

It was emphasized by the local advocates, however, that the government needed a clear, consistent policy that communities would not misinterpret and that it had to be firm. "If political pressures build up so that the suburbs can continue to flout low- and moderate-income housing and still get their money from Washington, there is little we can do," said a local official in Dayton to John Herbers of *The New York Times*.

And the local pressures did build up. The Warren debacle had raised the specter of the "forced" integration of suburbia, prompting officials in almost every metropolitan area across the country to demand clarification of the government's policy or nonpolicy. Confusion reigned at HUD, and reporters and columnists were having a field day. Kevin Phillips, the former Republican tactician-turned-columnist, portrayed HUD as "stalking suburbia through sewers" as it prepared guidelines designed to "force suburban communities to accept integrated low-income housing in order to qualify for much-needed sewer grants." Romney once again was up against a wall.

"As far as I'm concerned," Romney declared at a press conference, "a policy that involved forced integration of the suburbs or racial balance would fail; that it's not a sound policy; and this department is not undertaking a policy of racial balance or racial quotas, or forced integration, or anything of that character." Having stated what HUD's policy was not, Romney, however, failed to state what the policy was.

There was no such confusion at the White House. President Nixon and his chief political advisor, Attorney General John Mitchell, recognized well that much of the administration's political strength was in suburbia. As products of suburbia, Nixon from Orange County, California, and Mitchell from metropolitan New York, including a few years as a resident of Port Washington, they also recognized what a volatile issue racial and economic integration was in white middle-class suburbia. Having nurtured the suburban voter in 1968, they had every intention of nurturing the same voter again in 1972. The President made that fact very clear at a news conference a few weeks after the Warren incident, declaring that "forced integration of the suburbs is not in the national interest." At the same time reports from "White House sources" were appearing in the newspapers that Mitchell had suggested to Romney that he take another position in the administration. The message got through to HUD. The various memoranda proposing a clear and firm policy for open communities that had been circulating in the department disappeared into the dead files, and with them the careers of some committed civil servants.

Mitchell's role was critical. Even if HUD had persevered and had developed a policy using federal grants as a carrot to open suburbia, it would have fallen on the Department of Justice to coordinate its enforcement. The principal weapon in the federal civil rights arsenal is Title VI of the Civil Rights Act of 1964, which prohibits discrimination in any program or activity receiving federal financial assistance, on grounds of race, color, or national origin. (The other principal weapon is Title VIII of the 1968 Act, which states that it is "the policy of the United States to provide, within constitutional limitations, fair housing throughout the United States." Civil rights lawyers consider Title VI to have the most muscle.) All federal agencies, including HUD, Transportation, Health, Education and Welfare, Environmental Protection and others, have the duty to enforce Title VI as it relates to their specific programs. However, the Department of Justice is charged with coordinating enforcement, including the use of its legal staff to aid agencies that have few resources and little experience.

In one of its many understatements, the United States Commission on Civil Rights declared in its report on suburbia that the Justice Department "has exercised little leadership" in the coordination or enforcement of Title VI. The report further stated that Mitchell had taken a particularly narrow view of his department's role. When asked at a commission hearing in 1971 whether he could think of any way the government could develop a common approach to the implementation of Title VI, Mitchell took a puff on his pipe and replied: "I would not believe so, other than the fact that the law requires it, and of course the contracts and other documents require it. I think it is a matter of enforcement and policing by the different departments and agencies that do business in this field."

The commission's hearings also revealed that the Justice Department was not doing much about enforcing Title VIII of the 1968 Civil Rights Act. The commission cited as a reason the lack of staff assigned to the housing section of the department's Civil Rights Division, but it also hinted by its selection of testimony that a commitment also seemed to be lacking. One of the witnesses quoted was Donald Miller, a director of a Baltimore fair-housing group. When asked if he felt the Justice Department had been effective in moving against housing discrimination in the Baltimore area, Miller replied bluntly "No, definitely not." He continued:

"I have had to make personal trips to Washington to get them to even give me a little bit of information. I made repeated telephone calls on how they file correspondence, and yet I get very wishy-washy answers. Well, to the point where originally the first evidence is submitted. They said 'Oh, yes, good case. We will take action immediately.' It just means a form letter going. It takes a month—it took one particular case a whole month to get out of our local U. S. Attorney's office. Once it got on its way, it was lost at the Department of Justice in Washington. Then it took several more months trying to get any information out of them."

Whether for political or other reasons—if there are other reasons in Washington—the department also moved slowly to challenge local exclusionary zoning that has had the clear "intent and effect" to deprive citizens of their right to housing under Title VIII. As of 1974, the department had initiated only two such suits, leaving almost all the legal effort to fair-housing and civil rights groups, such as the National Association for the Advancement of Colored People, the Suburban Action Institute and the National Committee Against Discrimination in Housing. (It is interesting to note that the landmark Mount Laurel, New Jersey, case was brought by the Camden Regional Legal Services, Inc., a federally funded antipoverty agency cooperating with the NAACP.) And when the department did act, it was belatedly and only in the most blatant situation, as in the St. Louis suburb of Black Jack.

A site had been selected and plans nearly completed for a federally assisted low- and moderate-income housing project in the unincorporated suburb when in late 1969 a storm of protests began brewing. The project originally did have the blessing of the St. Louis County Council, which held the zoning authority for the community, but the opposition quickly changed that. Hundreds of letters of protest were followed by hundreds of housewives and their children picketing the county courthouse, carrying American flags, demanding that the council allow the small, 3,224-person community to incorporate itself. The council agreed, and before you could say "Black Jack, Missouri," the suburb became a legal entity, formed a zoning board and promptly banned all multifamily housing, including, of course, the proposed project.

The Civil Rights Division of HUD was reported at the time to have screamed discrimination, but its powers were limited to "conference, conciliation, and persuasion." Its reading of the situation was that it was beyond those stages, and therefore it strongly recommended that the Justice Department sue Black

Jack. Mitchell declined, despite the arguments of Romney and some of his own staff. The case just would not help the administration's image in suburbia, was the reported reasoning behind the decision. Little consideration was given to the thought that Black Jack just might have abused the law. The American Civil Liberties Union did join with the sponsors to file suit a year later, but the action was dismissed by a trial court. An appeal was pending when in June, 1971, the Justice Department in a surprise action reversed its earlier decision and filed suit, its first against exclusionary land-use practices.

The action coincidentally came on the same day the United States Commission on Civil Rights opened its widely publicized hearings in Washington to examine the role in suburbia of the federal government, including the Justice Department. The fact that at last the department had acted on the Black Jack situation allowed Mitchell, as one of the key witnesses, to fend off some embarrassing questions. The Black Jack action created as much smoke as Mitchell puffing hard on his pipe to cover what many civil rights leaders believed at the time was the department's lack of resolve to enforce the civil rights laws.

"I am not at all impressed by the lawsuit against the Black Jack, Missouri, situation," commented the then mayor of Cleveland, Carl B. Stokes, following Mitchell as a witness at the hearing. "I'm not impressed. I just don't know how much more blatant, how flagrant a situation could be, than the Black Jack case. My goodness, if a case such as that in which you literally almost have working drawings on a project, and then a community moves openly, deliberately, to rezone to stop it, well, my goodness, if a Government couldn't move under those kind of circumstances, then in fact there is no chance at all. It is not (action in the face of) this outrageously flagrant violation of people's rights that would assure me about the Administration's policy in this regard."

When pressed, Mitchell answered civil rights and housing advocates ambiguously, as was his style. "If we have responsibilities, we will carry them out, and if we don't have responsibilities imposed upon us, we won't assume them." Even when the administration was embarrassed into assuming responsibilities in the civil rights and housing area, as in the case of Black Jack, it displayed a lack of conviction and purpose. With no pressure from the top to expedite it, the Black Jack case crawled through the court system for four years, until June, 1975, when the United

States Supreme Court refused to consider, and thus left standing, a lower-court ruling declaring the town's antiapartment zoning law discriminatory. It was a Pyrrhic victory for the sponsors of the nonprofit subsidized project. At this writing the housing site remains vacant and the Black Jack population remains 99 percent white. It appears the six years it took to get the federal government to act and the courts to rule has killed the project.

As civil rights advocates noted, the laws were (are) there, but the commitment among the leadership of the administration was (is) not. Nixon and Mitchell had set the tone for the administration, and no one since has bothered or cared to restate and enforce the goals that so many people in the turbulent years of the sixties had fought, demonstrated and, a few, had died for.

With no real federal policy as a carrot, stick, or guide in the civil rights and housing areas, suburbia in the early seventies was left alone to face the increasing challenges of racial and economic discrimination. As expected, most of the communities reacted parochially, protecting the status quo. Hearing no moral or rational arguments from Washington, local politicians heeded with few exceptions the angry protests of their constituents over any attempt to open their communities. Project proposal after project proposal long in the development stages, some emanating as far back as the racial disturbances of the sixties, went down to bitter defeat.

In a special report entitled "The Battle of the Suburbs," *Newsweek* noted that the conflicts over subsidized low- and moderate-income housing in suburbia had become "the kind of close-to-home domestic war whose headlines dwarf all others in local newspapers. No corner of the nation is unaffected by the strife." The magazine cited as typical the battle in the affluent Los Angeles suburb of Woodland Hills over a proposal to rezone a site to permit a low-income project. When Mrs. Carleen Zawocki, a woman in her thirties holding a baby told a gathering of her neighbors in the suburb's American Legion clubhouse that she did not fear low-income housing, the magazine reported that the room exploded with fury:

"Shouts and epithets rang out. Several persons had to be sternly reprimanded by the hearing officer after they had jumped up to hurl personal insults at the speaker. One woman shrilly accused Mrs. Zawocki of having brought her eight-month-old baby with her to the meeting solely to create sympathy for her stand."

"I just didn't expect people who are so much like myself to get so violent about this," said Mrs. Zawocki later to the magazine's reporter. "But now I know that even these people can be terrible when they're afraid—and people here are afraid of any kind of poor people moving into the community."

A summation of those opposed to the project was offered by a young stockbroker, who declared away from the heat of the debates that "low-income housing represents all of the things I moved here to the San Fernando Valley to get away from. If we allowed it to be built, Woodland Hills could turn into a suburban slum. To be frank, I believe we should close the gates." The opposition prevailed and Woodland Hills closed its gates.

The stockbroker's statement was an unusually calm one for the opposition. With no moral leadership from Washington under Nixon and Ford, and most local politicians frightened for their careers, the opposition, usually a vociferous minority, has acted as if it has been given a license to intimidate. In report upon report from community after community involved in one housing integration battle or another the consensus quote from the "neighborhood spokesman" at the public hearings usually runs something as follows:

"I know I speak for my neighbors when I tell you that we all worked hard to move away from (fill in: Brooklyn, Philadelphia, Baltimore, Atlanta, Oakland, Chicago, or any other racially troubled center city or community). We moved here so we can enjoy some peace and quiet; so our children can go to good schools; so we can walk in our streets at night without worrying about being mugged. (Cheers erupt from the audience). And now (fill in a local nonprofit housing corporation, a multifamily project developer, a 'do-good' organization, a regional or local housing official, or a neighborhood masochist) wants to build a project (a chorus of catcalls reverberates through the hall) that, to add insult to injury, we are going to have to pay for out of our taxes. That project is the 'foot in the door.' It's going to destroy our community (affirmations echo from the audience). We don't need any housing for 'them' here. Let 'them' take 'their' project and (fill in: 'build it in Harlem' or similar city ghetto, or in the 'do-gooders' neighborhood,' or, simply and bluntly, 'shove it.')"

If the next speaker is the proponent of the proposal, he can forget about his prepared remarks or his attempt to explain whatever designs or models he brought along. He will be drowned out by an angry audience. I have witnessed it happen to others and have had it happen to me. The frustration is that you know that many people in the communities might be sympathetic to the need for the housing, especially if it is for the elderly, but they are reluctant to speak out strongly in the face of an emotional and at times irrational opposition.

Even when the immediate neighborhood for one reason or another is in favor of a project and does speak out, the fear of the broader community usually prevails, especially if it holds the power of approvals. Such was the case of Wyandanch, an unincorporated black enclave within the Town of Babylon on Long Island, which had developed with the New York State Urban Development Corporation (UDC) a proposal for a low- and moderate-income project. The history of the project is typical in many respects. The following chronology, prepared by the UDC, speaks for itself:

August 4, 1967. Midway through the "hot" summer that saw rioting in Detroit and Newark, four days of racial disturbances end in Wyandanch after government leaders, including Suffolk County Executive H. Lee Dennison, hold meetings with black youths to discuss their complaints and community problems.

August 7, 1967. Attacked because he allegedly overreacted to demands by blacks, Dennison responds by saying: "There are ghettos in Babylon Town, encircled by restrictive zoning regulations, and they exist because the town permits them. They have building codes and they don't enforce them."

September 28, 1967. Actual inspection of 422 homes in part of Wyandanch by the Suffolk County Health Department, in cooperation with the County Social Services Department and the Babylon Building Department, supports charges about bad housing in Wyandanch.

The report, entitled "Housing Survey: Wyandanch Area, Town of Babylon," finds that 194 housing units, or 46 percent of those inspected, had sanitary code violations; 96 units were deteriorating or dilapidated; and there were 156 violations of the Babylon Building Code.

The 1970 United States Census would disclose later that 500 of the 3,666 units in Wyandanch—13 percent—were overcrowded, and most were occupied by black families who comprised the majority of Wyandanch residents. The census found that Wyandanch contained seven percent of Babylon's poor, with 393 families living below the poverty level. It also found that 43 units had no plumbing; 12 had no toilets; that people in 24 units had to share bathrooms; and in 25 units they had to share kitchens.

October 21, 1969. After living in Wyandanch for a year, Father Andrew Connolly, Assistant Pastor of Our Lady of the Miraculous Medal Roman Catholic Church, invites several men from the parish to form a discussion group. Those who attend bring up housing.

November 10, 1969. Connolly and his parishioners meet with members of another congregation, Trinity Lutheran Church, and their pastor, David Swanson.

February 9, 1970. Connolly and Swanson, and 15 others representing both congregations, review alternate needs of the Wyandanch community. They decide to focus on housing and building code enforcement.

July 21, 1970. In response to a request for help from the Wyandanch community, UDC agrees to finance a study by Raymond, Parish and Pine, Inc., planning consultants, to identify what can be done to improve the housing situation in Wyandanch. It is agreed that the contract will be administered by the Suffolk Community Development Corporation (SCDC), an independent group established in 1969 to promote county-wide development.

October 27, 1970. Not wanting to wait for Raymond, Parish and Pine to complete its study, another public meeting is held by the people representing the two churches. More than 100 Wyandanch residents attend, including representatives of over 20 civic and social organizations working in the community. They vote to establish a Wyandanch Task Force. Its purpose: to study and activate programs to improve the existing Wyandanch housing stock, build new homes at prices residents can afford and generally better the hamlet's living conditions.

February 16, 1971. Task Force members and the Babylon Town Board begin meetings to review programs toward community development.

March 11, 1971. The Wyandanch Task Force elects Reverend David Rooks, a Baptist Minister, Chairman. Father Connolly is Secretary. Initially, 98 persons join. The same group will later incorporate as the Wyandanch Community Development Corporation (WCDC).

May 12, 1971. Raymond, Parish and Pine releases its study. It identifies several possible sites for new housing.

June 9, 1971. Babylon Town Supervisor Aaron Bennett writes to WCDC: "At meetings between the representatives of your organization and members of the Town Board we were favorably impressed and pleased with the progress you are making in your self-help program. We would greatly appreciate it if you would continue to keep us advised from time to time with updated reports of your activities and progress."

September 21, 1971. WCDC recommends Commonwealth Drive, one of the sites mentioned by Raymond, Parish and Pine, to the Babylon Town Board. The recommended site is in a level, wooded area close to shopping, transportation and a day-care center to serve working mothers. The plans are compatible with the Babylon Town Master Plan, which had labeled the Commonwealth Drive area as one of the most blighted in the entire town and added that "with proper treatment" the section could "become a very good residential area."

November 15, 1971. WCDC moves further toward development of the Commonwealth Drive site in a Letter of Agreement with SCDC and UDC. The agreement provides for a Community Advisory Committee (CAC), which can be a formal vehicle for local input, and that WCDC be able to recommend contractors.

May 25, 1972. Plans for the development at Commonwealth Drive move forward. UDC engages Gindele and Johnson of Poughkeepsie (N.Y.), leading black architects, to design the development.

June 8, 1972. The architectural firm completes a schematic design. It includes 29 clustered two-story buildings. Of the 182 garden apartments, 18 would be for elderly persons; 54 would be efficiencies and one-bedroom apartments; and 110 for families with children. The development would serve moderate- and low-income people. The housing units are designed to allow for the maximum development of open space and green area.

September 18, 1972. Negative reaction. The Deer Park Conservative Club holds a meeting to discuss the Commonwealth Drive proposal. Nearly 900 people pack the Veterans of Foreign Wars Hall in Deer Park, a predominantly white hamlet located about one-half mile from the housing site. One speaker, who will become a leading antagonist of the housing proposal, is Hermann Griem, President of the Joint Civic Taxpayers Association of Babylon Town. He says there are only 41 substandard houses in the Town of Babylon.

From Westchester comes a representative of the United Towns for Home Rule. He tells those assembled: "Your taxes must go up and your control must go down."

Like support for the project, opposition cuts across racial lines. Ted Williams, of the 25- to 30-member predominantly black Triangle Community Club, says the housing proposal would create an extra load "on the already overburdened taxpayer."

Reverend Rooks also attends the meeting. He answers assertions about high taxes by saying: "You're all excited about subsidized housing. Nobody talks about the subsidized roads we drive on, the subsidized airlines we fly on, or the subsidized trains—only the subsidized homes for poor people."

From somewhere in the room a voice responds. "Let them go to work."

October 17, 1972. The public debate intensifies. An estimated 1,000 residents, divided pro and con, jam a Babylon Town meeting. A petition presented to the Board describes the Wyandanch proposal as a "Forest Hills in Babylon Town." (Forest Hills was then very much in the news because of a New York City Housing Authority proposal to build a low income project there that would tower over the middle income neighborhood in Queens. The height of the project was eventually reduced and the project built, but not without bitter protests.)

March 6, 1973. Events that will eventually affect Wyandanch are happening in another place. In Albany, reaction to UDC's proposal to build 100 units of low- and moderate-income housing in each of nine Westchester towns triggers the filing of Assembly Bill 7323B. It would curb UDC's power to build in suburban areas by giving towns and villages veto power over proposed UDC housing developments.

May 27, 1973. Assembly Bill 7323B passes.

June 8, 1973. Because of the possible effect of the new legislation on the Wyandanch proposal, some reaffirm their previous position in favor. County Executive John Klein, an early proponent of the housing development, issues another statement in support.

Several groups go public in their support. These include the Long Island Mid-Suffolk Human Rights Commission, the Metropolitan New York Synod of the Lutheran Church in America and the Long Island Interfaith Council.

June 28, 1973. More church support for WCDC. Walter P. Kellenberg, Bishop of the Catholic Diocese of Rockville Centre, sends a public letter to Father Connolly. "The Wyandanch proposal," says the Bishop, "recognizes the demands for the common good and the local community's right to self-determination..." A follow-up editorial in *The Long Island Catholic* asks, "If you can't build housing for the poor in a poor community, where can you build it?"

July 13, 1973. A WCBS-TV editorial also homes in on the "home-rule" idea. It says "... neighboring communities are opposing the housing plan and have urged the Babylon Town Board to turn it down. Why, we cannot understand. The Wyandanch housing plan is a self-help effort and people in Long Island believe in home rule. So we urge the Babylon Town Board to approve the Wyandanch housing plan. All the people are asking is a way to help themselves."

July 22, 1973. An estimated 1,000 people attend a rally, sponsored by WCDC, at Wyandanch Park. Almost all of them sign petitions in support.

July 24, 1973. One of Long Island's employers joins those supporting the proposal. In a letter to SCDC, John B. Rettaliata, Vice-President of the Grumman Corporation, which, among other things, operates a 535-employee plant in Wyandanch, writes: "The WCDC, the SCDC and the NYSUDC... have Grumman's very fullest support in their efforts to erect sorely needed housing for ... Wyandanch families."

July 26, 1973. Before television cameras, radio microphones, and news media reporters, opposing sides converge on the UDC public hearing held in Wyandanch High School gymnasium. Attendees total more than 1,000.

There are 60 who speak in favor, 25 against. Of those attending the hearing, 467 sign cards stating their support for the project, 55 sign in opposition.

Opponents of the project present petitions with 4,931 signatures.

July 31, 1973. After covering the hearing and the events leading up to it, *Newsday* editorializes: "... this is a model program, a grass roots community effort to come to grips with an important problem. In addition to its backing among residents of Wyandanch, it has the support of the Governor, the County Executive and the local clergy. If that isn't home rule, then the term's a mockery."

August 7, 1973. Those in favor of the project present petitions bearing 4,217 signatures to the Babylon Town Board at its regular meeting. On this day, 140 supporters and 15 opponents attend the meeting. Of them, 26 speak in favor, nine against. Letters in support number 50. There is one letter in opposition.

August 26, 1973. Before 90 silent onlookers, the five-member Babylon Town Board votes 3-to-2 to reject the proposal. The Board notes, among other things, the "adverse impact" of the development on the community's high water table.

For many communities such as Wyandanch, it is not a question of assuming their "fair share" of the need for low- and moderate-income housing in their metropolitan area, but just providing housing to meet the needs of their own residents priced out of the local market or living in substandard housing. This had been the thrust of the study by the Port Washington Chapter of the League of Women Voters and its support of Cow Bay Green and the development of a master plan for the Town of North Hempstead. But as suburbia moved into the seventies the League and other housing advocates in Port and elsewhere sensed a growing opposition to any proposals and a reluctance at every level of government to assert itself.

If community resistance was not enough of a problem, Washington added a few more. Particularly crushing was the increasing red tape imposed on subsidized-housing programs by HUD, the confusion over the environmental impact statements now required by the Environmental Protection Agency, followed by the federal moratorium on subsidized housing. (The moratorium was officially lifted in the fall of 1974 with the passage of the Community Development Act, but confusion and politics in Washington delayed any funding until late 1975, and then only in dribs and drabs nowhere meeting the pent-up need.) It was recalled that as a Congressman, President Ford was one of the few strong critics of the Dayton "fair share" plan and other efforts to provide assistance for subsidized housing and regional planning in suburbia.

Ford's attitude has reinforced the attitudes of Nixon and his alter-ego, Mitchell, that had frozen in fear most of the federal departments from taking any affirmative action in suburbia. We now actually find the Justice Department not just standing idly by as the racial and economic segregation of suburbia continues, but in one critical case fighting a ruling of the United States Court of Appeals ordering HUD and the Chicago Housing Authority to cooperate in drafting a housing plan for that city and three adjacent counties. The plan would be similar to the Dayton plan in attempting to disperse needed low- and moderate-income housing outside ghettos throughout the metropolitan area. In an appeal of the decision in the spring of 1975 to the Supreme Court, which may eventually decide the issue, Solicitor General Robert H. Bork did not deny the pattern of housing discrimination in Chicago, but he argued that a "multidistrict remedy" like a metropolitan plan could not be imposed on both a guilty city and *innocent suburbs* (emphasis mine).

As the good sailors in Port Washington know, there is not much you can do when the wind dies down but pull in the sails and return to land. The CRC quietly passed away in the early seventies and the CAC and the League moved on to other causes. Among the groups left alone to wallow in the politics of housing were the senior citizens, who were being squeezed more and more by the local real estate market.

"What are we going to do?" asked one of the organizers of the Port Washington Senior Citizens Association, who came to me for advice in the spring of 1973.

"You have to build up a storm for subsidized housing," I replied. "You have to call attention to the problem. Prick the conscience of the community."

After some thought, I proposed to the senior citizens that they organize a dozen or so members to picket the local cemetery, Nassau Knolls, a large tract located in the middle of town. With signs stating "Land for the Living, Not the Dead," and "Give us land for housing NOW," they could garner wide publicity and perhaps prod the town to do something. I said I would draw the signs, write the press release and use my contacts to try to get coverage in the media. Much to my disappointment, they declined. "It would be too embarrassing," I was told. Three years later they are still quietly looking to the town to give them a site and some assistance for a housing project and help them win over local resistance.

11

The Politics of Suburbia

One of the hopes of mine upon moving to Port Washington, as expressed in an earlier chapter, was that being of reasonable size and distinct physical location on a peninsula, the community would lend itself to the healthy exercise of home rule. The political myth of the new America that I had been fed was that it was in suburbia where citizens escaping the alienation and anonymity of the cities supposedly could reassert themselves in the political process; where their voices could be heard and heeded among the policy and decision makers; where the democratic legacy of the miniature republics of Thomas Jefferson and the Founding Fathers had a chance of survival. I quickly learned that there was no political entity of Port Washington, but that it was just another Balkanized suburb within the vague Town of North Hempstead.

Jefferson had described townships in his writings as "vital principles of their governments (that) have proved themselves the wisest inventions ever devised by the wit of man for the perfect exercise of self government. Each ward would be a small republic within itself and every man in the State would thus become an active member of the common government, transacting in person a great portion of its rights and duties, subordinate indeed, yet important and entirely within his competence." It has not worked out that way in North Hempstead, where town politics is dominated by Republicans who view the exercise of power not as a public service, but as a business. There is little tolerance for citizen participation.

When we moved to Port Washington there had not been a Democratic supervisor or councilman on the five-member town board since 1917. The weekly meetings of the board were held on Tuesday mornings at 10 A.M., precluding any hope that I or other working citizens might participate, though there was a real question of what we could contribute. Agendas were vague and meetings were brisk, all important matters having first been discussed and decided in closed sessions, with perhaps a phone call or two to the town and county Republican leaders. The town was very much a part of a disciplined and dominant county party organization. In contrast, the local Democratic party, what there was of it, was in disarray.

Within a month my wife, Sherry, and I volunteered to ring doorbells, distribute literature, and make telephone calls on behalf of the local, state, and national Democratic slate. Not unexpectedly, we found that politics and its connotations of convictions and commitment seemed to put off some of our new neighbors and friends. They had accepted the political status quo of the community and did not want to be told that there was a chance it could be changed. In addition, there was a suggestion from friends that being an active Democrat in Port Washington displayed poor judgment as to how one could best contribute to the community. The Republicans had succeeded in their attempt to make the Democrats anathema to the suburban way of life.

"Vote for the Suburbs, Vote Republican," was the theme of the volumes of campaign literature we found in our mailbox that fall, and every fall since. The most flagrant bundle of literature usually arrives just a few days before election day, and most times includes a complimentary issue of the *Suburban Record,* a four-page newspaper extolling the virtues of the Republican slate and attacking somewhat hysterically the New York City-dominated Democratic party's "lust for power." Printed in the Republican party's own printing plant, the paper apparently is mailed to every voter in Nassau. A typical page 1 in the past had a banner headline declaring "High-Rise Threat to Suburban Life," beneath which was a photograph of a split-level home in the shadow of a monolithic high-rise apartment. The theme was amplified in the paper's editorial:

Nassau County today faces its most fearsome peril. We're not talking about air pollution or traffic congestion or some health menace, although these problems are related. We're talking about the very real threat to our suburban way of life posed by the relentless advance of high-rise housing.

Poised like a dagger at the jugular vein of the county, high-rise will surely become a reality if Democratic philosophy is allowed to take hold in our county. And that, friends, is what the county executive election is all about. . . . They want to create a "city of Nassau."

Democrats have a tough time trying to justify their existence in suburbia. They flourish best in the teeming wards of the inner cities, exploiting the frustrations of people who live on top of each other, who can't breathe because the air is befouled, who can't swim because the waters reek with slime, who can't travel because the streets are clogged with cars and taxis and buses and trucks. . . .

Ever since Nassau County was created on January 1, 1899, the Republican party has attempted at every election time to identify the local Democratic organization with the Democratic organization in New York City and the specter of all the city's ills that presumably many voters escaped from. When Nassau Democrats in 1904 charged the Republican officeholders with extravagances in the construction of county buildings, the Republicans did not bother to answer the accusation, but instead warned voters "to keep the Tammany Tiger out of Nassau County." The same cry was heard again and again obfuscating issues as the Republicans dominated county elections up through the fifties, recording pluralities in the towns and county of more than two-to-one. "Would you surrender your village government for a system of Tammany wards?" a Republican radio commercial warned voters in 1951. The *Suburban Record* and other Republican campaign literature has hammered home the theme to the present.

Nothing succeeds like success, and the repeated Republican victories in town and county elections have built up an organization that is one of the best financed, best disciplined and best organized in the nation, ironically matching the best the Democrats have produced in such cities as New York (with its Tammany Hall), St. Louis, and Jersey City, in the past, and Chicago, in the present. Appealing to the conservative predilection among new residents after World War I who were escaping the "hordes of foreigners flooding the cities," the Republican party established itself as "the" party in Nassau, just as rural Republican organizations were doing in other counties across the country undergoing suburbanization.

Like any political party in power, the Republicans in Nassau also were aided by the fact they could do favors for their friends, whether it was getting a road paved or providing a job for a relative. As a supervisor of the Town of Hempstead, and as county Republican leader, G. Wilbur Doughty was in a unique position in the twenties to do both while sitting behind one desk. The delivery of services to residents, therefore, was not identified as an act of government paid for by taxes, but rather a gift of the Republican party to be paid for by votes and donations.

The appeal of the party was to the privileged, and since most voters migrating to suburbia during the time felt privileged, they identified with the party. With the death of Doughty in 1930 and the depression, the party's appeal weakened for a few years, though it still controlled the towns and county. However, it was quickly and efficiently revived by the testy brilliance of J. Russel Sprague, a nephew of Doughty's. Using patronage to establish a disciplined organization, Sprague dominated the county for nearly 30 years, turning out some of the largest Republican pluralities in the nation. During this time Nassau was a Republican refuge from Roosevelt, the power base for the presidential campaigns of Thomas E. Dewey (which Sprague managed in 1944 and 1948), and a force for President Eisenhower. In recognition of Sprague's early support and power, Eisenhower, among other things, accepted Sprague's recommendation of Leonard W. Hall, a local congressman he had tutored, to be chairman of the National Republican Committee. Now not only did Sprague have the patronage of the towns and county to dispense, but also, through Hall, the federal government.

The pluralities Nassau and most other suburban communities gave Eisenhower in the fifties sent tremors through the Democratic party. If suburbia was the future, as political pundits were writing, then the future was bleak for the party of Roosevelt, Truman, and Stevenson. "The suburbs beat us," commented Jacob Arvey after Stevenson's defeat in 1952. (They would beat him again in 1956 and come close to beating Kennedy in 1960.) The Republican sage, Senator Robert Taft, magnanimously stated at the time that "the Democratic Party will never win another national election until it solves the problem of the suburbs." It was an overstatement, of course, for the Democrats did go on to win national elections. However, there is little question that suburbia has remained a major problem for the Democrats, for reasons we shall examine, just as it has remained a bastion for the Republicans, except when they occasionally slip.

The Republicans slipped in Nassau in 1961. Though Sprague

had officially retired as county leader in 1959, he continued to influence policy. The party had delivered a solid plurality for Nixon in 1960 and was confident it could sweep the county executive race in 1961, especially since the candidate for the traditionally divided and broke Democrats was a political neophyte, Eugene H. Nickerson, a Roslyn lawyer who had never held office. Despite some reported murmurs of protest from party regulars and the new county leader, Assemblyman Joseph Carlino of Long Beach, Sprague pushed the nomination of Robert Dill as the Republican candidate. A committeeman from Garden City, Dill had served Sprague well as a friend and as United States customs collector in the Eisenhower administration. If there is one weakness in the dominance of one party and one man in a political entity, it is arrogance. Sprague was arrogant, and the party paid the price.

Dill was immediately labeled by the Democrats as "Boss Sprague's candidate." Unfortunately for the Republicans, Sprague tried to answer the charge and was identified more closely with Dill. Even more unfortunately for the party, Dill also tried to answer the charge, and in one of his many diatribes termed the Democrats "greasy, slimy pigs." Nickerson, who had the engaging air of a patrician in the public service tradition, was stimulated to campaign harder, and his enthusiasm and that of young John English, the Democratic leader, ignited the party. Despite a 2-to-1 Republican registration and being outspent by an estimated 10 dollars-to-1, Nickerson won, 216,150 to 209,581. The Republicans, however, still controlled the towns and with them the patronage to feed the faithful. Governor Rockefeller also picked up the slack from Albany.

Thanks to a Republican ticket in 1964 headed by Senator Goldwater, Nickerson won again in 1964 in a Democratic landslide that also buried some Nassau state assemblymen, including Carlino. (Carlino went on to become a very successful lobbyist in Albany, and eventually gave up his political base in Long Beach to move to Port Washington.) Out of the debacle emerged Joseph M. Margiotta, a portly Uniondale lawyer, first as an assemblyman, then as town leader of Hempstead and, finally, as county chairman. While Nickerson was winning again in 1967 and looking toward a gubernatorial or senatorial nomination, Margiotta was tightening the party reins in the towns, "encouraging" employes to contribute one percent of their salaries to the party and building up the Republican county campaign chest.

In sharp contrast, the Democratic organization wallowed. With

Nickerson and English now moving in higher state and national political circles, the local party was torn over a variety of issues, not the least of which was the Vietnam War. Party regulars, who like their Republican counterparts, were primarily interested in, first, winning and, second, sharing the spoils, were disappointed in the seeming lack of concern of the county leadership over building up the party with patronage. They also were dismayed, and still are, by the party's issue-oriented liberals.

Though they can be imaginative and tireless workers when a candidate or an issue appeals to them, I have found liberal Democrats can also be unsteady and unreliable. Since few are dependent on the party for patronage, there is no self-interest to bind their loyalty. All the party holds for them are issues, which they are constantly debating and continually changing, exhausting the faithful. It gives the party spirit, but also saps it, leaving it weak at critical times.

So while the Democrats fought over issues, Margiotta dangled "favors" before the Republican workers. They responded, turning out victories with a heavy vote in the 1968 national elections and a heavier vote in the 1969 town elections. When Nickerson, his eyes on Albany, declined in 1970 to run again, Margiotta was ready with a well-oiled and fueled machine. Despite a lackluster candidate of limited ability, the Presiding Supervisor of Hempstead, Ralph G. Caso, the Republicans, without county patronage to feed on for nine years, were just too hungry to be denied. With Margiotta pulling the strings, Caso won over Anthony J. DiPaola, the mayor of Glen Cove. Though he had been outspent by an estimated 15 dollars-to-1, DiPaola proved a strong candidate with broad appeal; so strong that Margiotta eventually gave him a bipartisan endorsement for a seat on the state Supreme Court, thus eliminating him as a future candidate.

One of the few exceptions to the Republican sweep of the county in 1970 was the upset victory of Democrat Irwin J. Landes over incumbent Vincent R. Balletta of Port Washington for the state Assembly seat on the North Shore. The district had been considered safe for the Republicans. It included the Democratic voting communities of Roslyn and Great Neck, but they were outweighed by about two-to-one by the Republican communities of New Hyde Park, Williston Park, Searingtown, Albertson, Manhasset, and Port Washington. Though Balletta had lost conservative backing because of his vote for abortion reform, it was not supposed to harm him too much, for Landes also was for abortion reform. The difference was dedication.

Politics for the local Republicans was a business, from which many earned their living, and they conducted the Balletta campaign as they would a sales campaign. It was appropriate, for Balletta was a dull candidate. In contrast, Landes was issue-oriented and articulate, with a rare sense of humor. His bid attracted various good-government types, such as my wife, a county committeeperson, who conducted the campaign in Port Washington as a cause. Their enthusiasm was infectious and, despite the overwhelming Republican registration, they were able to ring enough doorbells and convince enough voters for Landes to slip in by about a thousand votes. It gave us hope for the future.

Following the disbanding of the Citizens Advisory Committee on the Master Plan in the spring of 1971, I joined my wife as a county committeeperson and threw myself into local politics. It had been obvious from the efforts of the citizens committee that a nonpartisan approach to the planning problems of the town would not work, especially now that Meade had been elevated to the bench, so I reasoned that perhaps a political approach would. At least it would put the issue within a context that the town administration would understand. I also was frankly outraged at what I considered the ignorance and arrogance of the administration as it bumbled along attempting to deal from the clubhouse backrooms with increasing and complex citizen concerns of housing, zoning, and the environment. Politics was a recourse.

The problem for the local Democrats was how to translate these concerns into issues; how to, with limited funds and volunteers, convey the issues to the public, and, not least of all, find candidates who could articulate the issues. The Democrats had won the congressional seat on the North Shore with Lester Wolff (in the Democratic landslide in 1964 and every other year since on his personal efforts) and the Assembly seat with Landes, both attractive candidates, but the alignment of their districts, though Republican, was somewhat better for the Democrats than the town lines. In addition, little patronage was involved in the seats, while much patronage was involved in the town administration. Simply put, the control of the town meant jobs, lots of jobs, which faithful Republicans had held since 1917. They would fight hard to keep that control.

The resolve of the local Republicans was strengthened by the intervention of Margiotta. The surprise Landes victory had revealed some flaws in the town organization, and Margiotta acted quickly to put it back in good running order. As noted in a previous chapter, the "soft-on-housing" supervisor, Meade, was replaced by a solid clubhouse councilman, Michael J. Tully. The town also got a new leader, Thomas Pierce, an old friend of Margiotta's who could be counted on to carry out the marching orders being cut at county headquarters. The euphoria among the Democrats over Landes' victory dissipated, so much so that the party's nominee for town supervisor, for whom I was to be campaign manager, withdrew after weighing the odds and calculating what it would take to mount a respectable effort. In November we were crushed in the town, just as Democrats were crushed in other town elections across the county. Margiotta would not be denied.

If 1971 was a difficult year for Democrats in Nassau, 1972 was a disaster. For my perseverance, I was elected an alternate delegate on behalf of Senator McGovern to the National Democratic Convention, falling into the rare quota of over-30, Jewish, suburban males. With that honor came the obligation to coordinate the McGovern campaign in Port Washington, from which followed my election as a zone leader for the party and a member of the county executive committee. The resulting meetings and more meetings, ranging from intraparty debates, encounter sessions to wakes, taxed my leadership. At times I thought the party was out to destroy itself, not needing any dirty tricks from anyone to do the job.

Despite a heartening turnout of volunteers, including some sons, daughters, and wives of stalwart local Republicans, it was obvious by September that McGovern would bomb in Port Washington. With his campaign beyond our influence, we turned our efforts to reelect Congressman Wolff and Assemblyman Landes, both of whose districts had been gerrymandered by the Republican state Legislature under the influence of Assemblyman Margiotta to favor the Republicans, of course. McGovern surprisingly did a little better than Humphrey did in Port in 1968, losing by about 3-to-2. However, our efforts for Wolff and Landes paid off, for they again slipped in, much to the chagrin of Margiotta, who had singled them out for defeat.

Margiotta was not hurting, though, at least according to a *New York Times* story shortly after the election that described him as "flourishing" as "the modern-day version of the old-fashioned political boss." It noted that the Nassau organization under his iron glove raises and spends at least $1 million every year (compared to about $50,000 a year by the Democratic county organization). Included in the expenditures is a $40,000 salary for himself and a chauffeured Cadillac, which is in addition to his salary and expense account as a state legislator and his income from a law practice. The funds come in large part from the annual contributions by the more than 17,000 county and town employees, and an average of $400 from each of the county's 971 election districts. That is about $6,000 from each leader. (As a Democratic leader I was able to raise about $200 from my districts, including $25 from my wife.) In addition, the leaders are expected to support a $500-a-plate dinner, a $125-a-person cocktail party and the $125-a-person Joseph M. Margiotta Invitational Golf Tournament. But being a Republican leader or county committeeman also has its benefits. The *Times* reported that 75 percent of the 1,800 committeemen were on the state, county, or town payroll. Also working for the county were Margiotta's sister, mother-in-law and sister-in-law.

Margiotta's command of a literal army of workers dependent on patronage and of a seemingly unlimited treasury fed by grateful government employes and "friends" further depressed the local Democrats, already divided on issues. I had pressed the party for a progressive stance on planning and housing, trying to balance the environmental concerns with social concerns. Having drafted in part the planning and housing platform for the national campaign in 1972, I had hoped that if the local party could do anything in the upcoming county campaign in 1973, it could at least take a strong stand and force the Republicans to debate the issue. If we were going to lose, I rationalized, we might as well go down flying on principles.

"That's a typical liberal death wish," sneered a party regular at a county executive meeting. The feeling was that housing was an issue too muddled with emotionalism fired by a constant barrage of Republican propaganda, as evidenced in its campaign literature, such as the *Suburban Record.* It was an issue to be avoided, just like civil or welfare rights. What constituency it already had were "gut" Democrats, the blacks, the liberals, and some senior citizens. To win in suburbia the Democrats would not have to appeal to these groups, but to the "swing" voters, who were more concerned with the environment, rising taxes, and the smell of corruption. I was reminded that the first and foremost rule of politics is to win. To some it seemed it was the only rule. Issues could only be considered a means to that end, according to the political professionals.

It was all talk, as so much of politics is. Any hope for a consensus, or even a debate, within the party on issues was lost in the spring of 1973 over a clash of personalities in an internecine leadership battle. The town and county meetings dragged on later and later into the nights and early mornings, testing my patience. I tried to avoid the meetings and concentrate on building up the Port Washington organization, but there too the frustration with the county organization's lack of resolve took its toll. With no issues or personalities to galvanize volunteers, the spirit of the McGovern-Wolff-Landes campaign dissipated. People were tired of politics.

"Who needs the aggravation," I was told by one of my committeepersons. "I'll cover my district on election day, but don't count on me for anything more." The intensity of campaigns and conflicting egos, it seemed, had burned out many volunteers, including, upon reflection, myself.

At the time my responsibilities as Director of Development of the New York City Educational Construction Fund were increasing, as neighborhood groups in the city fought our proposals for public schools combined with subsidized housing with the same fear and hate I had witnessed in suburbia. Evening meetings in the city were more frequent and demanding, leaving little time for my teaching, my family, and local politics. My frustration with the Democrats made a decision easy. I resigned my leadership that spring, content to be just a committeeperson with no political commitments except to cover my election district, which I shared with my wife. I would now have time to pause in my pursuit of causes and become an observer, or so I thought.

The Republicans, as expected, captured the Nassau town and county elections in 1973, but their victory celebrations were short. The clouds of the economy, Watergate, and other Nixon scandals were gathering over Long Island, as they were over the rest of the country. Margiotta or no Margiotta, few Republicans could stem the tide in the 1974 elections, which swept scores of Democrats into suburban seats and offices that had been held for generations by Republicans. About 24 of the 47 seats in the House of Representatives that the Democrats took from the Republicans were entirely or predominantly suburban. And the few Democrats who had tenuously held suburban seats, such as Wolff on the North Shore, got a firmer grip with heavy pluralities. Surveying the damage, Edward Maye of the Republican National Committee said that with all the issues favoring the Democrats, the issue-oriented, ticket-splitting suburbanites "just left us by the millions."

"You just couldn't organize them this year," said Maye. "People who went out and knocked on doors for Nixon in 1972 wouldn't do it for us again this year, because they didn't like the results of all their work. We had to go to paid operations, and, of course, that's not the same. If we don't get them remotivated, we're in some serious long-term trouble." If anything, Republicans in 1974 were motivated not to vote *for* Democrats, but *against* Republicans, especially in the "pale-blue-collar" suburbs where inflation was hurting.

The Republican discontent made it the easiest election my wife and I had ever worked in. Our feelings were that the national issues were so pervasive that all we had to do was deliver campaign literature (we had no money for mailings) and make phone calls to remind the registered Democrats to vote. We left the independents and Republicans to be swayed by the economy and the media. If a voter in Baxter Estates was not going to vote Democratic in 1974, we rationalized that there was little we could do to change his or her mind. With some guilt that I should have done more, I closed the polls on election night with my Republican counterpart, as was our custom, opened the voting machines and read the returns. The first line told me that the Democrats had taken Baxter Estates for the first time in my memory. And before the night was over the first Democrats since 1915, Barbara S. Blumberg of Great Neck and Richard S. Paige of Manhasset, were elected to the town council. The Republicans still held the majority with the supervisor's seat and two other council seats—they were not up for election—but it was a beginning.

Threatened with the loss of the towns and their rich source of patronage, Margiotta and the Republicans in Nassau dug in for the 1975 off-year local elections. With nothing else on the ballot, no gubernatorial or congressional races, their hope was that voter interest would fall off, as it usually does, allowing the solid base of paid Republican workers to pull out the party's majority of registered voters. The Republicans were confident that with no national disaster they could once again assert themselves on Long Island, attracting back into the fold the faithful, just as they had done after the 1964 disaster. With one eye on the economy and the other on the media, Republican leaders in other suburban communities were expressing similar hopes. A return to normalcy in suburbia would be a return to Republicanism.

As expected, the 1975 election in Nassau was "normal," with a light turnout of voters propelling Republicans to victories across the county, including North Hempstead where they defeated Mrs. Blumberg in her bid for reelection. (Paige remained on the board only because his seat was not up for election.) In Suffolk, however, the Democrats rode on the waves of local Republican scandals (noted in the next chapter) and took control of the county legislature for the first time in history, though John Klein, the Republican county executive, bucked the tide and won reelection. The results in most other suburban counties were mixed, but the Republicans seemed to have recovered somewhat from the debacle of 1974, at least enough to give them hope for 1976.

There is a basis for the confidence expressed by Republicans in suburbia. On Long Island, approximately 50 percent of the 638,000 voters in Nassau and 53 percent of the voters in Suffolk are registered Republicans, compared to 35 and 29 percent respectively for the Democrats. The spread between the two parties in the last decade has decreased (in the forties the Republican enrollment was about 75 percent), but it is still a healthy majority for the G.O.P. Similar figures can be found in other suburban counties, confirming the thesis of many political analysts that home-owning suburbanites tend to be conservative and vote Republican, varying only in elections in which there is involved a particularly strong personality or a major issue. The thesis, the variations and the exceptions, provides a steady source of grist for the academic and journalistic mills.

The Republican majority in suburbia has been explained by two conflicting theories, conversion and transplantation. The conversion theory contends that when a voter leaves a city for suburbia, he leaves behind his prior allegiances and wants very much to be accepted in his new community. According to the studies in voting trends by pollster Louis Harris and interpreted by Robert C. Wood in his book, *Suburbia: Its People and Their Politics,* "green grass, fresh air and new social status work their magic; class and ethnic appeals lose their potency. Differences in nationality, religion and occupation become submerged by a predominant identification with locality. The ownership of land, the symbol of community, these provide the sources for suburban loyalty and interest. Suburbanites shed their big city ways and embrace small town qualities of mind and outlook as quickly as they accept the backyard barbecue and the commuting schedule." The moment of truth, it seems, especially for Democrats, is the day that as a new suburbanite he or she receives the tax bill, or when he or she hears that a development is proposed that they think may threaten the value of their property. As we have seen on Long Island, the Republicans have skillfully played on these concerns.

However, there is a question of how committed the conversion may be. In explaining why the Democrats in 1974 had swept a suburban district in northwest Indiana that had been staunchly Republican, Robert Keefe of the Democratic National Committee observed that many of the voters there originally had been Democrats in such cities as nearby Gary. "Then they moved out because of the racial thing, and they kind of accepted Republican mores, kind of got to like the respectability of Republicanism. Then the economic crunch came, and they went back to their old voting habits."

The conversion theory also helps explain the split vote, at least in Port Washington. I have found when ringing doorbells in political campaigns over the years that some voters might prefer the more conservative approach of the Republicans on local issues that could affect taxes or property values, while preferring the more liberal Democratic attitudes on state and national issues. In recent elections Port Washington has split its votes, with Republican town and county candidates doing much better than Republican state and national candidates.

There are, of course, exceptions, but almost always based on strong issues, such as Watergate and the economy that sunk the Republicans in 1974, or exceptional personalities, usually negative, such as Senator Goldwater in the presidential race of 1964 and Senator McGovern in 1972. They both did poorly in Port Washington, giving the Democrats a rare majority in 1964 and the Republicans an overwhelming majority in 1972. Yet in the 1972 election Port strongly supported Wolff for Congress and gave enough votes to Landes for him to beat back a challenge by Republican Clinton Martin, Jr. for the state Assembly seat. Despite a 3-to-2 Republican registration edge in Port, the voting patterns are such as to allow hope to spring eternal in the breasts of local Democratic candidates.

According to the transplantation theory, most voters moving to suburbia actually always have been conservative—that is one of the reasons they moved to suburbia—and so when they get there they just come out of the closet and vote Republican. In support of the theory, political analysts note that with the migration to suburbia the vote there increased for Republicans while it decreased in the cities. This also bears out the theory that as voters move up the socioeconomic ladder—getting a better job, increasing their income, buying a bigger home, a new car—they also become more conservative, and thus tend to vote Republican.

As for most general theories, there are exceptions, such as I have found in the Town of North Hempstead, where the Democratic majorities happen to reside in the wealthier communities of Roslyn and Great Neck, while the Republican majorities are located in the more modest communities, as New Hyde Park, Williston Park, and Albertson. Here ethnic consideration also plays a role, for Roslyn and Great Neck are predominantly Jewish communities with a liberal tradition and New Hyde Park, Williston, and Albertson Irish and Italian Catholic with a conservative tradition.

The transplantation theory also can work for the Democrats, as has been noted in Bennett M. Berger's *Working-Class Suburb,* a study of autoworkers who relocated with their factory to the San Francisco suburb of Milpitas. Most were Democrats before they moved to Milpitas and most remained Democrats after they moved. But here again, and in the political pulse pieces in *The New York Times* and other newspapers and weeklies during presidential contests, we run into the problem of interpreting national trends based on isolated communities. ("Dateline: Suburbia. Stepping back from the neat pile of leaves he had just raked off his manicured lawn, a resident in this comfortable community did not hesitate to express his opinion, and the opinion of his neighbors, of next month's presidential election. 'We are Republicans and we are homeowners, and as such . . .' ") The connotations of being a Democrat or a Republican in, say, Great Neck, are quite different from being a Democrat or Republican in the suburbs of New Orleans, Dallas, Denver, Detroit, or Dayton.

The academic, journalistic, and clubhouse debates continue, heightened at every election time as pundits pore over voting returns. But if the returns have prompted anything among the pundits, it is caution. In their conclusion to *The Real Majority,* a study of contemporary voting trends, R. M. Scammon and B. J. Wattenberg declared: "Suburbia will indeed be the major psephological battleground in the years to come, but will probably be the major battleground only because so many Americans will be living there. Anyone who automatically deeds the turf to Republicans does so at his peril." After two decades of research, Timothy Schlitz and William Moffit stated in their bibliographical essay, "Inner-City/Outer-City Relationships in Metropolitan Areas," that we can "feel reasonably certain that the typical central city is Democratic-oriented and that the typical suburban area is more likely to be Republican, but it now appears that the disparity between the two has been considerably overstated." They concluded that "the final analysis of central city-suburban disparities can be only that we do not know exactly what they are" and that more research was "urgently" needed.

In what remains one of the more perceptive analyses, Wood observed that "whether [or not] more suburbanites switch votes than continue their old allegiances, one common inference seems possible on the basis of existing information: there is at work a political tendency toward homogeneity within each suburb compared to the social and economic homogeneity of each suburb. If assimilation is the major motivation on the part of the individual, the homogeneity comes about by conversion. If a desire to seek out one's own predominates, then the homogeneity results from transplantation. In either event, the end product is the same: an increasing differentiation in political sentiment among suburbs, a correspondingly wider range of voting behavior for suburbia in toto, and a dwindling minority group in any given suburb."

After nearly 20 years, Wood's observation seems more to the point than ever. The social and economic (to add racial would be a redundancy) segregation of suburbs also is resulting in the political segregation of suburbs. And with political segregation comes a one party dominance of government, in time with all its associated evils: graft, incompetence, and arrogance. It is not exactly the Jeffersonian ideal suburban governments purport to uphold.

12

The Price
of Politics

"It boils down to just how much the local taxpayer is willing to pay to support local pride, prejudice, and politics," H. Lee Dennison had told the Suffolk County Legislature in his farewell speech in 1971. It was a rhetorical statement, and the crusty, independent, outgoing county executive did not specifically answer it at the time. Dennison previously had bandied about the figure of a 20 percent reduction in property taxes if some consolidation and cooperation could be accomplished among Suffolk's 10 townships, 29 incorporated villages, and 527 special districts. It was not an unreasonable suggestion or estimate, for a number of consolidations to effectuate economies have taken place in suburban areas across the country, according to the National Association of Counties. However, few people think it will ever happen in Suffolk.

It was enough that Dennison, a nominal Democrat, had jolted the Republicans in 1959 out of the control of the county which they had held for 50 years. His election had followed a state investigation of land deals, shakedowns, incompetence, and misuse of county money that resulted in the indictment of 36 prominent Republicans and their associates and two business corporations. (Twenty-six convictions were eventually obtained, but most were subsequently overturned on appeal.) The thought that Dennison, or anyone, would attempt to consolidate and reorganize the patronage-rich townships had to be viewed with amusement, especially by such Republican leaders as Richard D. Zeidler, of Brookhaven, a portly, cigar-smoking auto dealer who reportedly became a millionaire in the years since 1962 when he took over the town leadership. (According to *Newsday,* Zeidler sells a lot of cars to the township and to aspiring Republicans.) Dennison's successor, John V. N. Klein, a Republican, has never broached the subject of consolidation, nor has Caso in Nassau County, which has 3 townships, 2 cities, 64 incorporated villages, and 280 special districts.

Four of Port Washington's seven-odd districts, water, sewers, garbage, and police, are independent bureaucracies, each providing its own local patronage and a few thousand dollars a year in pocket money for "volunteer" commissioners elected every year in December, ostensibly by the community. However, it is a rare year when a commissionership is contested, and when it is, maybe 500 votes decide the election, or about 3 percent of the eligible voters in Port. Little voter interest is ever expressed.

There have been occasional murmurs, none recently, from the League of Women Voters questioning whether Port could be better and less expensively served if the districts, particularly water and sewers, were consolidated on a town, county, or bicounty basis, but no one pressed the issue. The "concerned" residents always are too involved in school district battles over budgets and curriculum to worry about the special districts. But while they haggle at packed meetings over pennies and programs, debating the effect on the tax rate, the commissioners of the special districts in virtual obscurity are adding nickles and dimes to the ultimate rate, hidden in the town tax. During the spring of 1972 the battle over the school budget was particularly heated when I happened to notice a small item in the local paper obviously printed only because of a legal requirement. It prompted me to write a letter to the always receptive *Port Washington News:*

Editor:
Now that the community has succeeded in splitting itself over splitting hairs in the school budget, knocking neighbors over $10,000 items, I wonder if anyone had the energy or interest to read a little public notice last week in which the Sewer District proposed a modest increase over its original estimate for some improvements from $315,000 to $715,000— a rise of $400,000 or about 127 percent. Can you imagine if that had been an item in the school budget?

The District has scheduled the convenient time of 5:00 P.M., Wednesday, May 17, in its office on Harbor Road for a public hearing. If the School Board had conducted itself with similar decorum and dispatch in its handling of the budget, perhaps the community would have saved itself much aggravation.

The only person to attend the hearing in addition to the commissioners and the staff of the district was Ms. Amy Pett, the indomitable editor of the *News*. I was at work, as were a few other residents who had expressed curiosity over the operation of the district. No objections were heard at the hearing, though word did filter back to me that my letter calling attention to the hearing was not appreciated—by the school district as well as the sewer district. Both districts resumed their defensive postures and went back to their somewhat covert operations, while my attention was diverted to the fall elections.

In the following spring an item appeared in the *News* stating that the sewer district had been audited by the Office of the State Comptroller and that certain deficiencies had been found. I became curious again and contacted the comptroller's office in Albany for a copy of the audit. It turned out to be a very revealing document, stating, among other things, that "numerous restaurant and hotel bills were charged to the district through credit cards and paid by the district to the credit card firm," and that the expenses and the payment were "improper." It added that "advance lump-sum payments were made to district officials and employees for travel expenses" for which there was no accounting. In particular, the audit noted that "cash advances of $500.00 each were also made to Commissioner Vogt and to Superintendent Thomas for travel to Switzerland and England," adding that "hotel bills were paid by the use of a credit card, travel fares were paid by the district" and "several bills submitted with claims for reimbursement indicated charges for Mr. and Mrs." A few other abuses were noted, including failure to advertise for competitive bids as required by law, failure to record in the minutes proposed district budgets and financing certain construction without authority. It was a petty scandal, but one that to me illustrated the problems of a Balkanized government and its irrationale for existence, home rule.

Though the district reportedly was under the influence of the town Republican organization, it did not have a public identity as such. I therefore did not want any discussion of the "scandal" to become embroiled in party politics that might chill a reform effort, given the propensity among Port residents for nonpartisanship. As I viewed the alternatives, it seemed the matter would best be pursued by others than myself who did not have a strong political identity. In addition, I wanted to see some other residents pick up the cudgel.

I therefore decided to make only a half dozen copies of the audit, circulate them to some residents who I thought cared, sit back, offer no strategy, and see what happened. Though a few of the residents I gave the audit to expressed concern, the only person who volunteered to try to do something was Myron H. Blumenfeld, the founder and force of perhaps the community's most successful volunteer organization, The Residents for a More Beautiful Port Washington. Through perseverance and personality, Blumenfeld, an executive of Bloomingdale's Department Store, had led the organization in such efforts as having the train station landscaped, planting trees along the shopping streets and blocking road widenings, as well as riding herd on the town administration on everything from preserving wetlands and the shoreline to improving garbage disposal. Building upon the popularization of environmental concerns, the organization had about 700 members, ranging from flower club types to wilderness buffs.

Though Blumenfeld on his own stirred up some publicity, getting Assemblyman Landes to say he was looking into the matter, nothing came of it except a defensive statement from the district. The residents in the past had been successful in one concerted effort to elect one of its members to a commissionership for the garbage district, and Blumenfeld and I talked now of getting a "reform" candidate to run for the sewer district. A few persons expressed an interest, but all were concerned about being a single commissioner among three (one is elected every year for a three-year term) committed to cleaning up the district. No one stepped forward. The election came and went, with the old crowd still in control, though somewhat cautious, if not chastised by the publicity.

When I had first made copies of the audit, I gave one to Donald Christ, a lawyer and scion of one of the town's most influential families (his father had been a Republican leader and later a respected judge and his grandfather the last Democratic supervisor). Christ had commented at the time that the abuses in the district were relatively minor, nothing many residents in Port would get excited over. "Anyway," he added with some disdain, "no one really would want to embarrass Bob Vogt," (the commissioner who had gone to Europe on district "business"). Christ recognized that amiability took precedence, as it did for so many other community efforts.

Christ, of course, turned out to be right, for looking back on the incident, details of the "scandal" were accepted mostly with a shrug of shoulders or, worse, with a wink. "That's the way things work. Be glad it isn't more," said a neighbor. "If the county was involved, it would be worse," said another. Yet, however minor the abuses were, they were within a sphere where residents could take direct action, if they really cared, if home rule was more than rhetoric. But the convictions and commitment were missing.

It seems many of my neighbors, and other residents in Port (and I assume suburbia), have become inured to political corruption. The petty transgressions of the district, if that is what they were, were nothing in comparison to Watergate nationally and the almost daily exposures in *Newsday* of alleged violations of codes of ethics and election laws, influence peddling and flagrant graft amongst politicians on Long Island.

The exposures increased following the election in 1974 of Democratic district attorneys in both Nassau and Suffolk Counties. Within months, both offices were deep into investigations of alleged corruption. In Suffolk, the county's real estate agent—an office created to halt the hint of graft between department heads and builders—was charged with extracting $135,000 in bribes and the promise of $300,000 more from a contractor seeking to rent space in three office buildings in the county. The investigation also revealed that the contractor and others had done a number of favors for government officials and party leaders, such as free carpeting and paneling work at the county Republican headquarters, and selling homes to "friends" at below market costs. Other investigations included the examination of the records of the Republican administration in the township of Brookhaven during the construction there of a multimillion dollar Internal Revenue Service Center. County grand juries also were looking into such matters as the possible misuse of party funds by Republican boss Zeidler. Little items also kept popping up, like the Republican elections commissioner putting his family on the payroll and billing the county for travel expenses when driving his son to and from an upstate college.

In Nassau, grand juries were looking into, among other things, secret cash political contributions, falsification of records, and allegations of kickbacks to local Republican organizations. A federal grand jury also was investigating the kickback charge, which alleged that municipal employes have been forced to pay one percent of their salaries or face being passed over for promotions or pay raises. (The practice dates back to the Sprague days in Nassau, but the question now was whether the contributions were volunteered or forced.) The exposures can be expected to continue, as other investigations by the district attorney's offices dig deeper into the abuses of one-party domination over the last half century.

Long Island is not alone. It is only because I live there that I have been able to follow the history of its political corruption and document it more easily, just as I noted in Chapter 4 the Boyarskys concentrated on the Los Angeles area where they live. Random reports indicate the malaise abounds in other suburban areas, such as Fort Lee, New Jersey, where the mayor and chairman of the parking authority were charged with extracting $270,000 in bribes for the approval of a giant shopping center and office complex; in Greenburgh, a township in Westchester, New York, where federal agents and the district attorney are investigating allegations that organized crime and official corruption penetrated every government operation. The list goes on and on: garbage carting contracts, building variances, equipment purchases, and thousands of other daily acts of government that involve millions of public dollars.

I do not contend that reorganization or consolidation of special district, village, town, county, or regional services will eliminate corruption, only that it might increase professionalism, improve the delivery of services, effectuate economies, and better define the areas of responsibility so that an aware citizenry and, hopefully, the media could more easily identify and monitor the operation of government. Aside from the uncalculated cost of corruption, the present suburban system of government is from all accounts inefficient and wasteful. And of all the suburban systems of government, Nassau County appears to be the worst.

Two of the county's sharpest critics are Norman E. Blankman, a Sands Point millionaire who ran as an independent for county executive in 1973 and now heads a citizens' watchdog committee known as AWARE (Action Where Action Requires the Electorate) and Horace Z. Kramer, a Garden City lawyer who was as a Democrat the vice-chairman of the County Board of Tax Assessors from 1962 to 1973. Both have declared that Nassau residents have the dubious distinction of paying what are probably the highest local taxes per capita in the United States, with Blankman, a real estate developer, adding that the taxes "take up 42 cents of every apartment rent dollar, the highest ratio in the United States, resulting in the highest suburban rents in New York State and probably the nation."

Speaking at the budget hearing before the Nassau Board of Supervisors in December of 1974, Blankman noted while the county's population had increased by about 10 percent since 1960, the county's general budget had increased almost 700 percent, from $73 million to $579 million, under both Republican and Democratic administrations. And he added that since 1963 the population had only increased 4 percent, while the number of county employes increased 100 percent, from about 11,000 to 22,000. "This means that we added 1 employe for every 6 new residents." Deducting the large increases in social services from both the 1963 and 1975 general fund totals, Blankman said the increase in the remaining expenditures was still a whopping 430 percent. He conceded that inflation has had some effect, increasing during the same period by about 50 percent, but that it could not be made the scapegoat.

"Political opportunism, not the taxpayers' true needs, has shaped our budgets," he declared. "Faced with the longest and most severe depression since the 30s, we cannot tolerate the doubletalk and deception contained in Mr. Caso's budget and we cannot afford its expenditures, swollen by patronage, contract kickback and the ineptness of unqualified political appointees."

While Blankman has poked holes in the county budget, Kramer has done the same for the townships. He commented in an article in *Newsday* that "one would have expected that as the county's responsibilities increased (since the 50s), the responsibilities of the towns would decrease. Such has not been the case in Nassau County. As the county profile has grown, so has the role of the towns, and annoyingly enough in the same general housekeeping functions."

Kramer noted, as did Blankman, that the proposed county general fund for 1975 was about 700 percent larger than in 1960, but added that during the same period the general fund for the Town of Hempstead increased 800 percent. In particular, he pointed to a 315 percent increase to run the town supervisor's office and a 1,037 percent increase for the town board. Included in the costs of operation were five staff photographers and two press secretaries, traditional patronage plums. While the county's expenditures for parks and recreation rose from $2.2 million in 1960 to $17.8 million in 1975, a 685 percent increase, the town's park budgets, including special park districts, rose from $950,000 to $23 million, a 2,325 percent increase. He continued:

"Until 1961, the Town of Hempstead used to contract with the county public works department for road signs. The annual fee was $82,000. With the advent of a Democratic county administration, the town set up its own department with a budget of $158,000. The town has since developed a traffic control department with a 1975 budget of $949,000 and includes road signs in the department.

"Until 1965, the home for aged and incapable Republican party workers was the county sheriff's office. A Democrat was elected for 1965, and he fulfilled his promise to put the department under civil service. The Republican administration in the Town of Hempstead then established a department of safety whose 1965 budget was $250,000; its 1975 budget $1,812,000."

Kramer commented that he could understand the unwillingness of Republican town boards to sacrifice their power and patronage to a county Democratic administration even though it would have meant savings for the taxpayer. But he added that he could not understand why, now that there was a county Republican administration, the town supervisors and the county executive could not try to integrate services in Nassau, "especially since all recommendations for jobs came from the Republican headquarters at the Holiday Inn," (Margiotta's office). Kramer suggested:

"Why not have one highway department to service this county, one collector of taxes, one data processing center, one division for engineering, one drug and alcohol bureau, one planning commission, and one civil service department? Why should the towns and villages and cities give fat personal service contracts for work which could be performed for them by the county?" Why, indeed.

The need for reorganization and consolidation has become vital to the economic health of Nassau and other so-called inner ring, mature suburban counties. They cannot afford not to. Back when they were young suburban counties growing at the rapid rate of 5 to 10 percent a year, the increases in public expenditures were offset by the increases the growth brought to the assessment rolls. As the growth slowed in the older suburban counties within the last 10 years, so did the growth in the assessment rolls. Unfortunately, the growth of government did not.

This has led to the situation in Nassau in 1975 where the county's general fund expenditures increased 16.5 percent, while the assessment roll increased only .7 percent. The difference in part has to be made up by the towns and counties increasing property taxes, one of the more inequitable taxes since it is not based on income. (More money also is coming from the state and federal governments to localities, but that also is mostly out of the pockets of the majority of the middle class who reside in suburbia.) Homeowners are being squeezed.

One way the assessment rolls could be increased in older suburban counties is to develop what little land is left for its highest and best use. In addition, underutilized land also can be redeveloped for a higher and better use. But this takes imagination and planning, two ingredients that are all too often missing in local politicians. Again, I return to my county of Nassau for an illustration of how petty politics and inept administration among both the Democrats and Republicans have thwarted the realization of a potential of not only giving Long Island a needed "downtown" focal point, providing thousands of jobs, but also an estimated $100 million boost to its tax rolls. Such a boost could save an average Nassau County homeowner—me—about $200 a year in real property taxes.

It is difficult for Blankman to maintain his composure when he reviews the history of Mitchel Field, an 1,112-acre military airport in the heart of Nassau abandoned by the Air Force in 1961, with 576 acres going to the county government and the remainder to local educational institutions. First as a Republican civic leader, then as chairman of a nonpartisan task force, later as an independent candidate for county executive and most recently as head of AWARE, Blankman for years has campaigned for the rational development of the field, considered potentially the most valuable piece of real estate in all of suburbia. It is certainly the most valuable piece of real estate on Long Island. Located in the hub of the Island with easy access to mass transit and highways, the field has been appraised at up to $250,000 an acre.

Given its location and unmapped, unencumbered state, the field is seen as a rare opportunity. "It is like waving a magic wand over New York City and being able to start all over again from 34th to 59th Streets, and from river to river," Blankman has declared in his arguments for a comprehensive master plan, for which he has had the strong support of such diverse groups as the Regional Plan Association, the Long Island Association (of Commerce and Industry), the Suburban Action Institute, and the League of Women Voters. It is the opinion of Blankman, who by profession is a real estate developer, other developers, bankers, architects, and planners that if developed properly, Mitchel Field could have a worth of $1 billion, providing the county with an estimated $100 million annually in rent and taxes. After 15 years of studies, plans and provincial politics, the potential benefits are as elusive as ever.

When the federal government announced its intention in 1960 to abandon the field, Robert Moses declared the act "an almost miraculous opportunity . . . to advocate a practical plan, which will be in the best interests of the future citizens of Nassau County." The then Republican county administration formed a committee on development, with Moses its most prominent member, which in the summer of 1961 recommended a diverse, bland, low density plan including residential, cultural, industrial, commercial, community, and park uses of the land. However, the Democrats in the fall took control of the county under Nickerson and after nearly two years of haggling with the Republican-dominated Board of Supervisors formed a new committee to succeed the Moses group. The committee came back within a year with a proposal for a cultural center with all the trappings, including a coliseum, a theater, concert hall, and museum. It should be noted that the year was 1964 and everyone, including politicians and planners, was suffering from Lincoln Centeritis, a deadly and expensive disease caught at the glittering grand opening of the New York City complex.

It also was an election year, and soon after the committee had made its proposal, President Johnson was in Nassau County to break ground. But as soon as he put down the shovel work stopped, as civic groups and civic leaders, including Blankman, questioned the economic feasibility of the project. The county did approve funds late that year for the coliseum, but nothing else as the respected Regional Plan Association joined the debate by declaring that the field was an ideal location for a regional center to serve Long Island's growing residential, commercial, and transportation needs.

The debate among the civic groups, the county administration, the town supervisors and the political parties continued for nearly three years, interrupted only by a recommendation in 1966 by the County Planning Commission for 10,000 housing units, which brought into focus a major problem in the development of the field. Though the county owns the land, it is situated in the Town of Hempstead, which controls the zoning. With Supervisor Francis T. Purcell, a crusty conservative, supplying the invective for the past decade, the town has consistently opposed housing on the grounds that it would burden school facilities and because to get maximum tax yield from the land would require the housing to be high-density, high-rise apartments, which would destroy the suburban character of the community. There also is a strong local fear, expressed in no uncertain terms at public meetings, that a percentage of the housing would be for low-income families who, to say the least, are not welcomed in the struggling middle-income neighborhoods that border Mitchel Field. That Margiotta, the strong-willed Republican leader, is an assemblyman from the bordering communities, puts muscle in the town's resolve to oppose housing.

The commission's recommendation therefore was put aside as Nickerson finally reached a compromise in late 1967 with the Republicans to form an independent Mitchel Field Development Corporation, with Nickerson appointing six members and the Republicans three. Work on the coliseum finally got underway in 1968, as did another study by a planning firm with little expertise but some excellent political connections. The selection of the firm, Marcom, Inc., by the Democratic-controlled corporation in effect undermined what little hope Nickerson had in his nine years of office of realizing any comprehensive development of Mitchel Field. As a liberal Democrat, Nickerson had mouthed all the right phrases, heightening the expectations of civic groups. But when it came down to fulfilling his promise to do something imaginative with the opportunity presented by Mitchel Field, he failed. It appears his ambitions got in the way.

Marcom was just not up to the job. The plan it submitted in 1969, recommending a variety of uses, including housing, was, of course, attacked by the Republicans for including housing. But the plan also was strongly criticized by various civic and planning groups, including Regional Plan, for its many inadequacies. "Substandard" was a commonly used phrase to politely describe the studies for which Marcom received $121,000. "How could the well-intentioned Nickerson and the Democrats blow it by selecting Marcom, a firm that did not even have an architect on staff?" was a question asked by a member of a civic group that had been anxious to support a comprehensive plan and make the Nassau center concept of Mitchel Field a reality.

Newsday answered the question in a copyrighted story in 1970 by disclosing that while a fund-raiser for Nickerson's 1968 Senate campaign, Bertram Harnett, then president of the Mitchel Field Development Corp., had solicited contributions from the president of Marcom, Martin L. Ellis, a Democratic committeeman from Great Neck, between the time Marcom was awarded its first contract and three subsequent contracts. About $2,000 was contributed by Ellis and a major stockholder of Marcom, though Ellis and Harnett denied that the contributions were a factor in the contract awards. It also was revealed that during the time Harnett's law firm had been given a $25,000 personal service contract by Nickerson for legal work in a dispute between the county and the Metropolitan Transportation Authority. Less than a month later, on April 10, 1968, Harnett borrowed $10,000 from a bank so he could make a loan to the Nickerson campaign. Later that year Harnett was elected to the State Supreme Court, and Daniel T. Sweeney, a Democrat with little real estate or planning experience, became president of the Mitchel Field corporation. The following year, 1969, Marcom signed two more planning contracts with Sweeney, after which *Newsday* reported Ellis contributed an additional $2,000 to Nickerson's unsuccessful 1970 gubernatorial campaign.

The Mitchel Field corporation responded to the stories and criticisms by hiring the architectural and planning firm of Liu Urban Design to "clean up" the plan. The last minute efforts by the corporation were to no avail as Hempstead presiding Supervisor Caso, an outspoken critic of the corporation, was elected county executive in the fall of 1970 and almost immediately disbanded the corporation. Working under a contract for the now-disbanded corporation, the Liu firm submitted a revised plan early in 1971, only to have it shelved by Caso. However, after some strong protests, with Blankman's voice among the loudest, Caso stated that he might use the plan as a guide. An exasperated Blankman commented at the time that "if Mitchel Field is an example of how decisions are made in government then there is no hope." In retirement, Moses joined the chorus of critics to declare: "Too damn much politics and too little citizenship." And given the hand Moses has had in shaping the landscape of Long Island, he should know about both.

While Caso, Purcell, and Margiotta debated their next moves, the lame-duck County Planning Commission, which in 1971 was still controlled by Democratic appointees, adopted a county master plan, including some strong recommendations for Mitchel Field. Specifically, it proposed that 204 acres of the site be developed for 9,400 units of housing, 10 percent of which would be for the elderly and 20 percent for low-income residents. The proposal was consistent with the recommendations of the Nassau-Suffolk

Regional Planning Board, which had estimated the Island's need for low- and moderate-income housing at approximately 50,000 units. It noted that 1 out of every 10 of the Island's 700,000 units was substandard, and that the number was increasing. Particularly pressing is the need to accommodate the growing number of 1- and 2-person households—the childless couples, the elderly, the singles, and the young marrieds. The number of these households rose by 45 percent in the last decade, and is continuing to increase, with their obvious demand for apartments being reflected in the near-zero vacancy rate for apartments in Nassau. In addition, Blankman has noted that the housing shortage has resulted in at least 15,000 illegal double and triple occupancies in 1-family houses, which he warned would "start to decay whole neighborhoods into eventual slums."

Caso, Purcell, and Margiotta responded with blunt, declarative statements rejecting housing in Mitchel Field, with Purcell suggesting that it be built in Suffolk. (Eventually, they would acquiesce and allow 250 senior citizen apartments to be built, about 3 percent of the recommended total of housing). Blankman responded by forming a citizen group, the Mitchel Field Task Force, and joining with the Suburban Action Institute to file a court suit to force the county to develop a comprehensive plan for the field to include housing. They charged that the failure to plan for housing violated the constitutional rights of poor and blue-collar citizens, and violated the "general welfare" guidelines under which the state delegates its zoning power to local government. They eventually lost the case, though they are now considering another action, based upon the Mount Laurel decision in New Jersey.

Meanwhile, the county's strategy apparently has been to piecemeal the development of the field following a vague master plan that appears to be in a perpetual state of revision according to the latest political and promotional whim. With the coliseum completed and in operation, Caso declared 1974 the "Year of Mitchel Field," identifying a few parcels for light manufacturing plants, research and development centers, a shopping center, possible office buildings, a hotel, and various county projects, including a sports center, a science-aviation history museum, a central reference library, and a bus garage. Though 48 acres were leased to a developer for an industrial park, a year and a half later the developer admitted that the plans were "nebulous at the moment" and that he had "no idea yet" what they would eventually be. Caso did unveil in an early 1975 press conference a six-foot-square model that contained bits and pieces of numerous plans that had been suggested in the last decade. However, the model raised more questions than it answered, with the County Board of Supervisors requesting such details as costs, revenue potential and traffic studies. The model was sent back to the Planning Commission. Since then no details from the county or the private developer involved have been revealed, as Caso entered his sixth year of administration in 1976, with the field showing a net loss to the county in taxes and income, particularly from the coliseum whose management has become a repository for faithful Republican party workers.

The county's actions and inactions continue to prompt a chorus of protests from planners, civic groups, and the business community. They fear that the center will be spot zoned to serve an array of private and costly public developments, destroying any hope for a unified scheme and resulting in just more deadening suburban strips and sprawls that already deface the Island. "What they (the county and town administrations) are doing," says Blankman, "is taking the greatest real estate gem in the United States and smashing it to valueless fragments."

"Political provincialism," replied Blankman when asked to explain why Mitchel Field has not been developed anywhere to its potential after 15 years. "The people in charge have not understood development, things like cash flows, traffic projections, user requirements, and consumer generators. The concept also is too big. They have no frame of reference. They prefer small private deals that they can make and slip by the public without too much attention. If it is big like Mitchel Field, too many people start asking questions, like I have."

Blankman in particular expressed enmity for Margiotta's resistance to housing, which the developer said is the critical element in a proper and balanced plan for Mitchel Field. "I think he is opposed to housing because he thinks apartment dwellers will vote Democratic and, because the field is in his district, he could lose his seat," said Blankman. "It is a question for Margiotta of political survival; and that question outweighs everything else. It certainly outweighs for Margiotta the ultimate benefits of a properly developed Mitchel Field, including the desperately needed apartments and the reduced taxes for county residents."

There is some hope for Nassau. Following the one-man, one-vote edict of the United States Supreme Court in 1968, the courts directed the County Board of Supervisors to come up with a plan for equal representation. The board since the thirties had been based on the weighted votes of the four supervisors of the three towns and the two mayors of the county's two cities. By various deceptions the board delayed coming up with a plan for six years, thus perpetuating itself and its powers. When it did offer a plan in 1974, it was a warmed over variation of the board's structure, a thin attempt at keeping the status quo, and it was rejected by the voters. With the courts threatening action, the board finally came up with a plan for a county legislature based on districts of relatively equal population, but it was so gerrymandered that it too was rejected by the voters in a referendum in June, 1975. Exasperated, the court appointed a bipartisan citizens panel to draft a plan for a county legislature similar to others established in a number of suburban counties, including Westchester and Suffolk.

The panel recommended that a 15-member legislative body be selected from equal population districts; but before the court could impose the plan, the board agreed to put the issue before the voters again in the fall election. Two propositions were presented: (1) a minor variation on the court's plan for a legislature; and (2) the retention of the present board with a slight modification of the weighted votes. The board, backed by the Republican county organization, waged an intensive and expensive campaign against the plan for the legislature, contending that it was not needed and that it would cost more to operate than the present board. The economy theme was echoed over and over in a blitz of radio commercials, enough to convince the voters, and the weighted plan retaining the present board of supervisors won.

Nevertheless, more court action is expected and good-government groups hope that eventually a fair plan for a legislature acceptable to the voters can be developed. The charge of whatever legislative body evolves is still vague, but perhaps it will take up the issue of the development of Mitchel Field, as well as the complex and costly problem of the duplication of government services on the special district, village, town, and county levels. Perhaps. The problem that remains is that the villages and towns still hold fiercely to the status quo and their powers, especially zoning. A battle is in the offing, with the spur of the conflict, in my opinion, the inequities and inadequacies of the present property tax, the economic foundation on which home rule is constructed.

13

Taxes, Schools, and Taxes

If there is one major determinant that shapes the physical, political, and social character of suburbia, it is the property tax. Above all else, the effect on property taxes is the factor with few exceptions on which local governments decide whether they shall rezone a parcel of land for multifamily housing; allow a highway through a residential neighborhood to serve an industrial park; sell a potential park site to a developer; permit a landmark to be demolished for an office building; let a shopping center expand its parking lot to the back doors of adjoining homes; establish a media center in the public library; or put in a sewer system. The property tax also is the factor on which most local school districts decide whether they shall increase or reduce class sizes; hire a child psychologist for each school; expand its driver-training program; buy new books; compete in interscholastic sports; have a coach for girls' athletics; keep the heat on for evening adult courses; or simply keep their doors open. There are few school, community, or local government meetings where someone does not rise in anger and ask the president, chairperson, councilperson, or whoever is sitting in front of the hall what a particular action the gathering is considering will mean to the property tax rate. "Just tell me in dollars and cents what it'll be on my tax bill."

Local governments, including villages, towns, cities, and counties, generally must pay their own way; and that way is mostly through the income they receive through their property taxes. About 85 percent of all local tax revenues are raised by the property tax, with the balance coming from federal revenue sharing, permit fees, sales and so-called business nuisance taxes, and, in a few localities, income taxes. The percentage is even higher for suburban local government, for unlike some cities and counties it neither has the power nor the bureaucratic machinery to levy anything except the property tax. While the property tax has actually declined as a portion of all taxes paid by citizens, including federal and in some cases state income taxes and sales taxes, it is rising nationwide by about 10 percent a year. Close to $50 billion a year is now collected in property taxes, with about $30 billion from homeowners and $20 billion from businesses. The states are picking up more and more of the local education bill, but still an average of about half of the cost comes out of the local property tax, about $25 billion of the $50 billion a year national public education tab.

The property tax had an economic rationale when it was established in Colonial days, when wealth meant farm land, buildings, and livestock, items that could be seen, touched, and taxed. It was accepted then as a fair indicator of wealth, something government could tap to pay in turn for the services it rendered to the citizens, in theory, in just proportion to their property. (The larger the farm and lands the more roads government must build and the more soldiers are needed to protect it.) As people moved away from the farms and into the cities the property tax came under increasing attack. "There is nothing the matter with the property tax, except that it is wrong in theory and does not work in practice," wrote R. A. Seligman in his 1911 classic *Essays in Taxation*. "Practically, the general property tax as actually administered is beyond all doubt one of the worst taxes known to the civilized world."

Seligman's indictment was later echoed and enlarged by economist L. L. Ecker-Racz in his book, *The Politics and Economics of State-Local Finance*, in which he declared that the property today is "no longer an index of man's worth, income or taxpaying ability." He noted that people own stocks, bonds, saving accounts, and other intangibles often worth far more than their real estate, if they own any. The fact that the percentage of citizens in the United States actually owning land and homes has been steadily decreasing in the last decade reinforces the thesis of Ecker-Racz. (It should be noted, however, that the increasing number of renters indirectly pay real estate taxes through their rents, though deriving none of the benefits of the income tax deduction allowed for the payment of real estate taxes—a fact that some urban legislators hope to correct.)

Simply put, the property tax is a regressive tax. And according to economist Dick Netzer, of New York University, it "is the most regressive of the major forms of taxation used in the United States. Its burden, as a percentage of income, is much higher for low-income people than it is for high-income people. This is principally because housing is so large a component of spending for low-income families." There is some debate whether a more moderate form of a property tax would be equitable—that is, in relationship to the services a government performs for a parcel of land, such as providing roads, sewer service, and police protection. However, there is little question that the tax as now arbitrarily administered is unfair.

The inequities are further aggravated by the wide range of rules and practices of tax assessments in the no less than 71,000 local government units in the United States that have the power to levy property taxes. Thus, a house with a market value of $50,000 may be taxed $3,500 a year in California, which has the highest rates in the nation, and only $350 a year in South Carolina, which has the lowest rates. Rates also vary widely within states, within counties and within towns, boroughs and villages, depending on what makes up the tax base of the local taxing district.

One of the more glaring examples of tax disparities often cited is in the New Jersey suburban county of Bergen, where the boroughs of Rockleigh and Northvale, each a mile square, sit side by side. The owner of a $50,000 house in Northvale pays about $400 a year in property taxes, while the owner of a similar house in Rockleigh pays close to $2,000 a year. The staggering difference is due to the fact that Northvale's tax base is enhanced by a thriving 126-acre industrial park that pays to the borough about 90 percent of all local taxes. Rockleigh's tax base is almost all residential.

There also are similar tax disparities within towns and villages and on streets. The district line dividing the Lakeland School District and the Central School District 3 in the northern Westchester County town of Cortlandt runs along Buttonwood Avenue. The owner of a $40,000 house on the north side of the avenue and in the Lakeland District might pay $1,800 in property taxes, while the owner of a similar house on the south side of the avenue and in Central District 3 pays about $1,200. Their town and county taxes are the same, but the difference is in the school tax (special district, village, town, county, and school taxes are all part of the property tax). The Lakeland District has a tax base of mostly homes, while Central District 3 has been blessed with two $100 million, tax paying, Consolidated Edison power plants.

On the Port Washington peninsula, the village of Flower Hill is divided up among three school districts, Manhasset, Port Washington, and Roslyn. While the school tax rates (again, based on property assessments) of the Roslyn and Port Washington districts are about the same, the actual amount a Manhasset homeowner pays is about a third less, or about $400 less a year on a $60,000 house. The reason is the location in the Manhasset district of the so-called "Miracle Mile" shopping center that stretches along Northern Boulevard. While the center, with its major department stores including Lord & Taylor, Bonwit Teller, and Bloomingdale's, draws its income from the residents of the three school districts and others on the North Shore, the school taxes it pays benefit just the Manhasset District. (Even with this windfall, residents in the Manhasset District in 1975 voted down the school budget, as did nearly a third of the school districts on Long Island. The national percentage of school budget rejection is about the same.) What the shopping center does generate for the neighboring communities, if not the tax income, is a great deal of traffic.

The disparities and the spiraling increases in the property tax have created among most local governments a race for ratables. To avoid economic and political ruin, municipalities are constantly looking for developments, preferably "clean" industry or commerce, that will produce more revenue in proportion to the services they require, thus helping to reduce the tax burden of the voting homeowner. Only the most ardent arguments of environmentalists in the more affluent and tax-base rich communities have been able to stop such developments. The more economically desperate communities feeling the property tax squeeze will take almost anything, including the "not-so-clean" industry or commerce, despite the pollution, traffic jams, and ugly strip developments that may follow it.

Conversely, the municipalities will avoid if they can approval of "bad" ratables, the ones that create tax users instead of tax payers, such as subsidized apartments and most housing developments. Though racial and social considerations are certainly factors in the rejection by many suburban communities of housing proposals, as we have noted, the economic argument is the most persuasive. There is little doubt that in some cases the argument is just a cloak for racism and exclusivity. But whatever the motives, it is the economic argument most often heard in the establishment by local governments of highly restrictive zoning ordinances, so-called snobzoning, to keep out low, moderate, middle, and now upper-middle-income families.

I have calculated that given the rising cost of services, such as schools, garbage collection and disposal, and police protection, a $75,000 house in Port Washington will barely generate enough in taxes to cover its cost to the school and special districts, village, town, and county. The calculation was based on the assumption that there are only two children of school age in the house. If the house contains three children, all of whom will attend public schools, it will mean a net loss in revenue to the community. The figure quoted in 1971 for my previous place of residence, Princeton, New Jersey, was $60,000. In New Canaan, Connecticut, the break-even point is now projected at $80,000, and going higher.

To attract commerce and industry, most communities resort to what is called "fiscal zoning," which is zoning to encourage the use of land for developments that will produce a profit. If necessary, communities also will plan their public works program of roads and sewers or put political pressure on the county, state, or federal agencies to plan theirs to serve a potential local revenue producer. Regional planning and environmental considerations are definitely secondary as communities grapple for ratables. If anything, the competition encourages the further fragmentation of suburbia, with each community concerned with its own economic and political well-being. Thus, a civic leader in Port Washington could seriously suggest that a portion of the 1,200-acre sand pits lying vacant in the southeast edge of the school district should be developed for industry, arguing that "our" district would benefit from the property taxes, while all the traffic and much of the pollution would be borne by the neighboring community of Roslyn. (The major access road to the sand pits cuts through the heart of "downtown" and residential Roslyn.)

Despite the efforts of communities, industry and commerce have been becoming more and more selective in locating in suburbia, avoiding where they can high-tax areas. We therefore have in many regions a vicious cycle, with businesses not wanting to move into high-tax areas, which have high taxes for the very reason that there are not enough businesses on the tax rolls. There also is a tendency of businesses for marketing and identity reasons to locate in clusters, thus benefiting a single locality, such as Greenwich, Connecticut, for offices and corporate headquarters or Manhasset for retail stores.

Norman Williams, Jr., author of *American Land Planning Law,* a five-volume definitive study of zoning, contends that above all else the real powers in determining land use are those who could offer a "good" ratable and those in charge of siting highway interchanges and major sewer projects. "They are the true land-use control because once one of those projects comes in, everything else is mapped around it." Williams adds that "there is no point in revamping land-use regulations unless we're prepared to remove the fiscal pressures and provide a coordination between public-works programming and zoning."

Property tax reform is coming. There already are some efforts in metropolitan areas to develop a tax-sharing system to overcome the disparities and planning disasters caused by fiscal zoning. In particular, the Metropolitan Council of the Twin Cities of Minneapolis and St. Paul, known as the Metro Council, has put into effect a system that guarantees every taxing unit in the 3,000-square-mile Twin Cities area a share of 40 percent of the region's growth in industrial and commercial tax valuation. In effect, this means if a new office building is built in Minneapolis, or a new industrial park in Eagan Township, or a shopping center in Minnetonka Village, the community where the new facility is will receive 60 percent of the tax revenues it produces, with the remainder being shared by the other communities in the region. Each community's share of the 40 percent is determined mainly by its population and its existing per capita property valuation. If a community's property valuation per capita is below the metropolitan average, it will receive more. If it is above the average, its share will be smaller.

The tax pool plan (Chapter 24, Minnesota Legislature, Extra Session, Laws of 1971) surprisingly received strong support from most of the affected communities. Writing in *City* magazine, Paul A. Gilje of the Citizens League, a local non-partisan public affairs organization in the Twin Cities area, noted that "a contributing factor to the bill's passage was its avoidance of what might be considered 'radical' approaches, such as merging all communities into one metropolitan city or imposing a new metropolitan tax on commercial-industrial property." He added that the law works entirely within the existing framework of local government, with all localities continuing to make their own decisions on levying property taxes. The law created no new taxes or bureaucracies. What it did create was a sort of insurance policy for many communities that were concerned they might not be able to attract in the future enough of the industrial and commercial growth in the region.

The long term benefit of such a "share-the-wealth" plan is that it may stimulate communities to be more concerned with regional planning considerations than with parochial economic considerations. There already are some indications of this broader view in the Twin Cities area, where the Metro Council also establishes planning priorities and coordinates a variety of regional service agencies for the 120-odd municipalities in the area's 7 counties. However, the Twin Cities and its Metro Council is, unfortunately, very much an exception.

There are approximately 230 "metropolitan" areas in the United States, with 133 of them contained in a single county and the balance in two or more counties, including 24 interstate areas. Some attempts are being made in the regions to coordinate planning and a few interlocking services, such as transportation and air and water pollution control. Miami, Nashville, Indianapolis, and Jacksonville have moved in this direction, and San Francisco, Atlanta, Detroit, San Diego, and a few other cities are exploring possibilities. The only thing New York, New Jersey, and Connecticut can seem to agree on for the New York City region is improved transportation, and only then in a crisis, such as the threatened collapse of commuter rail service. Even in the regions where there is agreement concerning common problems, progress is slow and taxes are the typical roadblock.

The problem in almost all the regions is how to overcome the fear and selfishness of local communities hooked on home rule, especially tax-base rich communities. Some regional "governments" now have the power to review all local applications for federal grants, which gives them some teeth to put into a tax reform proposal. But so far the only region to nibble at the tax problem has been the Twin Cities. Though the inequity of the property tax has become a common lament in the rhetoric of local and state politicians, few are willing to take the initiative.

The real impetus for property-tax reform can be expected to come from the courts. A number of states are presently under court order to correct the disparities in expenditures for public education between school districts resulting from the dependence on local property taxes. In striking down the education finance systems, the courts did not outlaw the property tax, but rather held that the expenditures for public education should not vary from district to district because of the relative worth of the districts.

The court cases and subsequent reforms of varying scope now under way or being studied in a score of states were triggered by a decision of the Supreme Court of California in the case of *John Serrano, Jr., et al v. Ivy Baker Priest,* then treasurer of the state. The father of John Serrano, Jr. and the parents of 26 other Los Angeles County school children had signed a complaint in 1968 contending that the "plaintiff parents are required to pay a higher tax rate than the taxpayers in many other school districts in order to receive for their children the same or lesser educational opportunities as are afforded to children in these other school districts."

The parents had been recruited as plaintiffs by the Western Center on Law and Poverty, an offshoot of the Federal Office of Economic Opportunity, in Los Angeles, and a group of private lawyers and legal scholars that for some years had been considering challenging the property tax. No one was optimistic, for various suits in other states had in the past been rejected. As expected, the case was dismissed first by the Superior Court and later the Court of Appeals. To everyone's surprise, however, the state Supreme Court agreed in 1971 to hear an appeal. Hope was rekindled, especially in the heart of Sidney M. Wolinsky, then a partner in a prestigious Beverly Hills law firm, who had argued the case as a volunteer for the Western Center.

Aided by Professor Harold W. Horowitz of the University of California, an authority on equal protection, the lawyers refined their case. As reported by Robert Reinhold of *The New York Times,* the key tactic was to avoid asking the court to dictate how educational dollars should be spent; a concept the courts in two previous cases, in Illinois and Virginia, had found judicially unmanageable. What the Los Angeles lawyers were now asking was that the California court establish the principle of "fiscal neutrality," which is to say that whatever method is used to support schools it may not constitutionally be a function of wealth, other than the wealth of the state as a whole.

"The major strategy was to ask for a very restrained principle," Wolinsky told Reinhold. "We avoided concepts like 'need' and 'educational opportunity,' all those garbage terms that education has become overburdened with. We said we were not asking for compensation, only equality. All the court was asked to do was foreclose one of thousands of alternatives open to the Legislature. They could have vouchers, or could even give extra money to good school districts for special programs, as long as a rational choice is made in an educational sense."

On August 30, 1971, the court ruled in what is now a landmark decision that the state system of financing public education, by which each district supports in large part its own schools through local property tax revenue, "invidiously discriminates" against the poor because it makes the quality of a child's education dependent on the wealth of the district he happens to live in. "Recognising as we must that the right to an education in our public schools is a fundamental interest which cannot be conditioned on wealth we can discern no compelling state purpose necessitating the present method of financing." In plainer terms, the court noted that "affluent districts can have their cake and eat it too: they can provide a high quality education for their children while paying lower taxes. Poor districts, by contrast, have no cake at all." The court concluded: "By our decision today we further the cherished idea of American education that in a democratic society free public schools shall make available to all children equally the abundant gifts of learning. This was the credo of Horace Mann, which has been the heritage and inspiration of this country."

The decision in the Serrano case was followed less than two months later by a ruling of the Federal District Court in Minnesota *(Van Dusartz v. Hatfield)* that, under the Fourteenth Amendment of the United States Constitution (which forbids a state to "deny to any person within its jurisdiction the equal protection of laws"), public school pupils have a right "to have the level of spending unaffected by variations in the taxable wealth of their school districts or their parents." The court declared that if wealth does affect school spending, it must be the wealth of the state as a whole. "This is not the simple instance in which a poor man is injured by his lack of funds. Here the poverty is that of a governmental unit that the State itself has defined and commissioned."

The decisions in California and Minnesota were echoed on December 23, 1971, by a three-judge federal panel in Texas. Responding to a class action suit brought by a group of Mexican-Americans *(Rodriguez v. San Antonio)*, the panel ruled that local wealth cannot be the basis of school financing, especially since poorer districts "tax more, spend less." Three weeks later New Jersey's system of financing public education also was ruled unconstitutional.

As in the previous cases, the New Jersey action was brought on behalf of a student, Kenneth Robinson, who complained to the courts in 1971 that his hometown of Jersey City was spending only $890 a year to educate him, while 25 miles away the affluent suburb of Millburn spent about $1,400 on each of its pupils. It was noted in the brief that Jersey City could draw on only $27,000 in taxable property for each of its pupils, while Millburn could draw on $99,000. (The state average then was $1,010 expenditure per pupil based on a tax resource average of $41,026.) Not only did Superior Court Judge Theodore I. Botter rule that the state's method of financing public education out of revenues from the local property tax discriminated against young Robinson, but also against the taxpayer. Departing from earlier state decisions, which allowed differences in spending based not on wealth but on the "willingness" of citizens to tax themselves, Botter commented that education expenditures should not depend on the "mood" of the voters. He suggested that public education funds should come from "state revenues raised by levies imposed uniformly." The decision was appealed, but the New Jersey Supreme Court upheld the ruling in 1973, and ordered the state to enact a new education funding system by 1976, or the courts would.

Of all the states now wrestling with the problem of how to reduce disparities in public education expenditures based on the property law, New Jersey, lying between New York City and Philadelphia, is perhaps the most "suburban." It also has one of the wider ranges of disparities in school property taxes, illustrating the whims of fiscal zoning. We have noted previously the general property-tax disparity between bordering boroughs in the county of Bergen, where to receive the same level of municipal services a homeowner in Rockleigh pays on the average four to five times as much as a homeowner in Northvale. The disparities and their consequences in education are even more arbitrary and insidious. As an illustration, a comparison of the public school systems of Englewood Cliffs and Lakehurst is often cited.

Sitting on the Palisades across from New York City, Englewood Cliffs is a comfortable suburban community of homes in the $60,000 to $100,000 range, while Lakehurst is a modest exurban community of homes in the $30,000 to $50,000 range, 65 miles south, midway between New York City and Philadelphia. Though Lakehurst's tax rate is higher than that of Englewood Cliffs, its yield in 1975 was just $132 per pupil. The yield in Englewood Cliffs was more than $2,300. The difference was based on the fact that all Lakehurst has to tax is its homes, while Englewood Cliffs' tax base includes various corporate headquarters along Route 9W, a stretch known as the "Billion-Dollar Mile." The result is that Englewood Cliffs has three well-equipped elementary schools and Lakehurst has one, and that one does not even have a gymnasium. In addition, students at the Englewood Cliffs Upper School can choose among 77 electives, including video taping, photography, band, and other specialties, none of which requires an additional fee. The only electives Lakehurst offers are art and band music, for which there is a $5 a month extra charge for students. The differences are depressing, giving a clear advantage to the children of Englewood Cliffs at about the same relative cost to their parents in school property taxes as those paid by parents in Lakehurst.

Similar disparities abound in the Garden State, which, of course, is why the courts there have been so adamant in their rulings for the state to correct the situation. It is clear, however, that whatever tax equalizing plan is finally agreed upon, the taxpayers in communities such as Englewood Cliffs and Northvale will suffer. In a survey by *The New York Times,* parents in Englewood Cliffs were reported divided in their attitude toward a redistribution of school wealth. "You can't expect people who worked very hard to make a little money to pay for other people's children," said a dentist who moved from Manhattan to Englewood Cliffs. "That's why we moved here—to maintain good schools for our children. Look, I'm already paying for three kids and now you want me to pay more for somebody else's? Possibly this is being selfish, but I don't think so."

Others admitted that a redistribution of state aid, possibly to be financed by a state income tax, was fair, but they were concerned that it might affect the quality of their children's education. "I'd rather they did it some other way," said Ms. Ruth Hoffman, a mother with two children in Englewood Cliffs' schools, "but whatever happens, if it is a matter of my children's education, I'd want to pay to keep our quality high." In Lakehurst, Thomas Viracola, the school's principal, put it bluntly: "We're going to benefit from this thing [tax reform] no matter which way it goes. You know, we're way down on the totem pole and they're going to shoot at the guys at the top. They're the ones who are going to get hurt."

Similar concerns have been expressed in Connecticut, where the courts also have ruled that the state's system of financing public education on local property taxes violates both the equal protection and education clauses of the state constitution. While most persons involved in public education accept the concept of equal educational opportunity, the wealthier school districts are wondering if they will be penalized. "People move to New Canaan because of our school system," said Margaret Becker, chairman of the local school board. She wondered whether a plan to equalize education expenditures would harm the New Canaan system, which in 1975 ranked second (after Darien) in per pupil expenditures among the state's 169 school districts, and indirectly, the town's property values. "There's no question that we'll be paying more for education purposes and that we'll be paying someone else's school bills," said Theodore Meyer, chairman of the Board of Education of Easton, which ranked eighteenth in education expenditures. "But within certain limits this is not unreasonable. We recognize that there are some areas that you might call 'Connecticut Appalachia' that need help."

What will help acceptance of any plan to equalize public education expenditures in Connecticut is the fact that the state presently does very little for its school districts. The state in 1974 ranked forty-seventh in its level of aid to local education, though it was first in the nation in per capita personal income. "Anything that would provide more money than the present formula would be a good thing," said Norman I. Schmitt, assistant superintendent of schools in Newington.

The concerns in Connecticut and New Jersey are based on reports of various plans to equalize school funds already in operation in a few states. The first state to follow a court action was Minnesota, which acted just 18 days after the federal ruling in the *Van Dusartz v. Hatfield* case. The Minnesota plan provides for equalization of local school property taxes up to a state average for per pupil expenditures. Under such a formula, known as "power equalizing," the state guarantees that a poor school district will be able to spend the same amount per pupil that a rich district does at the same tax rate. If the poor district cannot generate enough income at the predetermined rate, the state will make up the difference. In Minnesota, this has meant on average a reduction in property taxes, but at the same time a sharp increase in income taxes, an increase in the sales tax and taxes on beer, liquor, and cigarettes.

If a local school district wants to spend more per pupil than the state average, it can raise its property tax above the state mandated levels. However, few districts have been willing to vote increases, and as a result some educators feel that what were once considered the better school districts in Minnesota are being pulled down to a lower academic level. Among the districts cited as suffering were the affluent Minneapolis suburbs of Edina, Bloomington, and Golden Valley, all of which defeated public referendums to raise property taxes above the state mandated levels so as to raise per pupil expenditures above the state average. With the defeats, some schools were closed, teachers laid off and enrichment programs cut back.

A similar reaction occurred in Michigan and Illinois, when those states initiated so-called "equal yield" laws designed to reduce disparities in educational expenditures based on local property taxes. Rather than raise their tax rates above state mandated levels, wealthy suburban school districts, such as Grosse Point, outside of Detroit, and New Trier, north of Chicago, have cut back their faculties and elective programs. However, the blue-collar suburb of Garden City, 15 miles away from Grosse Point, and other relatively poor suburbs in Michigan, Illinois, and Minnesota, have had their school revenues increased and have hired new teachers and expanded their curriculum. Problems, of course, persist, such as the need of some poor districts to spend more for "culturally deprived" students. The cost of operating schools also varies in different parts of states. And there always will be the debate among pedagogues whether more money actually means more learning. How far does "equal educational opportunity" go beyond the classroom and into the community and home?

Despite the questions and the problems raised in the equalizing plans, and despite the refusal of the United States Supreme Court, in an appeal from Texas *(Rodriquez v. San Antonio),* to uphold the Serrano principle on federal Constitutional grounds, state courts continue to rule in favor of school tax equality and state legislatures continue to approve varying reforms. As of 1974, reforms had been approved in Maine, Kansas, Colorado, Florida, Montana, Utah, and North Dakota, in addition to Minnesota, Michigan, and Illinois. Meanwhile, California, Connecticut, and New Jersey were under court order to reform. And a number of suits based on state constitutions of other states were pending before lower courts. In addition, a dozen other states were studying the problem or debating legislative packages.

The only state to avoid the school tax controversy seems to be Hawaii, simply because it does not rely on local property taxes to fund education and only has one school district. The entire system is state-run and state-supported, a tradition inherited from the time prior to statehood in 1959 when Hawaii was administered centrally as a territory. Local property taxes go only for municipal services, while the legislature battles each year with public education advocates, parent groups, and teacher associations over school budgets. While there is much debate over the level of educational quality on the islands, there is little debate over the equality of educational opportunity.

In New York, every aspect of public education policy is debated, as well it should be, for the state's problems are very similar to California's, with its property tax bite ranking just behind that of the Golden State's. A special state Commission on the Quality, Cost and Financing of Elementary and Secondary Education reported in 1972 "incredible disparities in wealth among New York school districts." Measuring the value of taxable real property that stands behind each pupil in Nassau County, a study conducted for the commission found that the ratio of value per pupil of the richest school district (Manhasset) to the poorest district (Island Trees) was 9.4 to 1. The study also compared Manhasset to Levittown, noting that in 1971 the taxpayers in Manhasset paid $21.83 in property taxes for each $1,000 of assessed valuation, while the taxpayers in Levittown less than 15 miles away paid $35.64. Even though their tax rate was about 67 percent higher than Manhasset's, Levittown could only generate enough revenue to spend $1,095 for each of its pupils, while Manhasset with its lower tax rate generated $1,721 for each of its pupils. The difference, as noted previously, is the location in Manhasset of the "Miracle Mile" shopping area.

Commenting on the public hearings the commission held during its two-year, $1.5 million study, Manly Fleischmann, its chairman, declared: "If I had to select any one subject that was most talked about, it was real estate taxes. The feeling was the real estate tax hit the little guy very hard. There was no concentrated attack on the income tax."

Answering the persistent fear among school boards that assumption by the state of education costs would mean a loss of local autonomy, the commission replied, as did some school board members, that autonomy would actually be enhanced by relieving the boards of the constant nit-picking at the budgets based on property taxes. As one observer said: "The availability of more money means more autonomy."

The commission in its comprehensive and voluminous report

eventually recommended, among many things, a five-year formula under which the state's poorer districts could be brought up to the level of the more affluent districts, with the state underwriting an increasing share of the education bill for all districts. It was a bold plan, and as such died quickly when the legislators started totaling up the cost and what it would mean in increases in the state income and other taxes. New York State raises about $3 billion a year for education through the local property tax, and as one legislative aide put it: "You'd have to go a long way to find another tax that can give you that kind of money."

Nevertheless, every year the legislature pressed by suburban representatives keeps increasing the state's share of local education. In 1974–75, the state funds accounted for 41.5 percent of local district budgets, with federal funds another 3.5 percent, still below the national average of about 52 percent. But the aid has not kept up with inflation, and as the state has added on to its share, the districts have had to add to their share through increases in the property tax. The result has been increasing disparities between school districts and increasing voter resentment.

Caught between the demands for property tax relief and more school aid, and larger state budget considerations and the suffering economy, New York legislators are in a quandary. Few observers are optimistic that any reform is forthcoming, noting an old saying that you can only equalize on a rising tide. So instead the legislators are providing fiscal bandaids to school districts while looking to the courts for a strong directive that would take them off the hook. Following the lead in other states, several challenges to New York's school financing system have been filed, but as of this writing the cases are still pending. And even if the challenges are successful, as I expect they will be, it is likely to be years before the state can comply with a decision and come up with an equitable plan to reform the system.

In California, five years after the Serrano decision, the legislature was just considering a $2 billion bill that would start to equalize public education expenditures. Though it would mean a reduction in property taxes for some school districts, it also would mean a sharp increase in overall taxes in the state, which few citizens seemed enthusiastic about. Not much hope was expressed for the bill.

Hope for relief in the near future also is slim in Port Washington, where every spring there seems to be a more bitter battle over the school budget, though with each year residents are having less control of the actual budget because of state mandated programs and fixed costs, principally teacher salaries. Nevertheless, the estimated 15 to 25 percent of the budget the local school board does have control over is debated fiercely and in recent years has split the community into two ill-defined camps of "progressives" and "conservatives."

Of all suburban activities—including partisan politics, environmental concerns, flower clubs, community chest and other charity drives, Little Leagues, the Boy and Girl Scouts, encounter groups, mental health associations, religious affiliations, tennis, bowling, boating, bird watching or just beer drinking, extramarital affairs, or gardening—school politics usually dominate. Keeping in mind that the rationale of many families for their move to suburbia was "for the kids," it has followed that the public school has become the major focal point of community interests, if not frustrations. In Port Washington, which in the past has prided itself on its school system, the interests seem just a little more intense.

As noted previously, the boundaries of the Port Washington Union Free School District come closer to physically defining the Port Washington community than any other district or governmental entity. In many respects, the school board is viewed as the governing body of Port Washington, directly affecting the lives of the residents more than any other local unit, with almost every meeting and statement of the board front page news in the local weeklies. "The lack of a government structure in Port seems to put unfair pressure on the school board, and just makes its job that more difficult," observed William Schall, an investment broker who with his wife, Paula, is active in school affairs. "They get blamed for everything, except, perhaps, the running of the Long Island Railroad." It also is noted that the school budget is the only government budget that most voters can actually vote for, and as a result many take out their frustrations with government on the budgets, just as they would if they could vote for, say, the budgets for the Department of Defense or the township.

Another reason for the intensity over school issues is the fact that unlike most suburban communities, Port Washington is heterogeneous. No one ethnic, social, or economic group dominates the peninsula. It is still very much a mixed bag of rich and poor, professionals and blue-collar workers, young couples and elderly, Catholic, Protestant, Jewish, and nonbelievers, and, surprisingly, many first generation immigrants. With the diversity of backgrounds comes a diversity of opinions. The various groups might socialize separately, but most have contact in one form or another with the schools, the common ground of Port Washington. Budget votes, bond offerings and elections in the school district, it seems, are the only occasions when most residents involve themselves in local campaigns.

The specific campaigns, of course, have varied over the years depending on what critical issue or program was dominating resident concerns and what personalities were running for elections. One year it was whether guidance counsellors for the elementary schools should be cut out of the budget; another year it was whether modular scheduling should be instituted in the high school. As for the candidates, the choices were between "conservatives" espousing discipline for students and caution for innovative curricula, and "progressives" pressing for flexible programs and more open discussions between parents, teachers, administrators, and the board. But the choices never were that simple, for emotions and rumors crept into almost every election. Candidates were accused privately of running so they could control patronage to local businesses; others were charged with being too "soft" with the teachers and dupes of the administration; and a few, it was whispered, were anti-Semitic or anti-Italian.

Above all the concerns, however, is the question of the budget and who should control it. The "progressives" have stated in one form or other that they are for "fiscal integrity," but that the "needs of the children" are paramount and that programs should not be arbitrarily cut. Most parents and the generally affluent population of Port support this position. The "conservatives" say they are concerned with the children, but that the budget and resulting school property tax has gotten out of hand. Their support mostly comes from the property owners without children, parents with children in parochial schools and the generally discontented. What makes the campaigns difficult is that the concerns of many "conservatives" are real. Taxes are hurting an increasing number of Port residents, and the school system does have problems that unfortunately the school administration and some "progressives" would like to hide, or at least try to resolve without fully informing the public. Though the maladministration of the district riles my wife and me, and we sympathize with a number of families being hurt by the taxes, the "conservative" candidates have tended to be residents of obvious limited ability and, worse, petulant. On the other hand, some of the "progressive" candidates in their desire to be amiable and reasonable have been weak and obviously manipulated by a school superintendent who has been less an educator than a politician. But at the same time, the "progressive" candidates have at least been open to reason, and we have supported them, as we have the increases in the budget.

Almost every spring since we moved to Port my wife and I, with some reluctance, have put aside whatever other community or family activity we might be involved in to help organize a campaign on behalf of a candidate or slate of candidates running for the school board. With the school board election and budget vote scheduled the first Wednesday in May, April in Port Washington is indeed "the cruelest month"; the month when the petitions for candidates must be filed, coffee "talks" scheduled, letters, flyers and newspaper ads written, neighborhood captains selected, voter card files for each area updated, telephone calls made and doorbells rung. It is a crunch, testing neighborhood friendships and acquaintances, and coming at a time when the budget is being proposed by the present school board, publicized and debated.

The elections have been close, with the "conservatives" winning one year and the "progressives" the next, depending on how loud the firebell is rung in each respective camp. They also have been costly (district-wide mailings and newspaper ads for candidates have run into thousands of dollars) and exhausting, and after nearly a dozen years of contested elections only two candidates filed for the two openings on the board in 1975. It appears that having won the majority in 1972 and holding it for three years the "conservatives" really could not deliver their promises to their constituency and hold the budget down. All they could do was nibble at the budget, but each time they showed their teeth the "progressives" would mount a concerted attack at public meetings, over the telephone, and in the newspapers. If anything, it has been a standoff, satisfying no one.

Typical was the proposed budget in 1975. Though there was to everyone's relief no contest among the candidates, the budget was very much in contention. After extended public hearings, the "conservative"-dominated board presented a draft budget which among many things pulled out for a separate proposition to be submitted to the voters the prekindergarten program. Serving about 100 "culturally deprived" students, the program for years has been controversial, with those opposed contending it is a "so-

cial service" that should not be carried by the schools. Its supporters consider it a legitimate and vital educational program, as well
as an important expression of the community's concern for its
disadvantaged.

Though the program was budgeted at $157,000, special state aid
beyond the normal contribution to the district covered $125,000.
Thus the cost projected to the district was $32,000, which trans-
lated into approximately $1.50 in the annual school taxes for the
owner of a $50,000 home. The board was immediately attacked for
selecting of all the items in the budget the pre-K program for a
separate vote, which many feared would invite defeat. "Why not
submit every educational program, music, athletics, languages,
for separate referendums? Why just pre-K?" asked a parent. John
Mueller, a member of the board and one of the sharper critics of
the program, replied there was no proof of the program's educational benefits, but his statement was contested by others, citing
various studies. Throughout the hearing Mrs. Gina Dissosway,
the president of the board, kept repeating that she did not want
emotionalism to enter the discussions, which in effect in-
timidated a group of pre-K mothers who had pleaded, some with
tears in their eyes and choked voices, for the program at an earlier
hearing. Speaker after speaker urged in moderate tones the resto-
ration of the program, though it was apparent their statements
were having little effect on a few members of the board, who
sneered and made sarcastic responses.

After hearing one speaker go down the list of budget items the
board considered vital, including $9,000 for new drapes in an
auditorium and $2,500 for brighter lights in a hallway, I could no
longer contain myself. I had outlined a reasoned statement based
on my experiences as an educator and as a developer of school
facilities, but I discarded it to declare that what the board had
done to pull pre-K, of all programs, out of the budget for a separate
vote was "damaging to the students" and "dishonest in their exercise of power." I was going to add that it also was a "discriminatory act," but scanning the smirking board I decided to make my
remarks stronger and call it what I really considered it: "a racist
act." One of the minority members of the board had called the
board's act "cowardly" with no real effect, but apparently my
accusation struck home, for the president of the board vociferously and self-righteously defended the board and put down my
remark, as did a number of other residents after the meeting. The
fact remained, however, that of all the educational programs in

the Port school system, pre-K had the largest percentage of blacks, 25 percent, as well as the largest percentage of foreign born. Nonetheless, it was clear that few residents wanted to confront the issue. "We have enough other problems with the schools," said a neighbor.

The controversy broiled for a couple of weeks, with pre-K supporters bombarding selected members of the board with pleas. Letters to the editor on the subject filled two pages of the *Port News*. Finally, a member of the board who had voted with the majority against the program took it upon herself to speak to the director of the program, which no one on the board had bothered to do up until then. Together they came up with a "compromise," which actually expanded the program to serve 144 children instead of 91 (by making half-day sessions) at less of a cost. With the district's share now at about $18,000 instead of the $32,000 originally projected (and the average cost to each taxpayer now less than $1 a year), the program was restored to the budget. Hard feelings persisted, but the budget squeaked through by about 200 votes out of 4,000, in the smallest turnout of voters in years. The Port Washington School District had survived another year.

14

The Corporate Landscape

A candidate for the Port Washington School Board in the early seventies seriously suggested that the peninsula's vast, vacant, and controversial sand pits bordering Hempstead Harbor be developed for a steel mill, which he contended with some quick calculations would generate enough taxes to substantially reduce the school tax bite being put on homeowners. The candidate cavalierly dismissed the problems of traffic and pollution that would be created if some steel company indeed would locate a mill there, contending that such a development was the only way for the school system to remain solvent without taxing many residents to death and splitting the community. Though the suggestion of the steel mill died quickly, as did the resident's candidacy, there is still some talk of an industrial park or office campus for a portion of the sand pits, holding out the faint hope to Port taxpayers that their burden may be eased. (At the same time, there is almost no talk of needed housing for the sand pits, though from a planner's point of view it is, combined with recreation, the most rational development.)

Another hope for tax relief as discussed in the previous chapter is the state approving some form of public school finance plan that would equalize expenditures among districts and somehow replace the property tax as the source of education funds. If the experiences of the few states that already have implemented in part such a plan are a guide, however, the expenditures will only bring the school systems up to some minimal level. The communities that have, or think they have, or want to have, superior school systems will continue to be under pressure from parents to add "enrichment programs," at additional costs to be borne most likely by the property tax. The battles over school budgets in the suburbs and more affluent communities of Minnesota, Michigan, Illinois, and Maine, among others that have some form of equalizing plan, have continued. And as long as budget battles continue, municipalities and other taxing districts will be looking for tax-producing commercial or industrial developments.

To take the hard edge off the race for ratables, there has been some talk among politicians and planners of counties or regions sharing tax burdens and ratables, such as experimented with by the Metro Council in the Minneapolis and St. Paul area. They contend that this would at last stimulate true regional planning and zoning, since the economic considerations would be secondary to human and environmental needs. Others are more skeptical what impact economic reforms really would have on zoning patterns.

"Everybody knows that, strictly speaking, you're not supposed to spot zone on the basis of how it will affect taxes," commented Dick Netzer, the public economist of New York University. "But short of openly stating that purpose, you can be pretty damn overt about it. But you can't be overt at all about other reasons." Arthur Kunz, of the Nassau-Suffolk Regional Planning Board, put it more bluntly: "You get rid of the economic argument and then, if you are opposed to certain people moving into your neighborhood, you have to say it. You can't hide behind another argument. It would pull the bigots out of the woodwork."

Netzer added that if suburban towns no longer need tax ratables, they also might change their attitude and zoning toward nonresidential developments. "You might find that nobody wants any factories anymore. If it's not going to do them any good, they'll say, put it in the next town."

Unfortunately, suburban resistance to industrial, commercial, and corporate development necessitating rational regional planning to accommodate the siting of businesses, is not a problem at present and in the foreseeable future. Businesses have been relocating to the suburbs at a pace equal to that of families since the end of World War II. And it seems recently the pace actually has exceeded that of families, apparently reflecting the shift towards "fiscal zoning" as towns grasp for tax straws in their struggle for economic and political independence.

The exodus of businesses from the city was led at first by manufacturing concerns, principally for technological reasons. With the decline of rail and water transport systems centered in the cities—indeed on which systems many cities had been created and economically flourished—and the ascendancy of superhighways and trucks, manufacturing could decentralize. It only had to be near a superhighway and in reasonable distance of its raw materials, labor, and product markets. In addition, suburbia, with its relatively cheap and available land, lent itself to the construction of new and more efficient single-story factories. No longer would manufacturing concerns have to compete for limited building sites or antiquated plants that of necessity had been clustered around rail or dock terminals downtown in the cities. The new technology of the fifties had freed them.

The statistics indicating the loss of manufacturing jobs in the central cities and the concurrent gains in suburbia in the fifties and sixties are staggering. Between 1947 and 1958, New York City lost 6.0 percent of its manufacturing jobs, while its suburbs gained 37.2 percent. In other regions, the figures were: Chicago, –18.5 percent and +49.4; Philadelphia, –10.4 and +16.4; Boston, –15.3 and +33.5; Detroit, –42.9 and +41.5; Pittsburgh, –25.3 and + 18.1; St. Louis, –21.1 and +41.7; and Cleveland, –22.4 and +98.4.

The trend continued into the sixties, with New York City between 1958 and 1967 losing another 10.3 percent of its manufacturing jobs, while its suburbs gained 36.0 percent. The trend was similar in other regions. In Chicago, the figures were –4.0 and + 51.6 percent; Philadelphia, –11.6 and +30.0; Boston, –11.8 and + 17.0; Detroit, –1.8 and +47.6; Pittsburgh, –13.8 and +3.7; St. Louis, –14.9 and +41.4; and Cleveland, –5.3 and +42.6. It has been estimated that 4 out of 5 new jobs created in the major metropolitan areas in the last 10 years have been in suburbia.

It is interesting to note that the increasing urbanization of suburbia, particularly in the so-called inner rings nearest the cities, is reported to have been pushing some industries further and further out into the far reaches of suburbia and beyond, where they are looking as they had nearly 30 years ago for cheap land to expand on and, in a few rural areas, cheap labor.

The trend in retailing has followed more closely the dispersion of population for the obvious reason: it makes good business sense for merchants to be where the consumers are. In the twenties and thirties most of the stores located on the old main streets of expanding suburban towns, near the railroad stations that served many of the new commuters. There were a few concentrations of shopping facilities in centers constructed prior to World War II, such as Country Club Plaza on the outskirts of Kansas City and Westwood Village in Los Angeles. But without the highways and cars needed to sustain them, the concept of shopping centers was just a gleam in the eyes of market analysts and architects. Then came the late forties and the freedom brought by the post war prosperity and the automobile.

The merchants following the first population waves engulfing the suburban towns filled in the gaps along the main streets. But when the new developments spread to the potato and corn fields where there were no old towns with established shopping districts, the merchants created their own by building along the arterial roads that their customers in more and more cars now drove on between their homes and jobs. The age of the automobile had come, and the seemingly endless neon strips stretching into suburbia, created to pander to the new consumer culture, caused havoc with both shopping and traffic. The roads became overworked and ugly.

"They could not fulfill two completely diverse and conflicting functions: that of serving the movement of thousands of automobiles and the function of stopping people in order to induce them to buy," observed Victor Gruen, the architect and planner. "Roads became hopelessly congested by those who parked cars along the curbs, by those who walked from stores situated on one side of the street to those located on the opposite side, and by trucks delivering and collecting goods. Finally the stores had to make some kind of arrangement to permit their customers to park their cars more easily, by arranging parking lots behind their buildings. This created a strange phenomenon. Most of the customers no longer paid any attention to the show windows and prestige entrances directed toward the main street, but entered the store from the rear parking lot, through a little back door which usually served also as entrance for employees and the place where merchandise was carried in and garbage carried out."

The outgrowth of this chaos was the shopping center, of which Gruen became one of the chief proponents and designers in the fifties and sixties. Growing from neighborhood centers to community centers to regional centers, this relatively new architectural concept accepted the dominance of the automobile and accommodated it in a design that has become the focal point, if not the symbol of the consumer oriented suburban lifestyle.

The centers were at first little more than a group of shops clustered around a branch of a single major "downtown" department store sitting in the middle of a huge parking lot, with easy access off a major highway. But with each new center the concept seemed to expand, embracing more stores and more services, paying more attention to the shopping "environment" by landscaping public spaces and designing seating areas and even playgrounds for toddlers, and ultimately enclosing entire complexes so that their climate can be controlled. Cultural, recreational, and social activities have been added in some centers to complement the retail functions and, of course, to generate more potential shoppers. Office buildings, motels, and most recently apartment complexes have been physically integrated into the centers and in the air rights above a few centers to form multifunctional megastructures, in effect new "downtowns" for suburbia.

"The more facilities you have going for you under a single identity, the more traffic you create for the retailer. It's a matter of volume and identity and suburban maturity," said developer Raymond L. Watson, of Southern California's Irvine Co., to *Business Week*. "We're finally getting some kind of skyline and developing a texture to suburban development." That is exactly what the Irvine Company's Newport Center south of Los Angeles accomplishes, with its more than 1 million square feet of retail space, a medical center, hotels, office buildings, and apartment complexes. It is distinctive, and it works, attracting residents from miles around. Even if they have nothing to buy, people seem to come anyway, to look, listen, and socialize along the center's pedestrian ways, just as people had done in the downtowns of years ago.

Many architects and planners consider these centers the "cities" of the twenty-first century, replacing every activity that had been performed in the old central cities. Not only do the modern centers now completely serve suburbia, they also are drawing shoppers from the cities themselves, with "branch" stores competing in some instances with the "home" store downtown. The developer of Woodfield, an enclosed, multilevel shopping center of about 2 million square feet, one of the world's largest, minced no words. Said A. Alfred Taubman at the opening of his center in Schaumburg, Illinois, about 25 miles north of Chicago: "We are competing against downtown Chicago. So we must come as close as we can to the strength and depth of selection you find in Chicago's core area."

The growth of suburbia as the major retail market for the country is indicated in the figures compiled by urbanologists Brian J. L. Berry and Yehoshua S. Cohen. Adjusting the figures for the general price increases from 1958 to 1967, Berry and Cohen found that the percentage increase in retail sales in Chicago went up during the 10-year period by 5.3 percent, while the sales for the Chicago suburban region increased by 86.6 percent. The figures for other regions were similar, if not more dramatic. Retail sales in Cleveland declined 15.2 percent, while its suburban sales soared 269.0 percent. The figures for New York City were +10.0 and +60.0; Philadelphia, +6.2 and +65.4; Indianapolis, +20.0 and +160.0; Detroit, +0.7 and +86.0; St. Louis, –7.6 and +76.2; Los Angeles, +22.2 and +75.4; Atlanta, +37.7 and +153.9; and Boston, –1.4 and +79.2. There is every indication that the figures for the present 10-year period will continue to show marked increases in the suburban share of retail sales. Since the above statistics were compiled, figures alone from the nation's 12,000 suburban shopping centers have nearly doubled to $150 billion a year, or more than a third of all retail trade in the nation.

The regional shopping centers are now not only squeezing the retail trade out of the cities, they also are squeezing it out of the suburban business districts. Hampered by the lack of parking, easy access to superhighways and the "draw" of major stores, if not the ambiance of landscaped, air-conditioned pedestrian malls, the shops along the old main streets of suburban towns are hurting. "Support your local merchant," is a constant theme heard on Port Washington's Main Street, where store owners do not hesitate to remind shoppers that they also pay local school taxes. "You might get the same thing for a few pennies less at Roosevelt Field (a regional shopping center with a selection of chain discount stores), but you'll pay those few pennies more in school taxes if I go out of business," a hardware store owner told me when I questioned him about the price of an item I was purchasing. Thanks to a "carriage trade," requiring such personal services as same-day deliveries, gracious acceptance of returned merchandise and credit, Port's merchants hang on to their customers and business. Other small merchants in other suburban towns not as well off as Port are not surviving, and vacancies and deterioration mark their once prosperous shopping streets.

The dominance of the regional centers also has affected the commercial strips along the highways, relegating to them the marginal businesses, automobile rows, motels, fast food shops, and bars. The strips have become the "grey" areas of many suburban counties, with the police and neighboring residential areas growing more concerned that in time the areas will become the slums of suburbia, just as the fringes of the downtown areas of the cities had.

The decentralization of manufacturing and retailing to suburbia has hurt the cities economically. But given the production and market factors that must be considered in the locating of manufacturing and retailing concerns, the moves have made sense to both management and consumer. Less rational and more disturbing has been the relatively recent phenomenon of corporations relocating in suburbia. If the cities have any functions left other than to house the poor and minority groups locked out of suburbia, it is their traditional role as the centers of business management, finance and professional and governmental services. The loss of corporations, the taxes they pay and the thousands of white-collar workers they bring into the center cities daily, cuts deeply into the foundation of metropolitan America.

The advertisements luring corporations to suburbia in *The Wall Street Journal* and the financial sections of *The New York Times* and other large metropolitan dailies present the proposition bluntly. "Join the Great Corporate Getaway to Connecticut," stated an ad in the *Times,* though it also could have been to Westchester, Santa Clara, or Orange counties, Elk Grove, Long Island, or any other suburban area in need of tax ratables and jobs, or where a speculator might have put together an office campus and was now seeking buyers or renters.

The ads look good to the weary executive reading them for a second time as his train limps along the New Haven tracks in the Bronx, or waits in the Jersey Meadows for a Penn Central drawbridge to unstick, or is sidetracked in the Sunnyside Yards again by a faulty Long Island Railroad switch. And at last as the executive stumbles off his train at Pennsylvania and Grand Central Stations hours late to fight his way into a crowded subway, or to try to catch an elusive cab, or even walk, the ads look even better and the city worse. Though less dramatic, the situation is similar for other executives in other cities, except instead of being stuck in a train, they might be stuck in their car on some freeway, or in city traffic, or backed up on a street waiting to get into a parking lot. Chaotic commuting, air pollution, noise pollution, crime, power shortages, bombs, strikes, payroll taxes—the list of city ills has become a litany to be recited over drinks at executive luncheons, the business clubs and in the commuter bar cars. Caustic comments become conversations, become company inquiries, become consultant studies, and soon another corporation is considering leaving a city for suburbia.

"By this autumn the managements of nearly 50 companies with offices in New York City had acquired property in suburban Westchester County with the idea of moving most or all of their general offices out of congested Manhattan," stated the lead sentence of an article in *Fortune* magazine entitled, "Should Management Move to the Country?" It appeared in December, 1952, indicating that corporations have for some time considered whether they should join the exodus to suburbia. A few corporations did abandon the cities in the fifties and early sixties, but at the same time many corporations moved in, causing little concern then among the city fathers. However, in the late sixties and early seventies the trend was definitely toward suburbia. Between 1965 and 1976, New York City's share of the nation's 100 largest corporations dropped from 19 to 10, and its share of 1,000 largest corporations from 198 to 120. It also lost hundreds of other major firms (and a total estimated 420,000 jobs), as did other large cities. The estimate of major firms leaving Boston was 75 in 2 years; St. Louis, 43; Cleveland and Detroit, about 2 dozen. Though the recession in the mid-seventies slowed the exodus, the list grows and the trend continues.

The cities are now worried, very worried, prompting many to establish agencies to counter the lure of suburbia by using high pressure sales techniques, public opinion and such "sweeteners" as additional police protection and more convenient parking. New York City a few years ago sent its Economic Development Administrator, D. Kenneth Patton, into the hinterlands of New Jersey to appear before the planning board of the hamlet of Bedminster to urge it to deny an application for a zoning change that would allow Western Electric to construct a $10 million office complex there. The company was then employing about 8,800 persons in New York City. Patton told the board that his objections to Western Electric's plan was not an effort to keep jobs and taxes for the city, but rather to preserve the rural character of Bedminster and discourage unplanned regional growth. He warned that if Western Electric and other firms continue to locate at random in the suburbs and ignore regional transportation, housing, labor, and tax problems, "we will Los Angelize our land, Balkanize our region's finances and South Africanize our economy."

Strong words and a stern warning, which has been echoed by

city politicians, professors, and planners at perpetual seminars and unending conferences sponsored by good-government groups. But when the words and warnings are filtered through corporate decision-making processes and paraphrased in memoranda and in deep tones in the anonymous board rooms high above city streets, they are dismissed as grandstanding. Private enterprise—what is best for the corporation—comes before public interest. "A few of our execs sit on this city board and that, and we support things like the Urban Coalition," confided a top corporation executive, "but if you look behind our corporate posture, we really don't give a damn about the city. In fact, some of our guys, especially the Midwest and South transfers, really hate it. They were big wheels in their towns, and here they are nothing." An executive with a company that moved from Midtown Manhattan to an office campus in White Plains, Westchester, put it more positively: "We were darn near lost in New York. Here we are an important part of the community." The discussion then in most corporations considering leaving the city is not whether their move is good for the city and the region—those are questions for their public relations men to deal with—but rather where to relocate and what can they expect to find in suburbia.

Corporations leaving the city generally relocate near the homes of their top executives, or in a community where the executives want, and can afford, to live. Of course, expensive studies are conducted by relocation consultants, but most persons in the business know the studies are shaped by subtle, and sometimes not too subtle, suggestions of the executives directing the studies. "What we are told, usually after the third drink at the contract lunch, is that so-and-so lives in, say Greenwich or Scarsdale, and wants to be within 10 easy minutes of his home and golf club," confided one relocation specialist who did not want to be identified for obvious reasons. "What we are asked is to survey the surrounding area and, with nice maps and charts, justify the selection, and to hell with any regional plans and projections."

Other consultants confirmed the approach. One even told of having his contract broken by a corporation president who lived in New Jersey when he strongly recommended an office location in Fairfield. He added that the corporation eventually moved to New Jersey—upon the strong recommendation of another consultant. An article by D. Young in the *Chicago Tribune* analyzing why corporations were fleeing Chicago cited prestige locations, as well as convenience to the homes of corporate executives:

Around the perimeter of O'Hare International Airport are any number of businesses that have O'Hare stuck in their name. The O'Hare area, which had no office space 10 years ago, now accounts for nearly 30 per cent of all suburban office space in the Chicago area. "Using O'Hare in the company name has the psychological aspect of giving the firm prestige," says Loren Trimble, an expert on the area's economic development. "O'Hare carries the connotation of being near the world's busiest airport, of being modern and in the jet age." Proximity to the airport explains part of the phenomenal growth of the northwest suburbs in the last decade. O'Hare has had a very direct effect on the building of fancy hotels, convention facilities and office buildings in the area.

But it is only one of many reasons for the rapid industrial and commercial growth and, most experts agree, not the main one. Most maintain that things would be booming in the area without the world's busiest jetport.

"I say that the principal reason we have 500 new companies in Elk Grove Village is that it is close to where the boss lives," said Marshall Bennett, a partner in Bennett & Kahnweiler, industrial real estate brokers. His firm developed Centex Industrial Park in Elk Grove Village, the largest of its kind in the nation. The northwest suburbs are now Chicago's biggest competitor for the dollar of the industrialist, conventioner and nightclubber. The area is one of the four fastest growing areas in the country.

The consequences of the corporate exodus to suburbia are obvious in the cities, which are losing taxes and jobs. The once thriving downtown stores that catered to the lunchtime and five o'clock shoppers also are hurting, as are the thousands of allied concerns that serviced the corporations. But the exodus also has consequences for both suburbia and the corporations that have moved there.

The grass of the suburban office campus might look good to an executive viewing it through the dirty window of a commuter train, but a closer look at the grass reveals that in spots it is a swamp into which corporations are slowly sinking, so slowly in fact that the corporations don't realize it, or at least they don't admit it. Few corporations will ever admit to any mistakes, least of all one as major as the relocation of its headquarters, a multimillion dollar decision. "There are, of course, strong arguments to remain in the city as there are strong arguments for suburbia," goes the palaver of corporate public relations. "But on balance, we feel the move is healthy . . ." Corporate wags add that the move of their company to suburbia was the greatest thing that happened since the 6:05 out of Grand Central was last on time—"and everyone knows it's never been on time."

However, a few of the corporate executives who had recited the litany of city ills and have since moved with their companies to suburbia now recite a new list of ills: transportation, housing, taxes, labor and management problems, and lack of essential services. In many respects, the list is a summary of the problems also confronting suburbia, as well as the corporations already there.

The most obvious problem is transportation. Corporations in suburbia are almost totally dependent on the private automobile, and the resulting traffic jams in and out of office campuses are getting worse every day. Traffic on the Cross Westchester and Garden State Parkways and the Long Island Expressway from 7 to 10 in the morning and 4 to 7 in the evening moves about as fast as Midtown Manhattan traffic, which is about an average of 15 miles an hour. It is not much better on the freeways of Los Angeles, Chicago, Boston, Detroit, St. Louis, Philadelphia, and Washington, to name a few cities in which I have been stuck in traffic jams. And it is not only a rush-hour problem. The average daily traffic per lane in many suburban counties now closely approximates that of the cities they surround, as a drive through a suburban business district or to a regional shopping center on a weekend will frustratingly prove. Communities are finding out through bitter experience that once an office or industrial development is approved, a vicious cycle of road widenings, highways, expressways, and more development follows, and soon a comfortable community is cut up into concrete ribbons.

Bitter lessons have not been lost on neighboring towns. When the town of North Castle in Upper Westchester was presented with a proposal by a developer to rezone 311 acres of residential land for office buildings, homeowners pointed to the west and the town of Mt. Kisco. A few years prior, Mt. Kisco had encouraged new developments and highways to serve them, only to be eventually engulfed by roads that destroyed the town's character. Though the proposal for North Castle held the promise of a substantial increase in the tax base without the need to provide schools, residents demanded that the town board commission a study of the impact the zoning change would have. An independent planning firm was hired and reported that although the new office campus would increase the town's tax income by $2.5 million a year, the town would have to spend about $4.5 million for new roads to handle the increase in traffic generated by the offices. While the town could in a few years pay off the cost of the roads and easily meet their maintenance and control costs, it was further argued that the roads and the subsequent developments sure to come once the zoning was changed would in time destroy the character of the town. The proposal died. Other communities also are casting a suspicious eye at similar proposals and are demanding sophisticated tax, traffic, and environmental studies before acting. The question seems to be just how much a community wants to sacrifice for tax ratables. "We frankly have become very wary of the 'benefits' of corporate development in suburbia," commented a member of a Long Island citizens group active in planning and environment.

Fears of traffic, with its noise and air pollution, also were cited by residents of Bedminster in eventually twisting the arms of the town fathers to reject the proposal by Western Electric to locate there. The residents were influenced by Patton of New York City, who had argued for an orderly regional development plan that would concentrate corporations in cities or satellite cities where they could be served by mass transportation. "Firms moving to auto-oriented campus sites are in fact moving backward toward a transportation technology of the nineteen-fifties," he said. "Our air, our senses and our countryside simply cannot support the further proliferation of such developments. In the next 25 years nearly 1 million new suburban office jobs must be accommodated. If everyone did what is proposed here (in Bedminster)," he concluded, "we would need 2,000 new lanes of roads, 20,000 acres of land, and we'd generate 750,000 new automobile pollutants into the region's atmosphere per day." Bedminster listened, but Western Electric did not. They took their plans to Bedminster's neighbor, Readington Township, which accepted them, and all the taxes and traffic they will bring.

The debates continue. Residents in the affluent Westchester community of Purchase fought a long and futile battle against plans by the Texaco corporation to build a huge office complex there, citing the detrimental effect the 1,500 to 1,700 cars coming into the community each day would have on the air quality. "Texaco pollutes air; wastes energy," read one of the signs carried by smartly dressed suburbanites who picketed the corporation's headquarters in New York City. "Texaco is a New York City Dropout," stated another sign, echoing the theme of city politicians. (When Texaco, the fourth largest corporation in America, moves to Purchase in 1977, New York City's share of "the top 100" will drop to 9.)

To block the plans, some residents tried to get the community to secede from the Town of Harrison, of which it is a part. Harrison controls the zoning of Purchase and had approved the Texaco plan, citing, among other things, the taxes it would generate. The secession effort failed, as did an appeal to the state environmental agency. Though a few residents privately admitted that the Texaco office campus was well sited, at the intersection of two expressways, and really would not harm the community, there was concern that other corporations would follow and turn Purchase into a "corporate superblock," to the tax benefit of Harrison. "The traffic will be unbearable, for us *and* the corporations."

General Foods, which led the parade to suburbia when it moved in the early fifties from Park Avenue to White Plains, considers traffic its major problem. Corporate planners there and in other corporations using the Cross Westchester Parkway have for some years been talking about staggering staff hours to ease the rush-hour jams. According to Richard Aszling, G.F.'s vice-president for public relations, General Foods moved out of New York City because it needed more space for its then 1,100 employees. Its headquarters now holds 2,500, but cannot be expanded as originally planned. The Cross Westchester took a chunk of G.F.'s land when it was built and later widened—to handle the increase in traffic generated in part by General Foods. So G.F. now has another 1,000 employees spread around the county in 4 satellite complexes, 2 in Tarrytown, another in Rye and 1 across the parkway in White Plains. It runs station wagons daily between the complexes, competing with the increasing suburban traffic. However, it is the rush-hour traffic that is most annoying. "I used to complain about commuting for an hour on a train and a subway," said a former city commuter now in a suburban office, "but I tell you it's less exhausting than 30 minutes of expressway traffic. I now have to fight my way through."

The top executives don't seem to mind the traffic because most of them live a short distance from their offices. They can afford to. However, the majority of middle-management and lower-echelon employes cannot afford to, given the spiraling cost of housing in suburbia, especially in the prestige communities where many of the corporations have settled.

One such community often cited is Greenwich, Connecticut, where more than 100 companies have relocated from New York City within the last 10 years. Besides being well-served by major highways, the railroad, and an airport, the town of 65,000 also has a tradition of being an elite, affluent residential community, with no less than 24 private clubs for yachtsmen, tennis players, golf-ers, or just plain socializers. Few homes in the town are priced less than $100,000. So when the American Can Company moved its headquarters there in the early seventies, a survey found that only 87 of the company's 1,800 executives also settled in Green-wich, despite liberal bonuses given to executives who moved. Few also could afford anything nearby, for when a corporation moves into an area the housing prices within a 10-mile radius skyrocket, forcing more and more employes to look further and further away in search of shelter. Canco employes looking for housing they could afford were directed to areas within "a 40-minute drive," though one wonders who the race driver was and at what time the routes were charted, since included as "acceptable locations" were Rockland County and North Jersey, a tough, toll-ridden hour away by most drivers' standards.

Only 60 percent of General Foods employes live in Westchester, though more would like to if they could find housing at the right price. According to the county planning department, however, there are substantially more low- and middle-income jobs in the county than there are low- and middle-income housing units. The last survey, taken in 1971, put the gap at 82,200. Officials now estimate it has passed 100,000, forcing more and more Westches-ter workers farther and farther away, to the exurban hinterlands of Putnam and Rockland Counties or back to New York City in search of homes or apartments they can afford. The gap between low- and middle-income jobs and comparably priced units in Nassau County was reported in 1971 at 139,000—and going higher.

There is a decided tax advantage to corporations moving to towns and counties with substantial gaps between jobs and hous-ing. The fewer residents in a town, the less taxes are needed to support municipal services and schools, which of course trans-lates into lower property taxes for the corporations. An extreme example in Bergen County, New Jersey, is the community of Teterboro, which in fact was conceived and incorporated as an industrial tax haven. With approximately $75 million in corpo-rate facilities and at last count only 22 residents, Teterboro has no school or welfare costs and one of the lowest tax rates in the state. At the Ford Motor Company's Mahwah plant in northwestern Bergen, only 20 percent of the company's 5,000 employes can afford to live in the county. The fact that 40 percent of the em-ployes are black only complicates the problem. The result is that

Ford at Mahwah has a high 5 percent of absenteeism and an annual turnover of 20 percent. The gap in Bergen County between jobs and homes has been estimated at 77,000.

Similar gaps appear to exist in other metropolitan areas, creating the relatively new phenomenon of reverse commuting. The traffic on the freeways during rush hours is now jammed both ways, with upper-income suburbanites who still work in the city passing in the opposite direction low- and middle-income city dwellers who work in suburbia. As an example of the situation in the Chicago metropolitan area, Young in the *Tribune* noted that 75 percent of the 25,000 employes at Centex Industrial Park in Elk Grove commute from the city, while the majority of Elk Grove Village residents work in the city. The expense of commuting for many low- and middle-echelon workers in suburbia and the frustration of trying to find an apartment or a home in reasonable distance to their job have taken their toll.

The prospect of the reverse commute cost the Pepsico and Lone Star Cement corporations a third of their workers when they moved from New York City to Purchase and Stamford, in Westchester and Fairfield counties, respectively. A consultant quoted in *The New York Times* said that unpublished private studies conducted for corporations considering leaving the city indicated that 75 to 90 percent of all nonexecutive level personnel did not retain their jobs after their companies moved to suburbia. On the executive level, 80 to 100 percent stayed with their companies.

In recognition of the problem, some corporations moving to suburbia have attempted to open up the local housing market. A few even tried to underwrite subsidized housing developments, including a noble attempt by the Johns-Manville Corporation to squeeze some housing into its corporate campus plans in Bedminster and get the town to buy the idea. But as we have noted, few, very few, suburban communities are willing to rezone to allow the construction of housing for moderate-income workers or even young executives and professionals low on the pay scale. Communities have allowed corporations to move in principally to ease their property tax burden, and they emphatically, if not hysterically, oppose any proposal that might mean more families with more children, which translates into higher taxes.

The lack of housing is aggravating an already serious labor problem for corporations in suburbia. There is a limited labor market among the dogwood and the cesspools, particularly in the secretarial and nonmanagement slots. "The crack executive secretaries just don't want to leave the city, and I really can't blame them," commented an executive who moved with his company to the suburbs. "We thought we could get some good re-entrants—former secretaries who got married, moved to suburbia to have kids, and are now looking for a second income to send them through college—but it really doesn't work out. There are not many of them. Absenteeism is high—their family always comes first. And so we are forced to hire younger, unqualified secretaries, but as soon as we train them they move on to the city or college." John P. Miraglia, a consultant and former personnel director of Johnson & Johnson in New Brunswick, New Jersey, added: "Given the demographics and nonexistent public transportation system in suburbia, there are just simply fewer available workers in the suburban labor market. The pickings are slim."

To meet the problem, corporations have taken all sorts of actions. In addition to putting out a magazine, Reader's Digest in Pleasantville spends more than $200,000 a year for buses to carry clerical staff to and from their homes across Westchester. Other bus services are operated by corporations in Fairfield, New Jersey, and Long Island; some even operate buses to and from New York City. IBM maintained an employment office in White Plains open Friday evening and Saturday to recruit workers from other suburban firms. American Cyanamid in Wayne, New Jersey, has been accused of "stealing" workers from nearby I.T.T. One result has been a spiraling of wages. Contrary to expectations, corporations are paying more for nonmanagement personnel in suburbia than they had in the cities, according to the Bureau of Labor Statistics. Added to this is the cost of company busing, employe cafeterias, and subsidized meals. When working in an office campus you just cannot run out to the corner luncheonette for a quick bite, let alone do some shopping. It is obvious that the total of personnel costs in suburbia is substantially higher than many corporations had anticipated. "We now value our help," said a suburban executive, emphasizing "value."

The competition is not only for nonmanagement personnel. Suburban corporations were said by consultants to feel a strain within their managements. A spokesman for a computer service company admitted that "our new people are less diverse than before we moved. I'm not sure this is a good sign." It seems that the younger and more aggressive and ambitious executives are hesitant about a suburban location for fear that they will limit their employment options by losing contacts with the city. And some add with a smile, their social options. The corporate man on the make who fought his way up the ladder from towns like Columbus, Ohio, or Webster, Missouri, to come to New York City, San Francisco, Chicago, or Atlanta for a juicy bite of the big apple doesn't want to give up his credit-card lunches. Moreover, corporate campus life may be great for golf, but it's lousy for quail hunting.

There also is another, even more subtle, management problem in suburbia, the impact of which cannot be measured by wage and employment statistics. It is motivation. Businessmen note a certain suburban lassitude—the loss of that look-British, think-Yiddish midtown beat—a fact that became very evident to the Royal McBee company when it moved from New York City to the suburbs some years ago. "At first it seemed stimulating and businesslike to arrange appointments in the city with salesmen, bankers, and foreign visitors," a spokesman for the company said. "Many of our executives even used to look forward to the enjoyable trips into Manhattan for meetings. But it soon became a drag. Psychologically, leaving the peaceful and serene suburbs to venture into the bustling city became much more of a task than commuting had ever been. We began feeling like farmers going into the marketplace with our wares. It was very demoralizing." The company returned to the city.

To keep in touch, many executives in suburban offices do make frequent trips to the city, which because of logistics become productions that more than kill a whole day for want of a business lunch. "Because of the hassle involved, some of the younger execs who need the 'lunch experience' don't come along, and in the long run that's bad for them and bad for the company," observed an executive trained at the IBM Poughkeepsie campus. "Instead, a few used to go home at lunch and mow the lawn. Bull sessions on 'campus' were more than likely to be about landscaping than new computer hardware. I felt that I would dry up if I stayed." Commenting on the move of American Cyanamid from New York City to Wayne, New Jersey, a president of a competing chemical firm declared that he felt "Cyanamid had lost important contact with the market and the intelligence network that plays such an important part in chemicals." A manager at Cyanamid admitted to a trade magazine that their marketing people since the move "seem to have lost some of their spark."

Basic communications for corporations in suburbia also presents problems. Firms have complained of the horrendous mail and telephone service in many communities not geared for the demands of corporations. Incoming mail has swamped the small Greenwich post office, forcing it to shift its outgoing mail to an already overburdened neighbor, Stamford. For awhile the U. S. Tobacco Company, which had moved from New York City to Greenwich, sent its mail privately by air from Chicago and had it delivered to Greenwich by company employes. With more corporations moving to Greenwich, a corporate executive there said service has gone from "horrible" to "impossible." Similar phrases were used to describe telephone service. When Pepsico moved to Purchase, it added at least 1,000 telephones to the small, local system. The result for Pepsico and community users was a constant busy signal, with waits up to 15 minutes for a dial tone. No one would guess how bad it will get when Texaco moves in.

There are other special problems and expenses for the suburban corporation. Strict zoning codes demand that companies develop extensive and expensive landscaping to hide their offices. The upkeep of the grounds requires a whole new staff, plus supervision. Similar problems abound in housekeeping. Companies also have found that it is nearly impossible to sublet additional space it is not using in its buildings, a common and sometimes lucrative practice of companies in cities. A company in suburbia therefore must carry the extra unused space that it needs for expansion, or not build it and hope it can when space is needed in the future. General Foods ran into this problem in White Plains, where it could not expand, and as a result is now spread all over the county.

Yet, corporations still rationalize their move, stating as one of their many reasons the need to climb out from under the various city and state corporate, real estate, and personal tax burdens. However, the suburban tax situation is getting very grim. It is to offset the tax on homeowners that many communities try to attract corporations into their areas. But taxes in suburbia keep increasing, and at a faster rate than that of many cities. Communities up against the tax wall can be expected to soon add additional levies on their industry and offices. "Since they are *not* voters they are the first in line to be tapped," said a suburban politician. "And if the tax picture gets any worse, I think special assessments, if not local corporate taxes, are coming. We don't want to kill the goose that lays the golden eggs, but we sure as hell want to get as many eggs as possible."

Lemming-like, corporations continue to relocate to suburbia, each convinced that their move is healthy for their business—if not for economic reasons, then for the amenities suburbia supposedly has to offer. And suburban communities continue to rezone away their open space and greenery—the amenities—in hopes of easing their increasing tax burden. It is the worst of unplanned and unbalanced growth, accentuating the division between the cities and suburbia and between the poor and the affluent, and further fragmenting suburbia itself into small, selfish garrisons.

Though the location within its boundaries of a rich, tax producing corporate headquarters or a shopping center might generate a smugness and a feeling of independence for a suburban community, it is only illusory. Despite their rapid industrial and commercial growth since the fifties, most suburban areas are far from economically self-sufficient. Their existence in large part is still dependent on their central cities for services and income.

Though Long Island's population is now more than 2.5 million, which would make it one of the world's largest cities if it was incorporated as such, it has no single comprehensive library, no important concert hall or art museum, no public zoo or aquarium, no major seaport or airport, no major legitimate theater, and no major league baseball or football stadium. For many, Long Island's proximity to New York City is what makes Long Island habitable.

In releasing an extensive economic study of Long Island, Lee E. Koppelman, executive director of the Nassau-Suffolk Regional Planning Board, commented that "there is absolutely no question in our minds that the future and economic well-being of Long Island is tied closely to the future and economic well-being of New York City." The study noted, among other things, that nearly a third of Nassau's labor force of 559,000 persons work in the city, and that their income of nearly $2.4 billion annually accounts for 43 percent of the total earnings of all county residents. Only 15 percent of Suffolk's labor force of 383,000 work in the city, but they generate 22 percent, or $725 million, of the total earnings in the county. In summary, the study found that the median income of Long Island residents employed in the city was about double that of those employed locally, giving the Island's economy a hefty boost. In addition, many of the industries located on the Island because of its proximity to the city and its marketplace for goods and services.

15

The Dream Deferred

We chose suburbia over the city because we felt for the comparative price of housing and its amenities it offered a better environment for us and our growing children. Unlike an increasing number of Americans, we had a choice, given our income and the year of our decision, 1968. We also sought in our move the old values of personal efficacy for our social and political concerns, which incidentally confirms a thesis by Robert Wood in his *Suburbia: Its People and Their Politics*.

There is some debate among sociologists over what has motivated families to move to suburbia. As early as 1925, Harlan Paul Douglas suggested in *The Suburban Trend* that the move was associated with a desire for family privacy and independence, concluding that suburbanites "are a chosen people separated from their fellow men." David Riesman indicated that suburbia allows families to become conspicuous consumers and indulge themselves, while Herbert Gans stated that moves are based largely on class and life-cycle stages. The respondents in a survey by William Dobriner stressed the themes of privacy, initiative, moderation, and upward mobility. However, Dobriner added in his *Class in Suburbia* that he felt people tended to give socially acceptable answers, such as "for the children," while their real reasons were more negative. He suggested that the "flight to the suburbs may be a polite assertion of the principle of white supremacy." The debates and studies continue.

An in-depth survey for *Newsday* by a team of sociologists at the New York State University at Stony Brook found that most families were motivated by the attractions of suburbia rather than dissatisfactions with the city. The respondents noted the "important" reasons they moved to suburbia were a "better place for the children to grow up," 72 percent; "to have own home," "needed more living space," "to live in a better neighborhood," and "better schools for children," all 64 percent. Other "important" reasons were "wanted a nice lot, larger or wooded," 60 percent; "too crowded in old neighborhood" and "better recreational facilities here," both 48 percent; and "character of old neighborhood changing," 45 percent. "Too much crime in old neighborhood" was rated "important" by 34 percent, while "didn't like some people in old neighborhood" and "many friends already had moved" received 16 percent.

The sociologists, professors Norman Goodman and Stephen Cole, concluded from these and other findings that "the reasons given for moving to a specific community relate mostly to the living quarters themselves, rather than to broad social or political considerations or even to such factors as the quality of the schools, tax rate level, racial makeup or proximity to friends, relatives, jobs and recreational facilities." In summary, Goodman and Cole contended that the desire to have a home of their own was the most important factor for the migration of families from the city to suburbia. The survey also noted that 91 percent of the respondents said they would advise their friends to make the same move if they could.

However, fewer and fewer people can now afford a single-family house, which since the founding of the nation has been an integral part of our standard of living and the embodiment of the American dream. About two out of every three Americans now live in a single-family house. But according to a report of the Congressional Joint Economic Committee issued in the spring of 1975, the median price of a new house as of 1974 had risen to $41,300. Applying a traditional rule of thumb that a buyer should not pay more than two to two-and-a-half times his annual income for a house, a new house is now unavailable to approximately 85 percent of all American families. The report noted that the median price of a used house was $35,660, putting it out of the reach of 80 percent of all families, and just at a time that the crop of the baby boom in the late forties and early fifties are forming households.

The fact is that the cost of housing is simply outpacing concurrent increases in income. Restrictive zoning pushing the cost of land up combined with higher construction costs and interest rates have resulted in an average increase in the price of a single-family house of more than 10 percent a year since 1970. Incomes during the same period have gone up at half the rate. "The rapid rise in the price of housing has locked out many potential buyers as the ratio of their incomes to the cost of owning a home has deteriorated," was the obvious observation of the United States League of Savings Associations.

Taxes, insurance, and utilities—the monthly carrying charges—also have risen sharply, as have nonhousing items such as food and clothing, prompting *The Wall Street Journal* to question whether most traditional yardsticks of how much house a family with a given income can afford are still valid. "A man making $20,000 a year can barely afford to buy a $40,000 house," commented Lewis Cenker, a builder in Atlanta and a president of the National Association of Home Builders. And there are fewer and fewer $40,000 houses on the market. The average price for a modest home in the better suburban communities is now about $60,-000, and going higher. In Port Washington the average in the Spring of 1975 was $70,000. One house that was on the market for $40,000 when we moved to town in 1968 was going for $80,000 seven years later.

Despite the substantial increases in value of their homes and the potential profit if they sold, few suburbanites are tempted to move unless they are forced to. In addition to having some of their profit nibbled at by realtor's fees and closing costs, whatever windfall a homeowner accrued would be swallowed up in the increased cost of another house. In fact, many homeowners recognize that they could not even afford to buy the house in which they now live. The result is that they have become more protective than ever over any public or private action that may affect their property values. And what they are protecting is becoming more and more of a relic. "Some young people are going to wonder how father could afford to own a single-family house when they're making twice as much as papa and they can't afford one," said Cenker. "That's going to shake them."

It already is shaking them each time they go out to look for a house in suburbia. Young couples making the rounds with realtors on weekends are reported "shocked" to learn how little their money can buy, even for the most modest and marginal houses. The realization is slowly sinking in that the American dream of a house of one's own in the suburbs is obtainable for only the upper-middle class and the rich. As noted in the report of the Congressional committee, people at lower economic levels are going to have to settle for rental or other forms of less expensive housing.

The building industry has responded by moving more and more into the multiunit market. The market share of the single-family house in the early seventies dropped below 50 percent of all housing starts for the first time in the reported history of the industry. Its share in the early sixties was 78 percent. Now apartments in varied financial forms—rental, cooperatives, and condominiums —and in varied physical forms—townhouses, attached houses, clusters, and mid- and high-rise apartments—are outpacing single-family homes. Industry economists have predicted that within 10 years the apartment share of the total housing market, including rural America and the vacation home boom, will reach nearly two-thirds. In suburbia, supposedly the bastion of single-family houses, more than half the new units now going up are apartments, despite the resistance in most communities to multiple-family housing.

"It's the strangest thing," said Clark Harrison, chairman of the board of commissioners of DeKalb County in suburban Atlanta, to *The New York Times.* "People around here complain when they can see a high-rise building through the trees." Yet, he noted that the apartments, construction of which in DeKalb was outpacing single-family houses by 2-to-1, were being filled up by suburban residents. According to studies of the Nassau-Suffolk Regional Planning Board, as many as 80 percent of the new tenants in apartment complexes on Long Island come from the same town they were built in or from an adjacent town. "It's a fantastic paradox," observed a local planner, noting the fierce opposition that had greeted various apartment proposals on the Island.

It must be added, however, that almost all the apartments going up in suburbia are so-called luxury developments, catering mostly to the more affluent retired or so-called empty nesters, couples whose children have grown up or who have no children, and the singles crowd moving to suburbia with the corporations. In some instances, town planning boards would approve proposals only if the apartments were limited to efficiencies or one-bedroom sizes, thus assuring no children would be generated to burden the local school system. The policy has become known as "zoning birth control." There is a vague formula among developers trying to predict the fate of zoning applications that says that the more bedrooms and the lower the price or rent, the less the chance of approval.

Some complexes allowing for family units are being built, usually further out in suburbia where more land is available at lower prices. These clustered developments tend to be better designed, offering central recreational facilities and retaining much of the surrounding greenery. This not only pleases the buyer, but probably as important pleases the local environmentalist, who may sit on the town board that approves the zoning. Many builders and their banks believe the clustered low-rise, multiunit complexes are the future for suburbia. With the help of design "teams" of architects, ecologists, economists, and sociologists, wrapped up by public-relations men, developers are getting needed zoning approvals in the more rational communities and are selling the concept to buyers.

However, the dream of the single-family house persists. A survey published by *Professional Builder,* a trade magazine, concluded that 92.7 percent of today's home shoppers want a detached house. Developers add that in particular the blue-collar worker is most resolute in his pursuit of a house. "The whole notion of condos, high-rises and clusters, however well designed, is basically a concept for the upper-middle class," commented Barry Bruce-Biggs, of the Hudson Institute. "Most people—particularly lower- and middle-income people—aren't attracted to these forms of housing and still consider a single-family house to be an integral part of the American standard of living. If they can't achieve this standard of living for their own family, they will be very angry indeed, and will look around for somebody to blame."

Given the harsh economic realities of today, there is little question that the dream of a house in a homogeneous suburb so long dangled before the aspiring residents of the cities is fading. At the same time, those realities for an increasing number of families already in suburbia are turning their dream into a dilemma. Escalating housing maintenance costs and taxes are consuming more and more of their disposable dollar. Making ends meet each month is a constant struggle. In our 8 years in Port our monthly housing carrying charges have gone up about 70 percent, from $350 a month to approximately $600, including a 67 percent rise in taxes, from $1,200 to nearly $2,000 a year (relatively low in Port because of the age of our house) and a 100 percent rise in fuel oil, from $600 to $1,200 a year (even though we keep lowering the thermostat). Our increases are typical. The crunch is on in the consumer-oriented, credit-extended society of middle-class suburbia.

We are keeping pace with the increases only because of additional income from my teaching and writing and from my wife's part-time family counseling. But living off a small fixed income and a modest salary as an assistant school librarian, my mother-in-law could not keep up her house in Port. Happily for us, she chose the alternative of moving into our rambling house, an increasingly common arrangement in suburbia where the elderly in particular have been hard hit. Also increasingly common is the legal and illegal conversion into apartments of basements and garages of detached houses by families in need of additional income to make ends meet. To planners the conversions are an ominous sign that a neighborhood is starting to slip. The "doubling-up" and rental of single-family houses make them more prone to deterioration. In addition, public services suffer, including schools as well as sewers. Also affected is a sense of community, for in its struggle to survive a family tends to become inner-directed. Questions of the effect on schools, sewers, and aesthetics are secondary to a family that must convert its garage into an illegal apartment for the rental income or be forced to sell and move into a rental apartment themselves. They may have argued vociferously against an apartment complex in their town, especially a subsidized one, but when their own needs are involved a different tune is played. To point up the contradictions at a hearing is just rhetoric when survival is at stake. It is difficult to blame them.

The conversions are one index of the problems of poverty in suburbia. Another index is the increase in welfare rolls in suburbia at a rate greater than in the central cities, according to the latest reports. Though dated, the last census also is revealing of long term trends. In a report entitled "Characteristics of the Low-Income Populations, 1970," the Census Bureau noted that 30 percent of the nation's poor, or about 8.2 million, lived in the central cities, while 21 percent, or about 5.2 million, lived in the suburbs. In comparison, in 1959, fewer than 1 percent of the nation's poor lived in the suburbs. It is not that poor people are moving to suburbia, but rather that the long-time blue-collar and elderly residents of the old villages engulfed by growth in the last decade are being squeezed by inflation and the dwindling job market. They are the residents of the "slurbs" reviewed earlier and those pockets of poverty hidden behind the greenery off the major road-ways and in the back streets of suburbia.

The last census reported that while the median income for Nassau's 359,638 families was $14,625, the income for 24,842 of the families, or 6.9 percent, was less than $5,000, which put them into a category of "poor." In Port Washington, the median income of its 7,905 families was $17,809, 22 percent higher than the county's. However, 558 families in Port, 7.1 percent of the population, were reported to have annual incomes of less than $5,000, confirming the opinion that behind Port's attractive North Shore facade there is indeed insidious poverty. In fact, the relatively high percentage of poor in Port qualified it as a "poverty tract" under the guidelines of the Federal Office of Economic Opportunity and the Economic Opportunity Commission of the county.

In the flush of the good years of the "Great Society," a group of concerned citizens in Port formed an antipoverty organization known as the Community Action Council (CAC). Under the direction of an imaginative organizer, David DeRienzis, CAC established itself as a model agency, creating such diverse services as job training and placement, family counseling, a credit union and co-op store, youth programs, a day care center and a transportation system of minibuses to get low-income residents to and from a hospital in Manhasset and to accommodate the elderly and handicapped. The CAC also helped form the Cow Bay Housing Development corporation to sponsor Port's subsidized housing project, as well as supplying support for a youth center in the existing low-income project. The organization flourished in the late sixties and early seventies, with substantial funds coming from a variety of sources, including the federal government, the county, foundations, and local fund raising. The CAC even generated some of its own funds by putting together a "plant" with local help and winning a contract to supply lunches to county-supported summer camp programs.

With federal funds dwindling and county funds tied up in red tape, however, the CAC found itself in 1973 struggling to survive. Its budget dropped from $120,000 a year to $56,000, and with it the scope of some of its services. At about the same time, local governments were finding in the mail the first of checks issued by Washington under its vaunted revenue sharing program. Though the Nixon administration had made some vague statements that some of the funds should go to social programs, since those were the very programs cut by the administration to gain monies for revenue sharing, few local governments were responding. And the administration was not pursuing any guidelines for social priorities, but was sitting back in a pose of benign neglect allowing the localities to do with the funds what they wished. An article in *The New York Times* reporting that one suburban community had used the funds to build a bridle path and that others were using them for such items as tennis courts, police weaponry, or just to lower taxes prompted me to action.

Without checking with the CAC, I appeared at a monthly meeting of the trustees of my village of Baxter Estates and, asking to speak at the end of that night's agenda, proposed that a portion of the $5,000 in revenue sharing funds coming to the village be given to the local antipoverty agency. I spoke long and with conviction that the revenue sharing funds had been drained from federal social programs and it was only correct that the funds should at least in part go back to those programs. I dismissed the argument that no other community had seemed inclined to divert any funds for such purposes, stating that it would reflect well upon Baxter Estates, one of the smallest incorporated villages in the nation, to establish a precedent. "Precedent or no precedent," I added, "it is the morally right thing to do."

To my surprise, pleasure, and pride, the trustees seemed inclined to agree. No one could take exception to the good works CAC had performed in the community; in fact the wife of a trustee, Pam Clapp, was one of the agency's numerous supporters. Yet, the issue was a sensitive one, for whatever funds were to be given to the CAC in an unprecedented action would in effect come out of the taxpayer's pocket: other villages in Port already were allocating funds to reduce taxes or pay for services such as public safety that they would normally pay out of property tax income. The politics of the proposal were deftly handled by Daniel W. MacDonald 3d, the mayor, who got from CAC all the backup information on services to village residents that he thought was needed to put down any protests. The trustees then waited until after the village election in the spring of 1974 to propose in the new budget that $1,000, 20 percent of the revenue sharing funds due the village, be allocated to the CAC.

With some anxiety I attended the budget hearing, expecting to hear a protest. However, MacDonald handled the hearing in his typical smooth style and not one of the dozen or so residents in the audience raised any questions. Only after the budget was approved did I stand up to say anything, and then it was an untypically brief statement congratulating the board. After six years in

Port I had finally pricked the conscience of a local governing body. It frankly was not difficult, for once the issue was presented to them the trustees responded well and in good faith. In particular, MacDonald had picked up the cause and was now convinced all the villages should be doing the same as Baxter Estates. "I hope this small gesture will inspire other villages to give to their social agencies that do such a good job," he declared. Unfortunately, various efforts to get other villages to do so have so far failed, though Baxter Estates has continued its support.

Meanwhile, the CAC struggles along, while its board of directors, of which I am now a member, somehow tries to sustain a community concern. It is difficult for us and other volunteer organizations, for the times are difficult. The hyper-volunteer activity so long a part of the suburban scene is abating. Though no statistics are kept on such activity, it is apparent from my own vantage point and that of others active in other communities that citizen groups, from flower clubs to great-book clubs, from little league to the League of Women Voters, are finding it harder and harder to keep up their memberships, programs, and financial support.

The reason most often cited for the difficulty volunteer organizations are having in suburbia is the economic squeeze on the middle class. A less obvious reason, but from my perspective as pervasive, is the women's liberation movement. An increasing number of women who had been the backbone of suburbia's concerned citizenry and its volunteer organizations are abandoning their traditional roles and are going back to school to prepare themselves for a profession or are going directly into the job market. It is not just for economic reasons, though they are certainly a consideration, but also a matter of personal and, in some cases, professional pride. Self-esteem is at stake for many of the more talented women in suburbia who have held leadership positions in their community.

For years my mother-in-law was one of the "good ladies" of the League of Women Voters, researching local issues and attending countless meetings. Her days are now devoted to running a media center in a junior high as an assistant librarian. My wife has worn many volunteer hats in Port, including those of the League, the local Democratic party, the North Shore Child Guidance Association and, it seems, almost every ad hoc committee on mental health services. Her days and most nights are now taken up with family counseling as a paid professional and the pursuit of an advanced degree in psychiatric social work.

Other women in Port that had supported various community

efforts with their volunteer time and talents also are now off pursuing their own careers. One past president of the Port League went back to law school, gained her degree and is now clerk for a judge. Another is now a management consultant, a third a travel agent, while other members of the League and similar organizations who had been active in the late sixties and early seventies are scattered throughout the professional fields of law, education, social work, and library science. A few even have become business executives, and one of the more imaginative women, Fran Zaslow, a successful caterer. The commuter trains have become co-ed. While community problems and conflicts during better economic times and before the rise in women's consciousness had been the focal points of local energies, they are now just passing interests. Life styles in suburbia are changing, with a resultant strain on traditional community institutions.

But if community interests may be decreasing, the social problems certainly are not. According to all indices—welfare cases, unemployment, divorces, mental health referrals, juvenile delinquency, and crime—they are increasing. And of all the problems, crime is getting the most attention. It is crime that many communities are channeling much of their revenue sharing funds to combat, beefing up their police forces, padding their retirement funds, and improving street lighting. Families that had left the city for suburbia to, among other reasons, escape the increase in crime there have found that it has followed them. In fact, for the last few years according to the Uniform Crime Reports compiled by the Federal Bureau of Investigation, crime in the suburbs has been rising nearly twice as fast as in the nation as a whole, far outpacing the cities.

Of course, raw statistics can be somewhat misleading. The increases for suburbia, such as approximately 20 percent in serious crimes in 1974, start from a smaller base, so if a community had 20 serious crimes in 1973 and 40 in 1974, it would show a 100 percent increase. In addition, the population of suburbia is growing while the population of the cities is decreasing. But there is little question among criminologists and demographers, and no question among suburban police departments, that crime in suburbia has become a major problem.

It is certainly paramount in the minds of residents in such communities as the Roslyn Country Club development in the North Shore village of Roslyn Heights. A former estate of Mrs. Charles D. Draper, a scion of a millionaire clothing manufacturer, it was bought in 1948 by Abraham Levitt and his sons and subdivided for 650 homes which sold for about $19,000 each. Twenty-five years later, and after much remodeling, additions and landscaping, the price of the homes had risen to an average of $80,000 and the community itself into an exclusive residence for lawyers, dentists, and doctors. Adding to its desirability was a country club with a pool and seven tennis courts and the excellent Roslyn school system. To a visitor, the community presented a picture of serenity.

In the summer of 1974, however, the serenity was shattered when a burglar broke into a house, held a man and his wife at gunpoint and robbed them. Two weeks later a burglar in one night broke into four houses, robbing the first three and raping a 15-year-old girl in the fourth. The sense of security suburbia had given many was replaced by fear. The community now supplements the Nassau County's police patrols with its own private guards, as do an increasing number of other communities where similar incidents have occurred. Burglar alarms have become one of the staples of suburban hardware stores and the work load of local electricians.

What makes the Roslyn Country Club development and other selected suburban communities prone to robbery is their convenience to major highways. Once considered an asset, the proximity to the highways is now a liability in the sale of houses to crime-conscious buyers. *Newsday* reported that according to police sources it appeared that the burglars who broke into the Roslyn houses had simply stopped off in the area, then got back on the adjacent Northern State Parkway for an eight-mile ride to the New York City line. The police added that this was a typical pattern all along the Northern State and other parkways and expressways, where adjacent communities were experiencing a marked increase in crime compared to the less convenient villages. It appears that along with the noise and air pollution, the highways also are bringing crime in the form of "commuter burglars."

Police have said that the pattern is for most thieves to work in the daytime, when the houses tend to be vacated with the husband at his job, the wife also at work or "volunteering" or shopping and the children at school. Working in pairs, the burglars pull off the highways into a residential area and cruise until they find a house that seems to be vacated. While one drives around the block, the other rings the doorbell. If someone answers, the burglar just asks directions. If no one answers, he or she tries the door. If it is locked, a rear door or window is smashed and the house entered. The other burglar returns in the car to the street and pulls into the driveway. Together they "clean out" the house.

A more ambitious pair may use a delivery van, which makes them less suspect to neighbors who might look out the window or to police cars cruising in the area. It also helps the burglars when they cart away heavy items such as television sets, high-fidelity equipment and, it has been reported, refrigerators, air conditioners, and freezers. During the summer when families are away on vacations the magnitude of the burglaries tends to increase. Some families have been reported to come home to find the entire contents, down to the rugs, missing. When the police investigated one such incident they learned that a moving van had pulled up to the house to empty it, but that neighbors thought that the family was moving and, for some reason or other, did not want to tell anyone. Dressed as moving men, the burglars went about their business.

Police in Westchester told the story to *The New York Times* of one couple in Briarcliff who went out to dinner one night and when they came out of the restaurant found that their car had been stolen. After reporting the incident to the police, they went home. The next morning they found to their surprise the car in their driveway. "There was an emergency and we had to borrow the car," a note on the windshield read. "Please excuse the inconvenience, but perhaps these two theater tickets will make up for it." The pleased couple informed the police that their car had been returned, and the next Saturday used the theater tickets. When they came home late that night, they found that their house had been burglarized.

Not all robberies in suburbia are being committed by such professionals. Reported thefts by juvenile delinquents also are increasing. In addition, the juveniles in suburbia account for a major portion of auto thefts as well as what police call incidents of nonconforming behavior, such as disorderly conduct and public intoxication. The rate of delinquency has been rising steadily, despite difficulty for county police to gain cooperation from local and village police on reporting offenses and offenders. Robert Lepanto, chief of research for Nassau County's Youth Board, estimated that 80 percent of the cases involving youthful offenders end in station-house adjustments in the affluent communities. In comparison, the estimate for poorer neighborhoods was 30 percent. The balance end in criminal charges. Any statistics are therefore flawed. But there is no denying the problem—and the irony.

"For the kids," is the common response of parents to the question of why they moved to suburbia. However, it seems from all indicators that the kids are having an increasingly difficult time coping. The problems of juvenile delinquency, as well as family conflicts, changing personal values and the response of local institutions, demand a more thorough review than I am prepared to present. It just remains to be noted that if the American dream of a house in suburbia has become clouded, so has the image of a home in suburbia.

An open discussion on "problems of the home" a few years ago in Port Washington attracted more than 200 residents, including about 50 teen-agers. One of the recommendations generated at the meeting by the teen-agers was a need "for a place where we can go if we have problems at home." Picking up on the concept, a few residents with the support of the North Shore Child Guidance Association and the CAC formed an organization called Group House to purchase a house that would be used as a temporary residence for local teen-agers who were unable to live with their families because of illness, disaster, divorce, or emotional disruptions. The house would allow teen-agers to stay in the community, continue in school and be with their friends while their problems or the problems in their homes were being worked out.

To make the concept manageable, it was agreed that the house would serve no more than seven teen-agers at one time; would have two live-in house parents, supported by a full-time director, a part-time social worker, and backup services from various community agencies. With a distinguished local board of directors headed by Lillian McCormick, Group House was able to obtain strong community financial support in 1974 to try to find a house and get the concept working. The county and the state agreed to help meet the operational expense once a house was opened.

When a house was eventually found and purchased in the unincorporated, relatively modest area known as Eastern Crest, however, some residents in the immediate neighborhood became hysterical. Flailing petitions and haranguing politicians, they eventually persuaded the spineless Town of North Hempstead to deny Group House a building permit for some needed renovations. The fear of the residents, of course, was that the house threatened the "residential qualities" of the area, though it was noted that some of the teen-agers who would be helped just might come from broken or troubled families in Eastern Crest. The house was finally opened, but only after a protracted court battle by the sponsors to force the town to grant the needed approvals.

Before taking the matter to court, the sponsors did attempt to win over the opposition, calling meetings and writing letters. The appeals failed, the vociferous minority refusing even to openly discuss the issue. Recognizing that public meetings probably would just generate more emotionalism, one supporter in Eastern Crest, Mrs. Toni Coffee, took it upon herself to walk the streets of her neighborhood, ring the doorbells of the opposition and try to reason with them on a person-to-person basis. A past president of the League and presently a member of the school board, Mrs. Coffee is one of the more respected members of the community, for her soft-spoken charm, as well as her intelligence. The reactions of her neighbors stunned her.

"They just would not listen," she recalled. "They were afraid to listen. There was fear in their faces." In reflection, Mrs. Coffee added that "for all the affluence and intelligence here, I worry that Port Washington will just become another selfish and hateful community." I worry, too.

16

Time Is Running Out

A discussion by a panel of experts on the problems of unfocused regional growth, uncoordinated public services, fossilized local governments, and economic and racial discrimination might attract 30 residents to the Port Washington Public Library on a good night. Add tax disparities to the agenda and 10 more people might show up. It is not that many Port Washington residents and suburbanites in general are not concerned with the problems, though they might put different, more direct labels on them and personalize them. It is just that most suburbanites feel there is little they could do about the problems, if indeed they could resolve in their own mind their own positions. And while they might be unhappy with the status quo, there also is the concern of what change might bring. The result is fear and frustration.

What has evolved out of this conundrum is a further undermining of the Jeffersonian ideal upon which our nation has rationalized its suburban institutions. Ironically, it is these very institutions that have created the conundrum. They have been unable to adjust to the problems and pressures created by the greatest migration in our history. New structures, if not a new ethic, are needed if the American dream of the good life is to be fulfilled. At present, selfishness and greed dominate, with 20,000 or so suburban governments and their 90 million residents denying their growing interdependency in the spreading megalopolis, ignoring the transactional hubs that are the cities and destroying their own environments, all to buy a little more time. But time is running out.

There are no easy answers, for whatever action is attempted will undoubtedly threaten vested political and private interests. But the situation demands action if we are to begin to face up to our responsibilities as a democratic nation supposedly responsive to the general welfare. Suburbia has tested our institutions and has found them wanting.

"If the metropolitan areas are to be made more efficient, their vitality released by the reduction of economic distress and racial tension, their mobility freed from the bottlenecks of inadequate and ill-coordinated transportation, it is essential to apply policies that are comprehensive, that treat the metropolitan area realistically as an organic whole. Disorder, crime, pollution, and overcrowding, housing shortages, the noise of aircraft and the congestion of roads—these and the host of other problems are no respecters of antique jurisdictional frontiers. They must be dealt with comprehensively." So stated the President's Task Force on Suburban Problems in its 1968 report. Nearly a decade later the confusion that is suburbia still reigns. If anything, it is worse.

In my odyssey it has become obvious to me as it has to others that regionalism must be pursued and structured to assume more authority for planning, zoning, and development, as well as for the implementation and coordination of *most* public services. For all intents and purposes, village and town governments within the suburban rings have become anachronisms, jealously guarding their jurisdictions at an increasing economic, social and political cost. At best their structures could continue and serve a ceremonial and communications purpose, garnished by some services.

However, if I have learned anything in my odyssey, it is that it is difficult to generalize. There are always exceptions in suburbia, given its amorphous state. It is not clear that *all* public services would benefit from consolidation on a regional level, as has been noted in a perceptive study by Elinor Ostrom and Roger B. Parks for the Center for Studies of Metropolitan Problems of the National Institute of Mental Health. They contend that certain services, in particular law enforcement, seem to be more effective in the present fragmented state, which includes 313 county and 4,144 local police forces.

I happen to agree, not because of any empirical evidence I have unearthed, but only because of my observation of the Port Washington Police Department and its responses to my calls, most of which involved reporting traffic accidents at the dangerous intersection in front of our house. I doubt very much that the Nassau County Police would respond as quickly, usually within five minutes. They also have been very polite, if not apologetic, when issuing a ticket. In addition, I believe my village clears the local roads after a snowstorm faster and better than the town or county would, though I suspect I pay a little more in taxes for that prompt service. Such are the incidents upon which exceptions are based. But I would agree with others that such services as law enforcement must be better coordinated on regional levels.

There also are questions of who would be served by regionalism. The political consolidations of such metropolitan areas as Indianapolis, Nashville, and Jacksonville have been viewed as successful attempts by conservative suburban and business interests to keep control of the central cities that were becoming increasingly liberal and black. The potential political power of those central cities is now diluted by a suburban majority. What benefits have accrued to the regions in general and the cities specifically are debatable. The parochial policies of the suburban communities regarding such issues as open housing persist, though at least the framework for reform has been established and some governmental efficiencies instituted.

Given the alternative of the status quo, however, I am convinced that regionalism is in part an answer. But considering that there are 230 distinct metropolitan areas in the United States, the evolving government structures have to be flexible, including a sensitive representative system to allow for responsible community and citizen participation. This should be instituted not only to encourage the valuable and necessary contribution of the many and various indigenous interest groups, but also as a check against the tendency of authorities to become self serving, just as most local governments have become. The democratic process must be served.

The federal government could help stimulate regionalism, if it wanted to, by enforcing Title IV of the Intergovernmental Cooperation Act of 1968, which requires "all federal aid for development purposes shall be consistent with and further the objectives of state, regional and local comprehensive planning." As noted by Charles M. Haar, an architect of regionalism and Assistant Secretary of HUD in the sixties, "The federal establishment, by virtue of being in and yet apart from any local situation is in a position to foster institutional arrangements which can be the hallmarks of a viable system of metropolitan governance and which can provide a response to the physical and human problems, the social and economic problems that know no fictitious local boundaries."

In response to the 1968 act, the 1966 Demonstration Cities and Metropolitan Development Act (Section 204, which Haar helped draft) and the Environmental Impact Act of 1969, the federal government has established a "Project Notification and Review System" (PNRS), (known as "A-95," because its definition was spelled out in an Office of Management and Budget circular dated November 13, 1973 and coded A-95) that requires regional bodies to review all applications for federal grants to insure that they are consistent with a comprehensive metropolitan plan. For all intents and purposes the process so far has been little more than a rubber-stamping act. But the potential for it to be used creatively is there, as demonstrated in the metropolitan areas of Dayton and Minneapolis and St. Paul.

If because of politics federal administrators or regional agencies are reluctant to use the grants as leverage to coerce local communities to accept comprehensive planning, civil rights advocates certainly are not. Following a United States Court of Appeals decision *(Evans v. Lynn)* in June, 1975, granting nonresidents legal standing to challenge federal grants to a community that allegedly zones out racial minorities, various cases are being prepared. The lawsuits are not based on zoning discrimination, but rather on the failure of the federal government to take "affirmative action" required of it under the 1964 Civil Rights Act, including the possible imposition of regional housing and public education plans. The lawsuits could tie up millions of dollars in federal grants, forcing local communities, if they want the funds, to modify their concept of home rule. However, the communities also could simply turn down the grants or not even bother to apply. And as in the case of Black Jack, Missouri, the lawsuits that are pursued could become interminable.

I am convinced that the real initiative will have to come from the states, for that is where the power now rests, as defined by the courts and the Constitution. The states have the authority to reform their tax structures and end disparities between communities and relieve the present burden on property. And they have the authority to impose land use laws superseding local zoning. In fact, in 1961 Hawaii took back all zoning powers from its local communities, while Maine, Massachusetts, Vermont, Delaware, Florida, and California recently have passed various environmental impact laws usurping some local powers. Other states and even Congress are beginning to recognize the need for land-use reforms.

However, land-use reforms are only part of the answer. Tax reforms also are needed. And not just property tax reforms, but a positive program of income redistribution coupled with a reordering of national priorities. Current efforts to open suburbia, encourage cluster developments and satellite centers and protect areas of critical environmental importances only can go so far, as conceded by the Regional Plan Association report on *Growth and Settlement in the United States.* The report states:

"In its broadest sense, the issue of managing physical growth is one of regulating the output of the economy and its distribution among different groups of the population, as well as its distribution in urban space. The two are highly interrelated. For when income growth accrues disproportionately to higher income groups, chances are that they will spend it on third cars, second homes, first motorboats, and long airplane trips—things that are highly resource-consumptive and detrimental to the environment. If that income is reallocated by government, it can be spent on public transportation, urban housing and urban parks, on mental and physical health, on community services, on education and cultural pursuits, on science and technological advancement. It can be spent on income support for the indigent and underprivileged. Most of these alternative economic outputs are quite expensive in terms of dollars or man-hours, but very economical in terms of the consumption of physical resources, and in terms of interference with the environment. Going one step further, curtailment of both unnecessary production and unnecessary consumption can provide more voluntary leisure time, a highly regarded aspect of the 'quality of life.' "

The report concludes that "the issue of growth management is not one of stopping economic growth, but one of restraining profligately resource-consuming sectors of the economy. Likewise, it is not an issue of stopping urban growth, but one of restraining urban dispersal. . . . Instruments for accurately targeting public and private investment in new construction on resource-conserving locations and urban forms will have to be devised. A broad range of taxation policies will have to be revised to the same end."

We are not at a loss for specifics. Congressional committees, public and private commissions and task forces, foundations, citizen groups, consultants, academicians, and journalists have for decades proposed a variety of programs, including some that are actually reasonable and feasible. What is needed is a commitment, which at the present time seems to be missing in most communities and on most levels of government.

The problems of our metropolitan areas are increasing. The spread of suburbia continues. It should not be stopped, for that would deny Americans their freedom of choice and opportunity. Indeed, it cannot be stopped, given the demands of our population and the willingness of our private institutions to respond to them in the marketplace. But the growth of suburbia can be controlled and focused to encourage rational development to conserve our resources and create a better environment for all. It is a hope.

And it is this hope that has sustained me through my various efforts in my community and in my profession, and through the writing of this book. It is my hope that it will sustain others, for the battle has really just begun.

Notes and Sources

1. A Nation of Suburbs

The ascendancy of suburbia is illustrated by a variety of reports issued by the United States Bureau of the Census, which periodically are being updated. An excellent summary of the census and its implications for metropolitan areas was *Growth and Settlement in the U.S.: Past Trends and Future Issues,* (New York: Regional Plan Association, 1975), prepared by the Regional Plan Association under a study financed by the Ford Foundation. Also useful was the *Research Reports of the Commission on Population Growth and the American Future,* (Washington, D. C.: Government Printing Office, 1972). *City* magazine, while it lasted, offered a valuable review of demographic trends, in particular its Jan.-/Feb. 1971 issue devoted to the suburban phenomenon. A more exhaustive and academic overview was provided by *The End of Innocence,* (Glenview, Ill.: Scott, Foresman, 1972), edited by Charles M. Harr, and *The Urbanization of the Suburbs,* (Beverly Hills, Calif.: Sage Publications, 1973), edited by Louis H. Masotti and Jeffrey K. Hadden. The latter contains an excellent and comprehensive bibliography.

My initial critical impressions of suburbia were influenced by *The Exurbanites,* (New York: Lippincott, 1955), by A. C. Spectorsky; *The Crack in the Picture Window,* (Boston: Houghton Miflin, 1956), by John Keats; and *The Organization Man,* (New York: Simon and Schuster, 1956), by William H. Whyte, Jr. A more positive view was offered by Herbert J. Gans' *The Levittowners,* (New York: Vintage Books, 1967). My enthusiasm for New York City was reflected in *The New York City Handbook,* (Garden City, N. Y.: Doubleday, 1966, 1968), which I wrote with Gilbert Tauber. My attraction to New Haven can be explained in part by Allan R. Talbot's *The Mayor's Game,* (New York: Harper and Row, 1967), an engaging report on that city and its mayor, Richard C. Lee. Fred Powledge's *Model City,* (New York: Simon and Schuster, 1971), takes a harsher view. Princeton was examined by George S. Sternlieb and associates in *The Affluent Suburb: Princeton,* (New Brunswick, N. J.: Transaction Books, 1971). There was no similar study of Port Washington when we arrived there, but helpful was *This is Port Washington,* a pamphlet published by the local chapter of the League of Women Voters.

2. A BIT OF HISTORY

The City in History, (New York: Harcourt, Brace and World, 1961), by Lewis Mumford, and *Cities in American History,* (New York: Knopf, 1972), edited by Kenneth T. Jackson and Stanley K. Schultz, helped to provide a perspective, as did the defense of suburbia by Scott Donaldson, *The Suburban Myth,* (New York: Columbia University Press, 1969). *The Suburban Trend,* (New York: Century, 1925), by Harlan Paul Douglas, was useful for comparisons to the present. Other interesting views of suburbia's past were Sam Bass Warner, Jr.'s *Streetcar Suburbs: The Process of Growth in Boston, 1870–1900,* (Cambridge, Mass.: Harvard University Press, 1962), and Stanley Buder's *Pullman: An Experiment in Industrial Order and Community Planning, 1880–1930,* (New York: Oxford University Press, 1967). The hope for the autonomous small community was expressed in the classic, *Garden Cities of Tomorrow,* (Cambridge: M.I.T. Press, 1965) by Ebenezer Howard. Roy Lubove's *Community Planning in the 1920's,* (Pittsburgh: University of Pittsburgh Press, 1964), examined the contribution of the Regional Planning Association of America and others of the day. Glimpses of suburbia were contained in Frederick Lewis Allen's *The Big Change,* (New York: Harper and Row, 1952), and *Only Yesterday,* (New York: Harper and Row, 1957), and in Max Lerner's *America As A Civilization,* (New York: Simon and Schuster, 1957). A different perspective was offered by the *Report of the National Advisory Commission on Civil Disorders,* (New York: Bantam, 1968) and *Building the American City: Report of the National Commission on Urban Problems,* (Washington, D. C.: Government Printing Office, 1969). Both reports were analyzed in Joseph P. Fried's *Housing Crisis USA,* (New York: Praeger, 1971). Excerpts and interpretations of the *Report on the President's Task Force on Suburban Problems* were contained in *The End of Innocence.*

A rich source of local history was the weekly columns, "Port Remembered," by Ernest Simon in the *Port Washington News.* Publications of the Cow Neck Peninsula Historical Society were helpful, in particular its *Port Recalled,* though a most thorough chronology was contained in a children's book, *Tales of Sint Sink,* (Port Washington, N. Y.: Port Printing Service, Undated), by Charlotte E. Merriman. Other notes and facts were culled from *Nassau: Suburbia, U.S.A.,* (Garden City, N. Y.: Doubleday, 1974), by Edward J. Smits, *Dynamics of Community Change: The Case of Long Island's Declining "Gold Coast,"* (Port Washington, N. Y.: Friedman, 1968), by Dennis P. Sobin, and *The History of the Town of North Hempstead,* a booklet by John E. O'Shea, the town's "curator," apparently published by the town and distributed around 1970. Some descriptions of Port Washington, identified as "East Egg," were contained in F. Scott Fitzgerald's *The Great Gatsby,* (New York: Scribners, 1925). A picture essay of the Baxter Homestead, including a photocopy of a property map dated 1743, appeared in the March, 1917, issue of *Architectural Record.*

3. BALKANIZATION

The description of a fragmented Port Washington and Long Island was based on my own research. Various reports of the Regional Plan Association and articles in *The New York Times* were useful, in particular two series on suburban America that appeared in *The Times* in June and August, 1971. The descriptions of Santa Clara County were from an article, "Urban Sprawl," by William H. Whyte, Jr. in *The Exploding Metropolis,* (Garden City, N. Y.: Doubleday, 1958), edited by *Fortune* magazine, and an article, "The Debris of Development," by Jack B. Fraser in the August/September, 1970 issue of *City.* The survey of Santa Clara County eligible voters was published in *Power and Land in California, Vol. II,* (Washington, D. C.: Center for Study of Responsive Law, 1972), by Robert Fellmeth. The problems of "localism" are clearly and fairly presented in *The Use of Land: A Citizens' Policy Guide to Urban Growth,* (New York: Crowell, 1973), a task force report on land use and urban growth sponsored by the Rockefeller Brothers Fund. A stronger study of land abuse is William H. Whyte, Jr.'s *The Last Landscape,* (Garden City, N. Y.: Doubleday, 1969). Dated, but useful, was Robert C. Wood's *1400 Governments,* (Cambridge, Mass.: Harvard University Press, 1961). Wood's *Suburbia: Its People and Their Politics,* (Boston: Houghton Mifflin, 1958), helped put my prejudices toward local governments in perspective.

4. PLANNING AND POLITICS

Patchwork or Paradise: A Call to Action was published by the Port Washington Chapter of the League of Women Voters in 1959. It is out of print. Minutes of the meetings of the Port Washington Citizens Advisory Committee on the Master Plan were kept by Mrs. Winifred Freund. I supplemented these with my own notes and interviews. There have been various studies of the growth of local governments; among the more readable are *Cities in American History,* (New York: Knopf, 1972), Kenneth T. Jackson and Stanley K. Schultz, eds., and *Chicago,* (Chicago: Chicago University Press, 1969), by Richard C. Wade and Harold M. Mayer. The development of Los Angeles is well documented in the studies by Robert M. Fogelson, *The Fragmented Metropolis, Los Angeles, 1850–1930,* (Cambridge, Mass.: Harvard University Press, 1967), and Winston W. Crouch and Beatrice Dinerman, *Southern California Metropolis,* (Berkeley: University of California Press, 1963). Bill and Nancy Boyarsky offer a penetrating view of planning and politics in *Backroom Politics,* (Los Angeles: Tarcher, 1974). I am indebted to *Newsday* for providing me with back issues of the paper dating to 1967 documenting the Suffolk County land scandals, the exposure of which gained it a Pulitzer Prize. For those interested in a more detailed review of planning and zoning recommended are Mel Scott's *American City Planning Since 1890,*

(Berkeley: University of California Press, 1969), and Stanislaw J. Makielski, Jr.'s *The Politics of Zoning,* (New York: Columbia University Press, 1960). Attendance at local zoning hearings also can be enlightening.

5. HOME RULE AND OTHER HOAXES

Who's Running This Town?: Community Leadership and Social Change, (New York: Harper and Row, 1965), by Ritchie P. Lowry, was a scholarly report of a California town that helped me put some of Port Washington's problems in perspective. More penetrating was Nelson Polsby's *Community Power and Political Theory,* (New Haven: Yale University Press, 1963). The study of the Lower Main Street area of Port Washington for the Village of Baxter Estates by Catherine Morrison and myself was, alas, unpublished and unpublicized. My skepticism of roadway widenings and highway planning was sharpened by Helen Leavitt's *Superhighway-Superhoax,* (Garden City, N. Y.: Doubleday, 1970) and later honed by Robert A. Caro's *The Power Broker: Robert Moses and the Fall of New York,* (New York: Knopf, 1974). The proposals and debates concerning the future of North Hills, Long Island were reported in *Newsday* and supplemented by personal interviews. Minutes of the Citizens Advisory Committee of the Town of North Hempstead were recorded by a township employee, and were often in conflict with my own notes. My article, "Will the Real Port Washington Stand Up?" was published in the *Newsday* weekend supplement of February 7, 1970.

6. FRUSTRATION AND FAILURE

The Survey of Concerns of the Residents of Port Washington was prepared, distributed, collected and collated by the Greater Port Washington Civic Council, Inc. A copy of the ill-fated report of the Citizens Advisory Committee of the Town of North Hempstead is in my possession, as are various reports to the town prepared by the firm of Community Housing and Planning Associates. My article, "The Balkanization of Suburbia," appeared in the October, 1971, issue of *Harper's* magazine. Supplemental reading was *Reveille for Radicals,* (Chicago: University of Chicago Press, 1945), by Saul Alinsky.

7. PLANS AND MORE PLANS

A review of planning proposals on Long Island was published April 13, 1972, by *Newsday,* which also has been conscientiously following the fates of the plans in its daily coverage to date. *The Comprehensive Development Plan for Long Island* was published by the Nassau-Suffolk Regional Planning Board (Hauppauge, N. Y.: 1970). Proposed plans for both Nassau and Suffolk Counties, as well as for the entire New York metropolitan area, have been published by the Regional Plan Association and can be obtained by writing the Association at 235 East 45th Street,

New York, N. Y. 10017. These and other plans have been reported in *The New York Times,* which ran an excellent series on the problem of planning and community growth controls July 28, 29, and 30, 1974, written by Gladwin Hill. The League of Women Voters devoted much of its Fall, 1974, issue of *The National Voter* to the same problem in an article, "No Pasaran...? Which Laws Will Prevail in the Land Use Struggle." A more detailed review appeared in *The Use of Land: A Citizens' Policy Guide to Urban Growth,* and in Norman William, Jr.'s *American Land Planning Law,* (New Brunswick, N. J.: Rutgers University Press, 1975). A problem with these reviews is that a variety of test cases are presently wending their way through the courts, dating definitive comments with each new ruling. Involved in and monitoring many of the test cases has been the Suburban Action Institute. I am grateful to Paul and Linda Davidoff of the Institute for alerting me to the significance of several decisions and providing me with transcripts of them. The ambitious program of the Institute was described in a booklet, *The Suburban Frontier,* by Delroy Hayunga, co-published in 1971 by the Institute in White Plains, New York and the Board of National Missions of the United Presbyterian Church, New York.

8. "Them"

Equal Opportunity in Suburbia, (Washington, D. C.: Government Printing Office, 1974), a report of the United States Commission on Civil Rights, was a most valuable resource. Much of the material on Pasadena was from a March 22, 1975, article in *The Times* by Jon Nordheimer. The problems of Oak Park, Illinois, were described by William E. Farrell in *The Times* of May 26, 1975. The portrait of Greenlawn, New York was from an article, "A Black Island in Suburbia," by Neill S. Rosenfeld, which appeared in *Newsday* February 10, 1975. The plan for North Amityville was contained in a report entitled, "Housing," published by the Nassau-Suffolk Regional Planning Board in 1968. It was supplemented and updated by personal interviews, as was the "History of Publicly Assisted Housing in the Town of North Hempstead," an undated manuscript reproduced by the town's Housing Authority. A broader perspective was offered by Leonard S. Rubinowitz's "A Question of Choice: Access of the Poor and the Black to Suburban Housing" and William W. Pendleton's "Blacks in Suburbs" in *The Urbanization of the Suburbs,* and Anthony Downs: *Opening Up The Suburbs,* (New Haven: Yale University Press, 1973).

9. Rare Occasions

The history of local efforts to build subsidized housing in Port Washington was based on my own research, personal interviews, and participation. The experience of the Miami Valley Regional Planning Commission (MVRPC) in metropolitan Dayton was reviewed in a variety of reports. National attention was first focused on the MVRPC by John

Herbers in a December 21, 1970, article in *The New York Times,* later updated by Paul Delaney, November 17, 1974. Dale Bertsch wrote with A. Shafor of his work with the Commission in the April, 1971, edition of *Planners Notebook.* A most thorough report on the MVRPC appeared in the Jan./Feb. 1972 issue of *City,* written by Lois Craig. Again adding perspective was Leonard S. Rubinowitz in *The Urbanization of the Suburbs.* The MVRPC also was reviewed in a Regional Plan Association study, *Implementing Regional Planning in the Tri-State New York Region,* (New York: RPA, 1975).

10. THE RULE OF LAW AND MOBS

The Warren, Michigan, conflict received intensive coverage in the *Detroit News* from July through November, 1970. The best summary of the conflict was an article by Martin V. B. Weston, "Warren Keeps Most Of Its Castle Intact," in the Jan./Feb., 1971, issue of *City.* Also appearing in the same issue were three other pertinent articles; "Open Communities: Frozen Federal Levers," by Simpson Lawson; "Musings on Suburbia," by Carlos Campbell; and "Why Worry About Loosening the Suburban Noose," by Don Canty. "The Battle of the Suburbs," a special report in the November 15, 1971, issue of *Newsweek,* was helpful. *Newsweek* also reviewed, November 6, 1972, the problems in Westchester of the New York State Urban Development Corporation (UDC) to which I added my personal interviews. Both *The New York Times* and *Newsday* covered the Wyandanch, Long Island, debate in the summer of 1973. The chronology quoted in the text appeared in the *1973 Annual Report* of the UDC.

11. THE POLITICS OF SUBURBIA

Suburbia: Its People and Their Politics; Who Governs, (New Haven: Yale University Press, 1961), by Robert A. Dahl; and *The Professional Radical: Conversations with Saul Alinsky,* (New York: Harper and Row, 1970), by Marion K. Sanders, were essential to my study of community politics. The history of Nassau politics was pieced together from *Nassau: Suburbia, U.S.A.,* (Garden City, N. Y.: Doubleday, 1974), back issues of the *Port Washington News* and *Newsday,* personal interviews and my participation. Different perspectives, all helpful, were offered by Bennett M. Berger's *Working Class Suburb,* (Berkeley: University of California Press, 1968); R. M. Scammon and B. J. Wattenberg's *The Real Majority,* (New York: Coward-McCann, 1970); and Scott Greer's *The Urbane View, Life and Politics in Metropolitan America,* (New York: Oxford University Press, 1972).

12. THE PRICE OF POLITICS

"The Report of Examination, Port Washington Sewer District, Town of North Hempstead, County of Nassau," can be obtained from the Department of Audit and Control of the Office of the Comptroller, State of New York. The section on Mitchel Field was adapted from an article I wrote that appeared in the Jan./Feb., 1972, issue of *City*. It was updated by personal interviews and a daily monitoring to date of *Newsday*. Problems of local politics were placed in a scholarly context by articles by Thomas M. Scott, "Suburban Government Structures," H. Paul Friesma, "Cities, Suburbs, and Short-Lived Models of Metropolitan Politics," and Joseph Zikmund, II, "Suburbs in State and National Politics," *The Urbanization of the Suburbs*.

13. TAXES, SCHOOLS AND TAXES

An excellent summary of the problems of financing local public education appeared in *The New York Times*, February 5, 1975. The annual January education reviews of *The Times* were helpful, in particular Robert Reinhold's January 10, 1972, report on various court cases. Also enlightening were the articles of Phyllis Myers in *City*, including "Second Thoughts on the Serrano Case," Winter, 1971, issue, and "School Finance: A Return to State Preeminence," March/April, 1972, issue. At hand as a guide was the report of *The New York State Commission on the Quality, Cost and Financing of Elementary and Secondary Education*, (Albany, N. Y.: 1972). The columns of Martin Buskin, the *Newsday* education editor, were, as always, pertinent and provocative. Supplemental reading included L. H. Masotti, *Education and Politics in Suburbia*, (Cleveland: Western Reserve University Press, 1967), Charles E. Silberman, *Crisis In The Classroom*, (New York: Random House, 1970), and the classic *Slums and Suburbs*, (New York: McGraw-Hill, 1961), by James B. Conant. I also am grateful to my colleagues at the New York City Educational Construction Fund and to the Educational Facilities Laboratories, Inc., a subsidiary of the Ford Foundation, for their travel grants and consultant assignments, which afforded me a broader view of the problems of financing public education programs, as well as facilities.

The Wall Street Journal and *Business Week* are a steady source of reports on the broader issue of property tax reform. "The Coming Change in the Property Tax," a most useful article, appeared in the February 12, 1972, issue of *Business Week*. The Fall, 1971, issue of *City* contained three pertinent articles, "Untangling Metropolis," by Simpson Lawson, "The Metropolitan State," by Richard P. Burton, and "Minnesota's Metropolitan Tax Pool," by Paul A. Gilje. The efforts of Minnesota and others also were reviewed in John Fischer's *Vital Signs USA*, (New York: Harper and Row, 1975).

14. THE CORPORATE LANDSCAPE

An examination of land use influenced by economic factors is provided in *City and Suburbs: The Economics of Metropolitan Growth*, (Englewood Cliffs, N. J.: Prentice-Hall, 1964), edited by Benjamin Chinitz, *The*

Emergence of Metropolitan America, 1915–1966, (New Brunswick: Rutgers University Press, 1968) by Blake McKelvey, *Urban Economics,* (Chicago: Scott, Foresman, 1972), by E. S. Mills. *Centers for the Urban Environment,* (New York: Van Nostrand, 1973), by Victor Gruen, looks at shopping centers in cities and suburbia. Pertinent to the issue of public interest as affected by business location was "City-Suburban Comparisons," an extensive position paper prepared by the New York City Economic Development Administration, "The Office Industry," a Regional Plan Association report by R. B. Armstrong and "The Suburban Lock-Out Effect," a report by the Suburban Action Institute. Among the more valuable articles reporting on the exodus of corporations were "Rise in Jobs Poses Problems in the Suburbs," by L. Greenhouse in the August 8, 1971, issue of *The Times* and "The Golden Days are Gone in Suburbia," in the September 5, 1970, issue of *Business Week.* D. Young's observations appeared in the May 7, 1972, issue of *The Chicago Tribune.* Helpful to understanding economic trends and their effect on suburbia was, "Decentralization of Commerce and Industry: The Restructing of Metropolitan America," by Brian J. L. Berry and Yehoshua S. Cohen, an article which appears in *The Urbanization of the Suburbs.* Other sources included various economic reports of the Nassau-Suffolk Regional Planning Board.

15. THE DREAM DEFERRED

Useful background for the study of the sociology of suburbia are Harlan Paul Douglas' *The Suburban Trend,* (New York: Century, 1925); P. H. Rossi's *Why Families Move,* (New York: Free Press, 1957); *The Organization Man;* William M. Dobriner's *Class in Suburbia,* (Englewood Cliffs, N. J.: Prentice-Hall, 1963); and *The Levittowners. The Suburban Community,* (New York: G. P. Putnam, 1958), edited by William M. Dobriner, contains an excellent collection of articles, albeit dated, including the observations of David Riesman. More current are "Suburban Life Styles: A Contribution to the Debate," by Harvey Marshall, and "The Family in Suburbia," by Scott Greer, both in *The Urbanization of the Suburbs.* The study of attitudes of Long Island residents appeared in "The Real Suburbia," a series of articles that ran in *Newsday* the month of April, 1973. These were all tempered by my observations, experiences and interviews.

The problems of the housing market in suburbia are the subject of numerous articles in *The New York Times, The Wall Street Journal,* and various professional real estate and construction publications. Other perspectives were provided by personal interviews and *Mortgage on America,* (New York: Praeger, 1974), by Leonard Downie, Jr., and *Housing and The Money Market,* (New York: Basic Books, 1975), by Roger Starr. *The Times* and *Newsday* are excellent sources for reports of crime and crime trends. An article on the allocation of federal revenue sharing funds by the Village of Baxter Estates appeared in *The Times* April 2, 1975, written by George Vecsey.

16. No Easy Answers

Many recommendations pertinent to the problems of suburbia were included in various government reports produced in the late sixties, among them the *Report on the President's Task Force on Suburban Problems,* (1968); the *Report of the National Advisory Commission on Civil Disorders,* (1968); the *Report of the National Commission on Urban Problems,* (1969); *Urban and Rural America: Policies for Future Growth,* a report of the Advisory Commission on Intergovernmental Relations, (1968); and *Poverty Amid Plenty-The American Paradox,* a report of the President's Commission on Income Maintenance, (1969). Other pertinent recommendations were noted in the *Reform in Metropolitan Governments,* (Washington, D. C.: Resources for the Future, 1972), edited by L. Wingo; *Population and the American Future,* the Final Report of the Commission on Population Growth and the American Future, (1972); *Equal Opportunity in Suburbia,* A Report of the United States Commission on Civil Rights, (1974); and *The Use of Land: A Citizens' Policy Guide to Urban Growth.* For specifics in the New York region, the Regional Plan Association has produced an excellent series of reports, including *Implementing Regional Planning in the Tri-State New York Region.* On Long Island a start would be the recommendations of the Nassau-Suffolk Regional Planning Board's *Comprehensive Development Plan for Long Island.* Donald Canty over the years has proposed a variety of provocative recommendations, some of which were included in his essay, "Metropolity," in the March/April, 1972, issue of *City,* in his book, *The New City: A Program for Nationalization Urbanization Strategy,* (New York: Praeger, 1969), and his comments as editor of *City* magazine and, most recently, the *AIA Journal.* Provocative also are the comments of Ada Louise Huxtable in *The New York Times,* a collection of which are included in her book, *Will They Ever Finish Bruckner Boulevard?,* (New York: Macmillan, 1971). And as relevant as ever is *Communitas,* (Chicago: University of Chicago Press, 1947), by Percival and Paul Goodman; and *The Last Landscape.* A broader perspective is offered in *Environment and Change* and *Environment and Policy,* (Bloomington, Indiana: Indiana University Press, 1968), edited by William R. Ewald, Jr.

On a broader level are the recommendations included in *The Seventies, Problems and Proposals,* (New York: Harper and Row, 1972), edited by Irving Howe and Michael Harrington; *Counterbudget: A Blueprint for Changing National Priorities,* (New York: Praeger, 1971), edited by Robert S. Benson and Harold Wolman; *A Populist Manifesto,* (New York: Praeger, 1972), by Jack Newfield and Jeff Greenfield; and *Setting National Priorities—The 1974 Budget,* (Washington, D. C.: The Brookings Institution, 1973), edited by Edward R. Fried, Alice M. Rivlin, Charles L. Schultze, and Nancy A. Teeters. They are a beginning.

Index